AFTER NEARLY SEVENTEEN YEARS
OF HUMILIATIONS, WAITING, FRUSTRATIONS,
EVA BRAUN HAD AT LAST REACHED HER
GOAL—HITLER WOULD BE HERS FOREVER . . .

The bunker was elaborately prepared with silver, champagne and whatever food they could find. Berlin was totally besieged so they had difficulty finding a justice of the peace. After the brief ceremony, everyone went to the study for the feast. Eva was radiant although Hitler had not even kissed her. She ordered her phonograph to be fetched and played her only remaining record, "Red Roses."

Hitler retired with his secretary to dictate his will. It was only toward five in the morning that Hitler and Eva found themselves alone.

NOBODY WILL EVER KNOW WHAT HAPPENED DURING
THAT BRIEF AND BELATED WEDDING NIGHT. BECAUSE
THE NEXT DAY THEY WERE BOTH DEAD.

D1359010

HITLER'S MISTRESS
EVA BRAUN

✠ ✠ ✠ ✠ ✠ BY NERIN E. GUN ✠ ✠ ✠ ✠ ✠

BANTAM BOOKS · · TORONTO · NEW YORK · LONDON

EVA BRAUN: HITLER'S MISTRESS

*A Bantam Book / published by arrangement with
Meredith Press*

PRINTING HISTORY
Meredith Press edition published November 1968
Condensations appeared in the DETROIT FREE PRESS *1969,*
ARGOSY *Magazine February 1969 and* LADIES HOME
JOURNAL *April 1969*
Bantam edition published August 1969

Preface

A few hours after my liberation from Dachau concentration camp by the American troops, my compatriots, I learned that on that same day, April 29, 1945, Hitler had married a certain Eva Braun. This coincidence (which in reality was an illusory one, for, as shown in this book, the wedding took place considerably earlier) has always intrigued me and made me profoundly curious about Eva Braun. This curiosity was further aroused by the fact that throughout the period when I was a war correspondent in Berlin for the neutral press, I was—like all the other members of the press and diplomatic corps—completely unaware of her existence, despite my aggressive curiosity, for which I paid an extremely high price.

A marriage, even *in extremis,* is a human gesture. Who was this Eva Braun who had persuaded the fifty-six-year-old demon of Berlin to make such a paradoxical decision?

In spite of all that has been written about her, Eva Braun is one of the most misjudged figures of the Third Reich. Historians have minimized her importance in the most cavalier fashion. She is grossly misrepresented, both in the five thousand articles concerning her and in various historical works treating events both great and small. The real culprits, those who contributed to this disguising of the truth, were Eva's own friends, the Speers, the Hoffmanns, the von Schirachs, those who owed everything—riches, fame, power—to the man whom, albeit misguidedly, she had loved.

Thus Speer declared to the eminent British writer Trevor-Roper, who adopted and firmly established this judgment: "Eva Braun will prove a great disappointment to historians."

Today, Speer regrets this hasty judgment. He told me this himself. Speer was something more than a simple minister for Hitler. "He's your only true friend," Eva Braun had told Hitler in the Bunker, when everything seemed lost. "He's the only one who won't abandon you. . . ."

When Speer, in fact, arrived by plane (the last arrival in the Bunker), Eva went to greet him with open arms and kissed him, radiant with joy, as though she had just seen St. George come into the dragon's lair. "I knew you'd come," she exclaimed, "you're our friend, the last of the faithful." To this Speer sheepishly replied that he was only passing through and had to leave again that evening, called away by his duties as minister of munitions—the nonexistent duties of a minister without a ministry! At Nuremberg, perhaps to influence the judges, he even claimed that he had contemplated poisoning Hitler in the Bunker, along with Eva Braun, who considered Speer her best and oldest friend.

Baldur von Schirach, whose grandmother was an American multimillionairess, was not given a severe sentence at the Nuremberg trials, and has just written his memoirs. He too tries to present a sensational picture of Eva Braun, who worked as a "shop assistant" for the photographer Hoffmann, whose daughter von Schirach married. He made this girl, Eva Braun's one-time friend, the first lady of Austria, while Eva was obliged to while away most of her time in an obscure villa in Munich.

Eva remained faithful to her lover even in death. Frau von Schirach, on the other hand, divorced her husband as soon as he fell into disgrace, and paraded lovers whose political and racial ideas contradicted everything Baldur von Schirach had ardently championed.

Eva, for her part, was a woman who blindly loved a man for seventeen years, the only man in her drab existence, and who, of her own free will, despite all the obstacles, all the warnings, all the prayers, followed this man to an ignominious death. History cannot dismiss her with indifference.

But why did she love such a man? Love is not a business transaction where the pros and cons are weighed, the advantages and disadvantages calculated by computer. Love is an irrational passion. If it were logically motivated, it would no longer be love.

Did his relationship with Eva Braun in any measure

humanize Hitler? I am not among those who subscribed to the absurd concept of Hitler as a monster who tortured flies, gnawed carpets in rage, and governed according to horoscopes. Yet it must be recognized that Eva Braun's great love, far from humanizing Hitler, damned him still further, for his first, his chief victim was the very woman who had loved him so much.

But history is a cynical lady who makes mock of the moral values of her heroes. No man was more hated and insulted in his time than Napoleon. Yet today strangers go and weep before his tomb. For two hundred years, the name of Oliver Cromwell was anathema in England, whereas today he is considered one of the greatest British heroes. I do not wish to trespass into the future by predicting that one day Berchtesgaden will become a place of pilgrimage, but it is beyond doubt that Hitler convulsed all our lives and that his influence on the history of this century has been colossal. Even today, nothing really important happens in the world that is not the outcome of Hitler's political activity or of his war. This is why the details of his private and sentimental life seem to me to be of the greatest importance.

Unfortunately, the most reputable historians have proved to be quite as inaccurate in this domain as the authors of articles for popular magazines. Thus I have not relied on them. I have done what they neglected to do. Whenever possible I went to the human sources, to the people who had allegedly made a certain remark or given a certain piece of information. I consulted police dossiers and registry office documents; I visited schools, convents, houses, hotels, parks, cemeteries. When a witness told me something, I asked for some proof, I checked and rechecked his declarations. I compared the evidence of two friends, of two sisters, of mother and daughter.

All this effort would have been fruitless without the active cooperation of those who actually witnessed the events. I must here express my gratitude to Hitler's secretaries, Traudl Junge, the beautiful Gerda Christian, and Johanna Wolf; to his former chauffeur Maurice; and to other collaborators, his barber, his later chauffeur, his maid; to Eva Braun's school companions; and above all to her only true friend Herta Ostermeyr, who for the first time for many years agreed to talk openly to an outsider about Eva Braun. I am certain that all these people did not consider me an inquisitor, an enemy, or a scheming reporter but a friend to whom they could confidently reveal the whole truth. I hope that they will ascertain that I have not betrayed their trust.

Thanks to the discovery of Eva Braun's thirty-three photograph albums and a few pages of her private diary in an obscure corner of the Washington archives, I was able to obtain the active collaboration of the members of the Braun family, who, after twenty-two years of silence, agreed to lay aside their reticence. Their silence was natural, for all this time they had been obliged to look on impotently while Eva's memory was violated, her most intimate possessions were sold to souvenir hunters, and innumerable pamphlets, not to mention the fake diary, were published. They themselves were ostracized for a time by their compatriots. It should be said here that today the Brauns are still reluctant to admit that they should have to pay the price of the days of luxury and safety that they spent at Berchtesgaden.

But I am no William Manchester commissioned by Mrs. Jacqueline Kennedy to write the history of her husband's death. I am therefore afraid that the Brauns will bitterly repent having confided in me when they read this book, because they care primarily about their own interests and their own image. I am only concerned with the truth.

I am convinced that this is how Eva Braun would have wanted historians to speak of the one and only great love of her life.

Nerin E. Gun

Acknowledgments

The author wishes to express his endless gratitude to Miss Cecily Fortescue who devotedly assisted him in editing this original version of the book. Without her knowledge and her talent it could hardly have been completed.

The list of people who helped the author is so long that space obliges him just to mention a few names, such as Dr. Wolf and Mr. Taylor from the National Archives, Dr. Hoch from the Institute of Zeitgeschichte, His Excellency the former Premier Daladier, His Excellency François Poncet, the former Chancellor Kurt von Schuschnigg, and the staff of the Public Information Department of the Pentagon.

It is also necessary to thank all those who, having known Eva Braun, agreed, sometimes very reluctantly, to reenter the past: Emmy Göring; Ilse Hess; Anneliese von Ribbentrop; Albert Speer; Hitler's adjutants, Fritz Wiedemann, Günsche, Brückner, Maurice; Hitler's secretaries, Junge, Christian, Wolff, Schroeder; and many others. Whatever this former concentration camp inmate thinks of their past, the historian knows that it was difficult for them to again risk notoriety and he appreciates their cooperation.

"A hero must be free"

—FRIEDRICH NIETZSCHE

"The worst feature of marriage is this creating of rights. It is wiser to have a mistress. Then there is no burden to carry and everything is simply a beautiful gift. This, of course, only holds good in the case of exceptional men." —ADOLF HITLER

Contents

CHAPTER ONE

The girl who laughed with her eyes . . .

From the bottom of the stairs behind her, only the legs of the young woman leaning over the banister were now visible. She was still gesticulating and shouting, *"Servus, Uncle Adi! Servus!"* in a crystalline voice that echoed down each landing of the staircase. The legs were extremely pretty—legs like those of a Staatsoper ballerina, and their attractiveness was amply revealed under the light skirt of her Bavarian dirndl dress as she strained over. This made the man whom she bade farewell linger unduly despite the impatient honking of the chauffeur, who was in a hurry to set off before the traffic grew too thick.

Adolf Hitler finally got into the long black Mercedes with its lights glistening like cannon mouths, a luxury car that the manufacturers had graciously put at the disposal of the man who, this seventeenth of September, 1931, was still only an ambitious politician of the lunatic extreme right wing.

The young woman was now standing on the main first-floor balcony of Hitler's home in Munich, a balcony that was to acquire historic importance a few years later, for from it Neville Chamberlain would announce to a delirious crowd that he had just signed with "Herr Hitler" the agreement that was to "guarantee peace in our time." Hitler looked toward the balcony once more and remarked, "Only Geli can laugh like that with her eyes."

Angela Maria Raubal, affectionately known as Geli, was Hitler's niece, the daughter of his half sister. She was also his ward, over whom he watched with the jealousy of a Don Bartolo. She was nineteen years younger than he was, and strikingly beautiful. "She was a princess who forced people to turn round and look at her, a thing that was not often done in Munich," I was told by Emil Maurice, who

1

thirty-seven years later is still nostalgically in love with her.

Usually Hitler went back upstairs to say good-bye to his niece again, perhaps out of affection or perhaps to give her some final injunction, for he showed himself very authoritative with the members of his household. That Friday, however, his mind was full of the cares of moving a part of his household to his villa on the Obersalzberg, a mountain near Berchtesgaden, of the difficulties of an impending tour that would take him as far as Hamburg, and of distrust of his new chauffeur Schreck, who was given to speeding. Hitler, who never in his life took the wheel of a car, preferred to be driven at a comfortable "middle-class" speed and did not wish to give Schreck a pretext for going too fast by leaving late.

Moreover, that Friday morning the "Föhn" was blowing over the town. The Föhn is a Munich phenomenon, a south wind that lifts the mist and reveals the mountains to the townspeople and that also has the peculiarity of making most people moody. Hitler was one of these, and it will be seen that nearly all the women whom he knew were also tormented by the Föhn.

He put on the leather auto helmet that was in fashion at the time and gave the signal for departure. The enormous Mercedes glided away from 16 Prinzregentenplatz, where Hitler had his bachelor's apartment, in the very heart of a rather aristocratic residential district. The building itself, which was at one corner, could be considered luxurious. By one of those ironical twists of destiny, during World War II it was not even grazed by the Anglo-American bombs that leveled five-sixths of the town.

The car drove around the square and headed for the town center in order to get onto the Nuremberg highway. The autobahnen were not yet in existence. Shortly before leaving the town, Hitler turned to his companion, the photographer Hoffmann, and murmured, "This damned Föhn. I have a nasty premonition. I know it's childish . . ."

Hitler's premonitions were usually connected with attempts on his life. The trip to Nuremberg proved uneventful, however. After spending the night at the Deutscher Hof hotel there, the party was about to start northward again when one of the hotel bellboys stepped in front of the car, forcing Schreck to brake so suddenly that Hitler was thrown against the folding seat in front. "An urgent telephone call from Herr Hess."

A summons of this kind from Hess, the general factotum of the party, meant something serious, especially as the hotel employee had added that the call was from Hitler's private apartment in Munich.

"Your niece has just been found in her room, a pistol, yours, in her hand; her condition is very critical . . . the police are here, in the foyer." When Hitler arrived in Munich, it was already too late. The doctors had been unable to save Geli, and her body had already been transported to the morgue and from there to the mortuary chapel.

The morning paper published the following paragraph:

According to a police communiqué, a twenty-three-year-old student fired a pistol aimed at her heart in a room of her apartment in the Bogenhausen district. The unfortunate young woman, Angela Raubal, was the daughter of Adolf Hitler's half sister, and she and her uncle lived on the same floor of an apartment house on Prinzregentenplatz. Friday afternoon the owners of the apartment heard a cry but it did not occur to them that it came from their tenant's room. When there was no sign of life from this room in the course of the evening, the door was forced. Angela Raubal was found lying face down on the floor, dead. Near her on the sofa was a small-caliber Walter pistol.

The motives for this action are not yet clear. Some say that Miss Raubal had met a singer in Vienna, but that her uncle would not allow her to leave Munich. Others affirm that the poor girl killed herself because she was supposed to make her debut as a singer but did not believe herself capable of facing the public.

The paragraph in the *Münchner Neueste Nachrichten* hardly did justice to the importance of the event and to the notoriety of one of the personalities involved. However, the serious newspapers of the time rarely devoted much space to sensational scandal. Later Emil Maurice explained to me that strong pressure was immediately exerted by the Nazis on the press in order to prevent the publication of undesirable details. Geli, for instance, was reported to be the tenant of a separate apartment, whereas in reality she lived in that of her uncle, in a room next to his. The hypothesis of the singer with stage fright is pure invention. Geli had no intention of appearing in public. Her uncle would never have permitted it, and besides she was far from giving the impression of being a timid girl.

I have managed to reconstruct the details of this suicide thanks chiefly to my conversations with Annie Winter, who had been Hitler's daily maid since 1929, when he rented his bachelor's establishment in the Prinzregentenplatz. Later she assumed the more dignified title of housekeeper. "Geli's mother was on the Obersalzberg and Geli was alone with me. But almost immediately after her uncle's departure she shut herself in her room with instructions that she was not to be disturbed. . . . Yet earlier she telephoned to a friend and I knew she wrote some letters. . . ."

These letters have never been discovered, and the friend whom she rang up, Elfie Samthaber, maintains that they spoke only about inconsequential things, a dress that was for sale in a boutique, an evening at the theater.

The room where Geli had locked herself in was richly and elegantly furnished with antiques imported from Salzburg; the sheets were embroidered, and the pastel-green color of the walls showed off the painted motifs on the furniture. Only the watercolor painted by Hitler during the First World War, a Belgian landscape, was out of keeping with this decor. The room was at the end of the passage, with a little anteroom leading to the room where her mother slept and to the bathroom. Hitler's bedroom, which was smaller, was centrally placed near another bathroom, while the kitchen and pantry were at the other end of the corridor, overlooking the courtyard. The main drawing room, a small library leading off it, and another room looked out on the street. The apartment was furnished in the style that characterized the rich bourgeois homes of Munich, with an abundance of armchairs, sofas, lounge chairs, pedestal tables, chests of drawers, writing desks, clocks, frames, light brackets, and other bric-a-brac mass-produced in factories in careful imitation of period pieces. The effect was completed by pseudo-oriental carpets, heavy velvet curtains, damask hangings, and vitrines full of statuettes. Some of these pieces of furniture, appropriated as trophies or booty, are still to be found in the houses of those who were once members of Hitler's entourage. Mrs. Winter, who now directs an antique shop, may show you some of the pieces that once belonged to the master, or supposedly so.

Mrs. Winter told me that Geli was delighted with her room and spent much of her time there. She therefore saw no cause for alarm that fateful Friday when the girl locked herself in.

"She had told me she did not want to spend the week-end with her mother on the Obersalzberg, as had been arranged, because she had no suitable dress to wear."

Geli was always extremely elegant, and her Viennese clothes caused a sensation when she visited Haus Wachenfeld, the villa that her uncle had rented in the neighborhood of Berchtesgaden. On Sundays, when she went to Mass at the Church of Jesus and Mary, in the center of the little town, everybody's attention, even that of the choirboys, was distracted from the service by her beauty and smartness.

"She told me that her uncle Adolf had refused to buy her a new dress, which also meant paying her fare to Vienna, for she brought her clothes only in Vienna and Salzburg. But she did not seem unduly disappointed. . . . Her moods changed so quickly. . . ."

That evening Mrs. Winter left the apartment as usual to go home. But a neighbor, Frau Reichert, who lived in a maid's room on the same landing, claims to have heard a dull sound and a cry early in the night.

Geli was afraid of this old woman, who was in the habit of going up and down the stairs of the building with a kitchen knife and a piece of bread in her hand. In fact, when she was alone, for fear of Frau Reichert, Geli would keep at her side one of her uncle's pistols, for Hitler had a real arsenal and encouraged his niece to handle his guns. "You must learn to defend yourself, living as you do in a politician's house."

It was only the following day, when she resumed her work, that Annie Winter began to worry. She knocked insistently at the girl's locked door and then, in alarm, summoned her husband. They forced the door together. It was a macabre spectacle. Geli was lying on the floor, her blue nightdress embroidered with red roses saturated with blood, her head resting on her folded arm; the other arm stretched toward the divan, where a 6.35 mm. caliber pistol was lying. She had shot herself in the heart.*

Annie Winter telephoned a doctor and the police, but first she had providently contacted Hitler's friend Rudolf Hess, who in this way was able to arrive on the scene before the authorities, accompanied by Gregor Strasser. Hitler had some bitter enemies at police headquarters, and the housekeeper had shrewdly realized that the authorities should not be given an opportunity to exploit this catastrophe as a pretext for searching the apartment and seizing documents. Geli's mother, Angela Raubal, returned on Monday morning, but only in time to follow her daughter to the Munich mortuary.

The girl's foolish action made a tremendous impression on Hitler. Subsequently, many of the women who loved him passionately tried to kill themselves in one way or another. But only his niece's death had such a deep effect on him. He even talked about committing suicide in his turn. He isolated himself completely, refused to go on living in his apartment ("I couldn't sleep just next to her room"), took no interest in politics and was within an ace of renouncing his "mission" altogether. If this had happened, Geli's suicide would not have been in vain: It might have saved the lives of millions of human beings. . . .

It is extremely difficult, even after all these years, to define the exact nature of Hitler's relationship with his niece. In the months that followed he only rarely alluded to her. As for her mother, she always maintained a discreet silence —and in any case mothers are often ill informed about their daughters' lives. The others close to the event contradict each other, either from memory failure or because they were intent on presenting a version of the facts that was favorable to them. This much is certain, that the relationship was not the usual one between uncle and niece. Hitler, although he did not completely disown his family, as he has often been accused of doing, was not excessively attached to his relatives. Thus, despite the exaggerated cult that he dedicated to Geli's memory, he allowed Geli's mother, his half sister, to be practically chased out of the Obersalzberg a few years later, without uttering a single

---

* Eva Braun gave her sisters a different version of the suicide, the one that Hitler had related to her: Geli had fired a pistol shot in her mouth after having wrapped the weapon in a face cloth in order to muffle the explosion.

word of regret. And when Leo, the brother of his beloved Geli, was encircled with the rest of the army at Stalingrad, he refused to authorize his evacuation, while granting this favor to certain officers and many dignitaries of the party.* One of Hitler's companions, Esser, even remembers that when they were assembled after dinner round the *Stammtisch* in the Café Heck, with the radiant Geli Raubal presiding as usual, Hitler, ignoring her presence, or perhaps because of her, condemned nepotism roundly as "dangerous and offensive." "Napoleon"—Hitler never lost an opportunity of comparing himself with Napoleon—"contributed to his own downfall by placing his relatives on thrones and bestowing power and riches on them. Moreover, in this way he made himself appear highly ridiculous."

When, on September 5, 1929, Hitler moved into his new and spacious apartment in Munich, he offered hospitality to his widowed half sister Angela, who wished her daughters Angela and Elfriede to study singing and painting in Munich. His chief motive was a desire for company rather than fraternal generosity or a wish to repay the help that his half sister had given him for a short period when he was a penniless student in Linz. In his situation, he was afraid of living with wastrel companions who might one day abuse his hospitality and betray him. He knew that he could trust his half sister.

Angela, accompanied by her two daughters, arrived just before Christmas of 1929. Hitler was dazzled by the beauty of young Geli, who was then twenty-one but had the sharpness and zest of a seventeen-year-old. Her sister Friedl, on the other hand, although younger and quite as pretty, left him completely indifferent. Geli was slim, with an oval face that betrayed her father's Slavic origin, for in 1903 her mother had married a tax collector in the service of the Austrian crown who hailed from Bohemia. "Her big eyes were a poem and she had magnificent black hair," according to Emil Maurice's description. She would no doubt have been mortified had she known that much later, distinguished historians, heedless of the accuracy of details, would present her as a "blond Gretchen." She was very proud of her Viennese citizenship and of her dark complexion and despised the "stupid blond Bavarian

---

* Leo returned from captivity in 1947 and died a few years later.

girls." Her Viennese accent was delightful. All this, combined with her rebellious character and her impertinent ways, made her the exact opposite of the ideal type normally preferred by Hitler, who liked his women to be well endowed, very blond, and above all essentially Prussian.

He adored Geli from the first moment. He had known her, of course, when she was still very small, but he had unpleasant memories of his visits to the Raubal household in Linz. The master of the house showed only contempt for this ill-clad and impoverished student, who came to beg meals from his half sister.

"He liked to go out with Geli," Maurice told me. "He liked to show her off everywhere, he was proud of being seen in the company of such an attractive girl. He was convinced that in this way he impressed his comrades in the party, whose wives or girl friends nearly all looked like washerwomen. Hitler, incredibly enough, even accompanied her on shopping expeditions. True, he was obviously embarrassed at having to follow Geli out of a store, laden with parcels."

Emil Maurice had been Hitler's chauffeur for a long time and also was his companion from the very beginning. "We chased girls together and I used to follow him like a shadow." Maurice was a former partisan, had taken part in the first displays of force and had even participated in an attempted assassination of one of Hitler's adversaries. He came from an old Huguenot family and subsequent rumors about his Jewish origin are completely unfounded. Hitler and he were inseparable, and with Geli they formed a trio worthy of a trashy adventure novel. Hitler, who was an incorrigible matchmaker (he even organized a wedding a few days before his death), tried to persuade Maurice to find himself a wife. "I'll come and have supper with you every evening when you are married," he promised.

"Following his advice, I decided to become engaged to Geli, with whom I was madly in love, like everybody else. She gladly accepted my proposal."

But when Maurice announced this agreement to his master, there was a tremendous upheaval. Hitler flew into a tantrum and heaped reproaches on Maurice. He immediately dismissed him, although the separation must have been very painful to him, for he was extremely attached to Maurice, and he was the only chauffeur in whom he ever had complete confidence. Later on he avoided any contact with Maurice,* who, having become a watchmaker, was not summoned to share the glory of his master and companion as he had shared his hardships. This incident is sufficient proof that. for Hitler, Geli was much more than a niece whose virtue had to be protected.

"He loved her," Maurice affirms, "but it was a strange affection that did not dare to show itself, for he was too proud to admit to the weaknesses of an infatuation."

"His affection was that of a father," Annie Winter contends. "He was concerned only with her welfare. Geli was a flighty girl who tried to seduce everybody, including Hitler, and he merely wanted to protect her."

Hitler found it difficult to hide his feelings, and some of his friends in the party were worried about the influence that Geli had acquired. Friends reminded Hitler of the verses of Dietrich Eckart the poet (who died a drunkard in 1923) on the theme "A Führer Must Be Alone," and much later on, Rudolf Hess, when commenting on one of Geli's whims, advised Hitler to follow a precept of Goethe: "One must know how to train women." Hitler protested obdurately and insisted that he had not the slightest intention of getting married. "I have no desire to complicate my life still further, with Geli or anybody else."

There was another reason for caution. Geli was his half niece; marriage with her would have been perfectly legal, it is true, but Hitler, who was himself the offspring of complex intermarriages, had a marked dread of excessively close blood ties. His sister Paula was feeble-minded, and he did not want to run the risk of having cretinous children by Geli.

"I love her," he allegedly confessed to his friend, the photographer Hoffmann, "but I don't believe in marriage. I make it my business to watch over her until such time as she finds a husband to her taste."

So Geli was almost his captive. Her uncle satisfied her slightest fancy, but she could no longer go out alone. When she went for her singing lessons (Hitler admired her

---

* Emil Maurice, now the father of two married children says today: "It was luck that I did not marry Geli. She would have taken me with her into a bottomless pit!"

voice and was greatly in favor of these studies), she had to be accompanied by his henchmen or by her mother. She was not allowed to accept an invitation to a ball or a party, and when she wanted to go for a swim in the Königsee, Hitler, overcoming his dislike of all sporting activities and his terror of showing himself in public in a bathing suit, went bathing with her. He sometimes had her watched by the party police and asked Mrs. Winter to keep him informed about the letters she received.

Any young girl would have revolted under these circumstances, and in fact Geli was in a constant state of insurrection. But at the same time she was completely fascinated by Hitler, whom she found strange, attractive, mysterious, bizarre, and because he declared himself inaccessible, she had resolved to captivate him.

"Geli loved Hitler," Annie Winter affirms, "she was always running after him. Naturally, she wanted to become 'Gnädige Frau Hitler.' He was highly eligible . . . but she flirted with everybody, she was not a serious girl. . . ."

Probably no great importance should be attached to the judgments of Annie Winter, who shows the same cynicism when talking about the other women in Hitler's life. I suspect that Annie, who was the same age as Hitler, never forgave these women for the indifference that her employer showed toward herself.

By all accounts Geli was flirtatious, and her brief engagement to Maurice proves that she was not capable of staying faithful to Hitler indefinitely. But, like all the women who lived in the dictator's immediate vicinity, she must have been dominated by the man's demoniac charm or, if one prefers, hypnotized by his magnetic personality. In a letter to a friend she speaks of "O.A." [Onkel (Uncle) Adolf] as of a strange creature whose slightest action, whether it concerned a lawsuit about some mysterious funds from Italy, or the administering of a dose of poison to an old Alsatian dog (odd that Geli should have been struck by this detail), assumed the vast proportions of an event in a Wagner opera. Geli was also impressed by Hitler's popularity. When they went to the Café Heck, admirers thronged round him, he was acclaimed, women kissed his hands. Probably she considered that a match with her uncle would be a personal triumph, a challenge to her powers of seduction. Undoubtedly her mother, who was also totally under Hitler's influence, favored this union, with its excellent financial prospects.

But was there a real liaison? An affair? I greatly doubt it, for Hitler was too reserved to court a woman openly, especially his niece, and although he was not lacking in sexual initiative, he was not a man who would take the risk of having a mistress living with him in his own apartment. Geli, for her part, had no such scruples. It should be remembered that in 1931, Germany was in the depths of economic depression and that moral standards were considered to be at a low ebb. The young girls of Munich were not slow to find some pretext or other for wandering in diaphanous nightdresses in the immediate vicinity of a bachelor's room. Some of Hitler's entourage insinuated that Geli, who lived alone with her mother and her uncle (and maternal vigilance in such cases usually proves to be completely ineffectual) must have been tempted more than once to frolic in the corridor at night and that Hitler, for all his avuncular and bourgeois principles, would have found it difficult to resist such an invitation.

After his niece's suicide, Hitler lived for many weeks in total retirement at Gregor Strasser's house, refusing to speak to anybody and even to eat regularly. He came out of this torpor to go to Vienna, where his half sister had managed to persuade the Catholic authorities to grant Christian burial to her daughter. Austria had banned Hitler from its territory, but a special dispensation was obtained, and Hitler, who had made a vow to return to Vienna only as a conqueror, went humbly, for love of Geli, to the capital of the country he had deserted. He went to the cemetery, placed flowers on her grave, and returned the same evening to Berchtesgaden to continue to cry and to mourn her death for some time.

I have succeeded in finding Geli's tomb. At the time of the *Anschluss,* it occupied a central position in the cemetery. The Austrians, however, who have long been masters of the art of opportunism and who even manipulate burials in order to escape their responsibilities, have since relegated the grave to an out-of-the-way corner, and the Viennese authorities even officially deny its existence. But a custodian let himself be persuaded, and so I was able eventually to find the marble slab, streaked with brown stains, on which one can still read:

HERE SLEEPS OUR BELOVED CHILD

—GELI.

IN ETERNAL SLUMBER

SHE WAS OUR RAY OF SUNSHINE

BORN 4 JUNE 1908—DIED 18 SEPTEMBER 1931

THE RAUBAL FAMILY.

Hitler wore mourning for his niece for several years. Geli's room had to stay exactly as it was, and nobody had the right to enter it except Mrs. Winter, who was responsible for keeping it clean. "Hitler asked me to put fresh flowers there once a week," she says. He went there every Christmas Eve to meditate, this being his way of keeping the vigil, and he remained faithful to this commitment until the beginning of the war. When, in 1938, foreseeing an armed conflict with Czechoslovakia, he made his will, he devoted a whole paragraph to provisions for the furniture that had belonged to Geli. "Nobody must touch it; it must be returned to her mother." Geli still belonged to him undividedly, since he had this power to dispose of her furniture, her clothes, and her personal effects. A bust of Geli carved by Professor Thorak occupied a place of honor in the New Chancellery in Berlin, and Adolf Ziegler was commissioned to paint a portrait of her, which was placed in the famous main drawing room of the Berghof, in Berchtesgaden. Until the very end, there were always flowers in front of this picture. It is said that Hitler wept when he saw the portrait for the first time. He named the artist—whose only claim to fame was this portrait, done from a photograph—president of the Academy of German Art, a position that enabled him to bar from the museums dozens of Picassos, Matisses, Renoirs, Cézannes, Van Goghs, and Gauguins. . . .

The National Socialist Party had to exert considerable pressure to prevent the Bavarian police from making more thorough investigations into Geli's death. The strangest rumors were abroad. Rudolf Hess himself did not believe that it was a case of suicide but of a killing by a jealous rival who had penetrated into Geli's room at night and shot her. Others talked of an execution by the SS, motivated by Hitler's horror of the consequences of an incestuous relationship or by his desire to hush up a scandal, Geli being pregnant and refusing, as a good Catholic, to have an abortion. According to another speculation, it was the desperate deed of a girl who had been flouted, violated, deceived. Hitler, it was also alleged, had come back to Munich at night unbeknown to his entourage and, beside himself with jealousy, had killed his unfaithful niece. At the Nuremberg trial, it was vaguely mentioned that a document, now lost, seen by a Fräulein Breit, secretary to the Munich journalist Michel Gerlich, proved Hitler's guilt. But all others who had seen the document are dead, shot by the Gestapo or killed at the Russian front. For a long time there was talk, too, about a great love of Geli's in Vienna, variously identified as a doctor, a painter, or a music teacher. It is probable that Geli had flames in many different places, one of which may have been Vienna. But she could hardly have carried on a great love affair while her uncle kept her practically a prisoner. . . . And if this had been the case, could she have become engaged to Maurice?

It is difficult to explain why a girl of twenty-three should decide to commit suicide. However, the reason may well be connected with an incident that took place on the morning of Friday, September 18, 1931, soon after Hitler's departure. "Before shutting herself up in her room, Geli had helped me to tidy up the Führer's room," Mrs. Winter relates, "and I saw that she was searching in the pockets of one of his jackets. She found a letter. Later I was able to read this letter, handwritten on blue paper, which she had torn into four pieces and left well in view on the table, no doubt so that her uncle would see it."

The letter, as Annie Winter remembers, read more or less as follows:

Dear Mr. Hitler,

Thank you again for the wonderful invitation to the theater. It was a memorable evening. I am most grateful to you for your kindness. I am counting the hours until I may have the joy of another meeting.

Yours
Eva

Geli Raubal could easily guess that this Eva was Eva Braun, the *Dirndl* (girl) who for months had been hovering around Hitler. He had written something at the bottom of the letter, but Annie Winter did not manage to decipher it. Geli had probably realized then that this Eva Braun could become a dangerous rival. She closely resembled Geli, except that she was fair, and she had the same supreme asset, her youth—Eva Braun was even four years younger than Geli.

This is not sufficient motive for a suicide, even on a day when the Föhn is blowing. But the reason for her action may have been the realization that she was losing her hold on Uncle Adolf, the realization that she would never be able to force him to marry her, the realization that this tyrannical uncle did not behave in this way toward her solely out of love—since he had the desire and the time to take an interest in Eva Braun—but because he had put his brand on her, because he considered her as part of his goods and chattels, his absolute property.

CHAPTER TWO

A convent-bred young lady

A pipe in his mouth, a beer glass in his hand, the cat on his lap, this is how people thought of Herr Lehrer Fritz Braun, who was a Württemberger by birth but a good Munich bourgeois by character. Yet that night, he seemed to have cast aside the celestial serenity that at the time was an essential quality of a Bavarian. The reason was that he had been forbidden to smoke. His mother-in-law objected to the smell, and as the temporary mistress of the house, she was issuing orders to everybody, even to the midwife. He had long since drained his beer jug, at a time of night when all the taverns in the vicinity had put up their shutters hours ago and when the cat Resl, outraged by all the bustle, had gone in search of a little peace on the neighbors' rooftops. For, despite the lateness of the hour, a certain confusion reigned in the three poorly furnished rooms at 45 Isabellastrasse.

The baby was slow in arriving. Mrs. Braun had felt the first labor pains on Saturday morning, and it was now in the early hours of Tuesday. They had summoned the doctor three times in spite of the protests of Granny Kranburger, who had come specially from the province of Oberpfalz for the occasion. "There's nothing to worry about; my daughter may be small but she's as strong as a horse. She'll give birth to a fine boy and he'll grow up to be a doctor like his grandfather." Grandfather Kranburger was not, strictly speaking, a doctor; he was the veterinary surgeon of the province, but for the farmers of those parts, a vet was more important than a mere M.D. The latter tended only human beings, while the other treated cows, and nothing is more valuable to a peasant than his cow. Moreover Herr Kranburger was an official who wore a uniform with epaulettes and the royal arms embroidered on it, and when his wife went to the *Kaffeeklatsch* on Wednesdays, the other ladies who formed part of local society greeted her with a respectful *Frau Bezirkstierärztin* (Mrs. District Veterinary). Even Fritz Braun had a petty official's deference for this title and therefore grudgingly tolerated his mother-in-law's presence.

Of course, he was expecting a boy. He already had a girl, Ilse, born in 1909, and it was now incumbent on him to present the good king of Bavaria with a male offspring. He had already chosen a name, Rudolf. The choice had been inspired by a romantic story that was being serialized at the time in a Munich newspaper: the tragic love of the Archduke Rudolf of Hapsburg and his mistress the Baroness Marie Vetsera, who had met their death together in Mayerling. The paper was beside Mr. Braun, who had just looked to see what was new in the world this eve of the sixth of February, 1912—a cursory look, for he was not interested in politics. A group of English intellectuals had launched a stirring manifesto in favor of lasting peace, a proclamation that did not prevent the Italians from waging war against the Turks in Tripolitania, the Aegean, and even the Red Sea, where their fleet had just shelled an unknown Ottoman fort on the Strait of Tiran. But the talk of the day was a new dance, the turkey trot, which had been banned for its downright salaciousness from the genteel drawing rooms of London, New York, and Berlin. Kaiser Wilhelm II was about to announce at the Reichstag that the German navy would soon be the most powerful in the world. Thanks to the invention of a new combustion engine, this navy would boast the fastest battleships in the world, beside which those of the other fleets would seem like floating metal carcasses. A certain Gregory Rasputin was reported to have caused a scandal at the czarist court.

The baby was born at twenty-two minutes past two in the morning, while outside, according to the same *Münchner Neueste Nachrichten*, a dismal, persistent drizzle was falling, and continued to do so for several days. Fritz Braun had dandled the small body, which was light as a feather in his arms, and the baby girl, for a girl it was, had fallen asleep almost immediately. They woke up little Ilse, who, in her new position of seniority, promised to watch over her sister for the rest of her life.

Fritz Braun was admittedly a little disappointed and also worried. His wife came from a family where there had been only daughters, four of them in all, and what if she also was destined to give birth only to girls? He was still too overwrought to go to bed, and therefore started feverishly to make a list of all the Brauns in various parts of Germany and in North and South America to whom he must straightaway announce this news. There were quite a few, the most famous of whom is Wernher von Braun.

Much later it was flippantly claimed that the name Braun was merely chosen by Hitler's favorite in order to symbolize her unity with the sacred cause. The brown shirts, the brown house, the brown movement—a brown girl was clearly needed. In spite of all the questions I have asked those who lived in Hitler's immediate entourage and despite having read *Mein Kampf* from cover to cover, I have not succeeded in finding a logical explanation for this particular choice of color by the Nazis.

The idea of using colored shirts as the uniform of a militant party was first adopted by Mussolini, who had borrowed it from the "Arditi," a special unit of volunteers in the First World War. Hitler himself declared that he considered the choice of a color symbolizing a political idea as an essential question, for this was the only way of impressing the masses. He would have preferred red, but it had already been appropriated by the Communists. White was too effeminate and had royalist connotations. Blue was the Bavarian national color, and therefore too regional. "Perhaps the Führer had run out of colors," explains his beautiful ex-secretary, Gerda Christian. "He was forced to choose brown, which was the only shade still available. In fact it was a practical one for people who had to lie low all the time to escape from the police. . . ."

What was the new baby going to be called? Was Rudolf to be replaced by Marie, the name of the Baroness Vetsera in the newspaper story? There were Maries in both families, but Fritz Braun wanted something different, as he did not favor too Catholic a name. Slightly anticlerical, he had given his first daughter the pagan name Ilse and decided that Eva sounded just as irreligious.

Unfortunately, he had omitted to consult his wife's calendar: Eva is also a Catholic name and his daughter was later to reproach him frequently for his choice. Saint Eva's Day, or more precisely Saint Genevieva's Day, falls one day before Christmas, and since in those parts name days are celebrated rather than birthdays, Eva was regularly deprived of festivities and presents. Relatives and friends alike, out of parsimony or forgetfulness, combined the two dates, to Eva's extreme vexation and despair. She always attached the greatest importance to the respecting of all her prerogatives, especially in the matter of presents.

Eva grew up in an idyllic atmosphere. The Brauns, by the standards of the time, were an almost perfect couple. Although the young schoolmaster's modest resources were considerably strained by the arrival of this second daughter, the family lacked nothing.

Before her marriage, Eva's mother, Franziska Katharina Kranburger, called Fanny, had been a very athletic young girl. While she was still in her adolescence, she became a ski champion, a feat that was considered rather audacious at the time (this was in 1905). She was also an admirable swimmer and was on one occasion the heroine of a life-saving episode that was reported in the local papers. She must have been remarkably beautiful because even now, at the age of eighty-three (she was born on December 12, 1885, at Geiselhoering, in the province of Oberpfalz), she dazzles the visitor with the delicacy of her features, her young-girl's legs, her vivacity and alertness.

The marriage lasted fifty-four years. Fritz Braun died on January 22, 1964, at Ruhpolding, and his wife has remained there in order to be closer to his tomb. "There was not a single cloud, not even a real quarrel," Franziska Braun assured me, "and this in spite of the vicissitudes of two world wars, two financial recessions, two inflations, and the catastrophic years that followed the Nazi debacle. Fritz was the only man in my life; I never even kissed another and never had the slightest flirtation. And I am certain that he too never took any interest in any woman but me."

Fair-haired like her mother, Eva, or Effie, as she was called, was a pink-cheeked, chubby baby whose laugh brightened the house and who crawled everywhere in search of mischief. Later horoscope readings reveal that at the moment of Eva Anna Paula Braun's birth, the Sun and Venus were entering Aquarius and the Ram, respectively, while Saturn confronted the Bull, all of which signifies great expectations. Mama Braun, however, never concerned herself much with horoscopes and fortune telling. She had already decided her daughter's future: She would become a famous dressmaker with a salon in Berlin, just close to the Kaiser's castle.

The Kaiser meanwhile had decided to wage war, and Fritz Braun was sent, with the rank of lieutenant, to the Flanders front. I have taken considerable pains to discover if his path ever crossed that of Adolf Hitler; there was only a difference of ten years in their ages, and Hitler also fought in Belgium for a good part of the First World War. But they were both insignificant combatants, and few traces of their war peregrinations have survived.

Mrs. Braun and her three daughters (the youngest, Margarethe, known as Gretl, was born three years after Eva) underwent hard privations like everybody else, but the family accepted them with patience and great solidarity. The mother made army uniforms, as well as shades for table lamps. She dismissed their maid and took in a lodger. Ilse, the eldest, looked after her little sisters with loving care, and they played with dolls and enacted fantastic fairy tales in which Eva was the enchanted princess and the cat her Prince Charming.

As butter was extremely rare, their mother buttered their evening slices of bread very parsimoniously, so much so that sometimes it was impossible to tell if the bread was coated or not. Eva remarked in Bavarian dialect to one of her sisters who was complaining of this fact, "Put your slice of bread under the light and if it shines, it means it's buttered." This childish remark, whose humor I must admit escapes me, became a classic in the Braun household. It was repeated on the occasion of every family celebration—and God knows they abounded—and it was even quoted later in the drawing rooms of Berchtesgaden.

Eva was a capricious child. Once her mother had tried to overcome her obstinacy by plunging her head in a basin of cold water . . . in vain, for Eva did not give in. Her father was even stricter, and Eva received more than one dressing down for playing truant. But punishments made no impression on her, and she repeated her misdemeanors without the slightest hesitation. She completely neglected her homework, and it was only in the morning, when she was dressing, that she started to learn her lessons. Her sister still remembers how, kneeling in front of a chair, she wrote her German composition with one hand while she combed her fair hair with the other.

The punishments were short-lived, and their mother, al-

ways frugal in her housekeeping, managed to buy innumerable toys for her daughters and took them to the
operetta, the theater, and later the cinema. Their father,
for all his apparent surliness and his pedantic theories,
adored his daughters, especially "Evamierl," and once he
made her a miniature dolls' house, complete with furniture, bedding, and cooking utensils. It cost him six months
of hard work.

When Eva was afraid that one of her pranks might be
discovered or when she wanted to avoid some irksome
task, or again when she refused to swallow one of those
wartime culinary concoctions such as rutabaga puree or
oatmeal porridge, she pretended to have a stomachache.
This trick, which she had first tried successfully at the age
of four, was repeated indefinitely, and she was always to
complain of a delicate stomach. Dr. Morell tried in vain to
diagnose her trouble, and Hitler was terrified when she
had gastric attacks, which she finally came to believe in
herself. In reality, she enjoyed extremely good health and
did not even suffer from headaches during her monthly
periods.

Conditions in the Braun family having considerably improved, they moved in 1925 to a vast apartment on the
second floor at 93 Hohenzollernstrasse. The house still exists, its wartime bomb damage repaired, and even today
the apartment once inhabited by the Brauns gives the
impression, by its location and dimensions, of being a solid
bourgeois dwelling.

The three girls reached the age of adolescence, took
music, painting, and dancing lessons, attended the Teng-
strasse secondary school, and started to attract the attention
of boys. There was a maid again, the subtenant had disappeared, and visitors could now be received properly. Life
was gay, full of distractions, of high jinks on the stairs,
and the neighbors talked of the *Drei Mäderl Haus,* the
house of the three young girls, an expression borrowed
from the operetta about Franz Schubert.

Her parents had taught Eva to become a good skier, but
her forte was ice-skating. She had once announced that
she was preparing for the Olympic Games, especially since
she had discovered that the athletes traveled at the committee's expense. She would swim for hours, and despite
her father's interdictions, she did not hesitate to go a long

way out from the bank of the Starnberg Lake, where the family went for Sunday outings.

The secondary school archives prove that Eva Braun obtained her diploma with a profusion of credits. "She was a terror, it's true, the troublemaker of the class, but she was intelligent and quick to seize the essential aspects of a subject, and she was capable of independent thought," her former teacher Fräulein von Heidenaber informed me.

When, rarely, she was forced to stay still, Eva read the Wild West novels of Karl May, a German author who specialized in this genre. She was not interested in love stories, but her professor had made her a devotee of the *Tales of Oscar Wilde*. She always carried the book with her, even later at the Obersalzberg, although Hitler had banned all the author's works. In spite of her mother's enthusiasm for the opera, Eva preferred jazz and American musicals. Her favorite actor was John Gilbert (the cinema was still predominantly silent), and she had a boundless admiration for the star of *Metropolis,* Brigitte Helm, chiefly because her father had once facetiously declared that she looked slightly like her.

The Brauns had made a rule of sending their daughters to a convent school in order to complete their education. In Bavaria, to become a real lady, it was necessary to pass through one of these specialized institutions where girls were taught the social graces and in this way could subsequently claim the distinction of having been brought up in a *Kloster*. The English Sisters, a Catholic order founded by a fugitive from English persecutions, undertook the education of young girls from the middle class who wanted both to acquire good manners and learn a profession, so they could earn their living. For it must be remembered that in 1929, poverty and unemployment prevailed in Germany, and it was essential, even for a girl of good family, to be equipped to support herself.

The convent was on the banks of the Inn River, a stone's throw from the Austrian border, at the entrance to the little town of Simbach. Eva was unhappy there from the first moment, amid so many girls and so much discipline. She was not even comforted by the fact that the nuns made excellent desserts and little delicacies, with the result that she gained nearly twelve pounds in as many months. The courses normally lasted two years, but she refused to stay as long and even intimidated her mother by threatening to run away and seek her fortune in Vienna or Berlin.

The nuns have kept a register, where her name appears and a medical report, which gives gynecologic confirmation of the virginity of the pupil Eva Braun. One of the nuns, sister Marie-Magdalene, agreed to talk to me about the past and generously affirmed that "Eva was ambitious and intelligent and had a pretty voice. She excelled as a performer in the modest amateur theatricals that were staged in the convent. . . . She had no close friend among the girls. She regularly attended the religious services."

Brought up in Bavaria by a very devout mother, following a set tradition, Eva had been confirmed, had received her first communion in great style (her white dress was the prettiest of the neighborhood, and her grandfather had given her a little wristwatch), and, like all the Braun girls, she went to church every Sunday. At the convent, she was obliged to go to confession twice a week. She belonged to the Children of Mary and occasionally had the privilege of decorating the altar.

The convent is still flourishing today, with four hundred pupils and a building enlarged by the recent addition of two new wings. When I visited the Mother Superior, I was afraid that the nuns might refuse to give me any information, preferring to ignore a pupil who had achieved such notoriety. But far from it. They crowded around me, asking innumerable questions: "Did she love him?" "Is she really dead?" "How did she meet him?"

Yet they had small reason to be grateful to their former pupil Eva Braun. "When, in 1940, the National Socialist Party decided to requisition our convent in order to install a school for party propaganda here," the Mother Superior explained, "I did my utmost to avert this catastrophe. In some way or other, I knew that Eva Braun was at Berchtesgaden and I telephoned her, which was no easy feat.

"She listened to me a moment and then said dryly, 'I'll speak to Party Member Bormann about it; he's here in the drawing room with me. . . .' She put down the receiver, and I heard the sounds of a conversation followed by masculine guffaws and a crystalline laugh, which I took to be Eva Braun's. She came back to the telephone and continued in a reassuring voice, 'Don't worry, everything will be all right; I'm seeing to the matter.'

"But our convent was taken over a few weeks later and

was only restored to us after the liberation, by the Allies."

At the end of July, 1929, Eva Braun left her convent. She waited demurely on the platform of the little station in Simbach, her cotton dress, with its small blue and white checks, rather strained over her round hips, the skirt almost above her knee, her thick woolen stockings only half masking the shapeliness of her legs, a big moon-shaped hat emphasizing the fullness of a face fattened with fancy cakes and sugared noodles flavored with thyme. With a big bag and a box crammed with books on the ground beside her, she was waiting for the Munich train, a diploma in her pocket, but without any experience of life, a cheap novel that she had bought at the station newsstand under her arm. Never having kissed a man in all her seventeen years, she waited for the train that she hoped and prayed would carry her into a world of dizzy discovery, of great and beautiful adventures. . . .

CHAPTER THREE

The boy who toyed with the sun

When the rising mist clears from the Inn River, it is quite possible to see the old main square of Braunau from the dormitory window of the Simbach convent school. A narrow street prolongs the end of this square like the neck of a bottle. On the right side of the street, the first floor above an eating house called the Pommer had been let to the chief customs official of the place (the frontier line bisected the bridge linking Simbach and Braunau). Here Adolf Hitler was born.

There were no remarkable omens on Saturday, April 20, 1889, at half past six in the evening, when Klara Hitler, née Pölzl, the daughter of peasants, gave birth to a seven-pound son. The father was away, and the mother had been seized by panic at the onset of strong labor pains. The following Monday, at three o'clock in the afternoon, in the presence of Alois the father, Johanna the hunchback aunt, the godparents Johann and Johanna Prinz from Vienna, and the father's subordinates, the Braunau customs officials, the Reverend Ignaz Probst christened the baby in the traditional religion of its parents and of the Austro-Hungarian monarchy, with the name Adolf. The first name was, in fact, hardly Catholic, being essentially Germanic and pagan. It meant *edler Wolf*, Noble Wolf, and later Hitler often used the name Wolf as a pseudonym or code, and his sister adopted it toward the end of her life.

I have not the slightest intention of embarking on a full biography of Hitler. I merely wish to point out the particular aspects and episodes of his youth that were directly to influence his sentimental life and his relations with Eva Braun. The complications that preceded his birth, for example, explain at least partially his decision to marry Eva.*

These complications began in the second year of the reign of his Catholic—if simple-minded—Majesty the Emperor and King Ferdinand I of Hapsburg.

That year, 1837, the servant-girl Maria Anna (known as Marianne) Schicklgruber gave birth to an illegitimate child, Alois, who was brought up on a farm and became a gooseherd. For four years this Alois, the father of the future Adolf Hitler, bore the name of his mother, Schicklgruber. The unmarried mother was one of the eleven children of Johann Schicklgruber, who had married in 1793. Certain historians have appropriated a quip of the photographer Hoffmann, who even in prison wanted to maintain his reputation as "the Drunkard of the Third Reich" or "the Berchtesgaden Jester" and therefore speculated that if the Führer had remained a Schicklgruber he would never have come to power, for who would have shouted "Heil Schicklgruber"?

It was not his family name that was to hamper Hitler's relations with women, but rather the cloud that lay over his father's birth and therefore, indirectly, over his. For when his grandmother Marianne Schicklgruber returned home pregnant in 1837, at the age of forty-one, it caused a scandal in the little Lower Austrian village of Doellersheim. Her father refused to take her in and she was forced to take refuge with a sympathetic peasant.

On May 10, 1842, Marianne married a certain Johann Georg Hiedler. According to the records, the name dates from 1435 and was pronounced in many ways, among them Hitler. Johann Georg, who earned his living as a miller, had already been married, to a certain Anna Maria Bauer, who died after three years of marriage. This Hiedler lived in the Schicklgrubers' house, which explains how he came to marry the unmarried mother. The bride-

---

* I feel that the popular works by William Shirer, Heiden and others are not always an adequate source of information for this part of Hitler's life. They are all incomplete, if not inexact. Everything must be taken into consideration, and for my part, the only book that seems to me well documented is that of Franz Jetzinger (*Hitler's Youth*). Unfortunately Jetzinger, who shared my prison cell in Vienna in 1944, finished his book in 1956, and had not yet had time to free himself of his aversion for the man who had victimized him, an aversion which is fully justified but which impairs his historical objectivity.

groom's brother, Johann Nepomuk Hiedler, who was fifteen years his junior, is believed to have taken in the little boy Alois, in which case it was on his adoptive uncle's farm that this illegitimate child grew up. The mother died in 1847 and her husband, Johann Georg Hiedler, in 1857.

The child Alois could not be present at his adoptive father's funeral, having gone on foot to Vienna to seek his fortune. And he found it: He became a customs official, with a right to a uniform, a pension, and the respect of his fellow citizens. He was now somebody. Yet despite the fact that he was a very important personage who had precedence over the police superintendent, the schoolmaster, and the tax collector, his name was still Schicklgruber. It was only in 1877 that, to the stupefaction of his subordinates in Braunau, he declared that from then on he would call himself Hitler.

Records show that in 1886 the adoptive uncle, Johann Nepomuk, presented himself with two witnesses before the parish priest of Doellersheim and officially declared that Alois was the illegitimate child of his brother Johann Georg. He asked for the legitimation of this child, who meanwhile had reached maturity and become an honored servant of his royal and imperial Majesty. The legitimation was duly carried out.

But were these witnesses speaking the truth? Was Johann Georg Hiedler really the father of Alois and had he married the mother for reparation's sake? Then why had he not legitimated the child immediately? This is an insoluble mystery.

Alois, true to his birth, showed himself an extremely precocious Don Juan. He became the father of a little girl Theresa, whose mother was a certain Thekla from Vienna. The girl Theresa subsequently had a son Fritz, whose striking resemblance to Adolf Hitler caused people to stop in the street. It is possible that on occasions he played the role of Hitler's double.

In 1873, Alois married a certain Anna Glassl, the daughter of a tobacco merchant. The bride was fifty years old, but she had a sizable dowry. Alois nevertheless wished to have something younger about the house. He lit on the idea of summoning Klara, the daughter of his adoptive aunt Johanna Hiedler (the sister of Johann Georg and Johann Nepomuk). This cousin was seventeen—an age that seems to have haunted the male members of this family—

and not unnaturally her presence does not appear to have been welcomed by the lady of the house. Frau Hitler asked for separate maintenance on November 7, 1880.

Meanwhile Alois, who was then forty-three, had found another mistress, the peasant girl Franziska Matzelberger, who was also seventeen. Franziska, known as Fanny, came to live at Alois's on condition that Klara were sent away. This new cohabitation caused even more gossip in Braunau, the more so as on January 15, 1882, Fanny also gave birth to an illegitimate child, Alois. It was only after the death of his legitimate wife Anna in 1883 that the customs chief was able to marry Franziska and legitimate his child Alois.

On July 28, 1884, Frau Franziska Hitler gave birth in Vienna to a baby daughter who was given the unusual name of Angela. This was the future mother of Geli Raubal, the niece who committed suicide in the apartment on Prinzregentenplatz. The birth weakened Fanny greatly, and she died a year later of an unknown illness.

Klara, the young adoptive niece, the daughter of Johanna née Hiedler and of her husband Johann Baptist Pölzl, who had been displaced at the time of Franziska's intrusion, had come back to live with cousin Alois. She did the housekeeping during Fanny's illness, brought up the children, and probably gave nocturnal comfort to poor Alois, who must have been saddened by the absence of his wife, who was in hospital. However that may have been, Klara certainly became his mistress after Fanny's death, but she demanded almost immediately to be led to the altar. But alas, the parish priest found himself unable to give the nuptial blessing. According to the parish register, Alois was the recognized son of Johann Georg Hiedler and Klara Pölzl was the daughter of Johann Hiedler's sister, Johanna. The betrothed were therefore first cousins. A dispensation had to be obtained, and this was declared to be outside the competence of the diocese. An application had to be made to the Vatican and finally Rome gave its consent. And so on January 7, 1885, Alois Hitler married his blood cousin (if Alois is considered to be Hiedler's son), Klara Pölzl, the future mother of Adolf.

Hitler was certainly aware of these antecedents, and this explains his middle-class prejudices, his struggle against the feminine element that tended to dominate him as it had dominated his father, his reluctance to father an illegitimate child, his crusades in favor of unmarried mothers, his puritanical and artistic tendencies and above all the terror that seized him when he found himself in the presence of certain ailing women. He must have thought that the incest of which his father and mother had been guilty would have fatal consequences for his descendants. "A genius can give birth to an idiot," he is supposed to have said one day to his table companions at Berchtesgaden. This fear was not unfounded: Alois' and Klara's first child, born in 1885 and christened Gustav, died at the age of two. Then came Ida, who also lived for only two years. Otto, the third child, only survived a few days. Adolf, the fourth, was the first child to resist this blood curse. Five years later another boy, Edmund, was born, but he too died prematurely at the age of six. The sixth and last child was Paula, who outlived her brother until 1963. But Paula was a retarded child, and although the secret was extremely closely guarded on the occasion of her rare visits to Berchtesgaden, the Braun sisters realized that she was not in full possession of her faculties.

It could be argued that the most patent proof of the consequences of this marriage between first cousins is Adolf Hitler himself. But this would be digressing widely from the subject.

Hitler did not grow up in needy circumstances. He had no cause to feel ashamed of his father's profession, far from it. He did not love his father, it is true; Alois was violent and selfish, terrorized his family and spent much of his time in taverns.

But all the testimonies confirm that Klara Hitler was an extremely gentle woman, a slave to her duty and devoted to her children, especially "Adi," who never raised his voice and was hardly ever moody. She was pretty but frail. Hitler lied about almost everything in *Mein Kampf* but not about his mother, whom he described as a good fairy forever watching over her children. Hitler certainly loved his mother greatly, and perhaps loved only her in his whole life. He perhaps searched all the women whom he met for a reflection of his mother, who was for him the ideal woman.

On May 2, 1895, at the age of six, little Adi, dressed in a dark-blue sailor suit and holding his half sister Angela's hand, went to school in Fishalm for the first time. The family had left Braunau to live two years in Passau, on the German side of the border, and then in Linz. On his retirement the father had bought a small farm at Lambach, and young Adolf went to a neighboring village school. But the farm was a financial drain, and Alois was soon obliged to sell it and buy a house at Leonding, near Linz.

Hitler learned to play the piano at the age of eight and studied singing for two years with the Benedictines in Lambach, where they had a singing school; his teacher was Father Bernhard Bruener. Hitler himself wrote that he had been greatly impressed by the Catholic liturgy and that he even contemplated taking orders. Much later, he often talked to Eva Braun about religious ceremonies and even sang a few church melodies for her benefit. Hitler never prevented Eva, who had also been brought up a good Catholic, from attending Mass when she so wished.

Hitler was a rather mediocre pupil, and even repeated a class. Many teachers have passed judgment on him, enthusiastically in the days of his triumph and critically at the time of catastrophe. "Hitler behaved like any other boy of his age; he played truant, went on madcap expeditions, had his own crazy gang, and took absolutely no interest in girls."

One evening in the Berghof, Hitler fell to reminiscing and told how he had been severely punished on more than one occasion because during religious instruction he was caught playing with a mirror, reflecting the sun's rays on the trees and benches in the courtyard. Eva's sister, Ilse Braun found this detail strikingly revealing and significant —Hitler, still a child, toying with the sun, waiting for the day when he could really juggle with the universe. . . .

In 1903, Alois Hitler succumbed to a fit of apoplexy while drinking his usual liter of beer in a tavern at ten in the morning. At this time the eldest son Alois emigrated to France, where he worked in a café in the rue des Pyramides, in Paris, while the other daughter Angela married the tax collector Raubal, leaving Adi alone with his mother and the semi-imbecile little girl, Paula.

At the time of puberty, Adolf was a rather unsociable boy, brusque in his manners and rebellious in his speech, but attractive to women. He was pale and gleamy-eyed. "Your friend has a burning look," the mother of his close friend Gustl was one day to say of him. He was a visionary, ambitious and impatient of his surroundings.

His mother had sold the Leonding house and had come to live in Linz. She had no financial problems, her husband having left her a pretty inheritance on top of her pension; but she wanted to live near her daughter Angela as well as enable Adolf to attend the *Realschule,* or secondary school, without undue traveling. And so shortly after his confirmation on May 22, 1904 (it was a fine celebration and young Adolf behaved exemplarily in church), he made the acquaintance of Gustav Kubizek, otherwise known as Gustl, who was later to be described in a letter as "his only childhood friend."

Kubizek's evidence is the only one of an intimate nature that remains from this period, and it would have been valuable had it been sincere. Unfortunately, for a variety of reasons, Kubizek allowed his imagination free play and concocted a fictitious account which has been proved to have no connection with reality. One is even led to doubt Hitler's statement concerning this best friend. Hitler was often guilty of intentional exaggeration, and in this instance it was politic for a man who had been accused of inhumanity to have "a childhood friend."

Gustl Kubizek was nine months older than Hitler. His father was an upholsterer but, although he also worked in the shop, his real interest was music. He had met Adolf at the theater, at a time when Hitler was still attending the school in Steyr, for he had been forced to enter another institution outside Linz in order to get his class promotion. The two young men shared the same passion for the theater; they went there almost every evening. Hitler was drawing a lot and talked of becoming a great architect someday; he had already planned the reconstruction of Linz. Their conversations consisted of endless discussions of Wagner and his works.

A seat at the opera, even in the top balcony—and Hitler refused to go anywhere more modest than the first balcony or mezzanine—is an expensive item, especially for an unemployed adolescent. Hitler cannot have had much money left for running after girls, and the rumor that he had a mistress in Linz is unfounded. The girls looked at him, to be sure, for he already had a certain exciting aura, a detached way of visually undressing a woman. He cut a striking figure, when, with his check suit, his broad-brimmed black felt hat pulled down over his eyes and a

small cane with a black ivory knob in his hand, he saun-
tered down the main street of Linz with Gustl.

One evening many years later, in the Berlin bunker,
Hitler described how he had had an affair with a peasant
girl in Leonding. She was in the cow shed milking the
cows; there was a sudden noise; they knocked over the
lantern, and it was only by a miracle that they did not set
fire to the place.

Later, on another of his promenades, young Hitler was
suddenly captivated by a tall, blond girl, with her hair
knotted on the nape of her neck, a silk dress, and a red
parasol. After this, Hitler walked every evening with Gustl
in the hope of again meeting this girl, who was called Stephanie. He would never have the chance to speak to her,
but she was his ideal, his madonna; for her he would
make a name for himself, be a second Michelangelo; for
her he would build a magnificent villa; for her he would
go to war, become Pope, millionaire, minister. All this for
Stephanie Jansten, a young girl of seventeen who lived in
Urfahr.

Adolf realized that he was not so elegant as the young
lieutenants who surrounded Stephanie. "I am only Adi; a
nobody . . . but one day. . . ." He wrote poems for her.
He even thought of kidnapping her—and killing her and
himself.

Stephanie, who at that time was seventeen—all the
women Hitler was to love would be seventeen—and had
just come back from a Swiss finishing school in Geneva,
did not give too much importance to this strange young
man. Only much later, when she had married a lieutenant
of the Linz regiment, she confided that she vaguely remembered a young harum-scarum who gazed at her ardently. One day she had received a letter from a young
man announcing that he was going to study at the Art
Academy in Vienna and asking her to wait for him, for he
intended to come back and marry her. Stephanie's mother
read the letter and tore it up.

In May of 1906, Hitler set off for Vienna, no doubt
with the idea of making Stephanie notice his absence. Several years before he had intended to enlist as a volunteer
to defend the Boers in the Transvaal. It is interesting to
think that he might well have met Winston Churchill there
and have studied on the spot the system of concentration

camps, which the English used in the Boer War but which Hitler carried to such perfection.

On his return, he prepared his mother for an important decision: He intended to study at the Academy in Vienna and become an architect. Klara was very ill with cancer of the breast and had to be operated on in Linz (Hitler was to be haunted all his life by the fear of cancer and was constantly undergoing medical examinations). She left the Linz house at 9 Humboldstrasse and moved to Urfahr, where Stephanie lived, to 9 Blutenstrasse. In September, 1907, Hitler, then aged eighteen, rented a room for ten crowns a month from Maria Zakreys, a Polish lady who lived at 29 Stumpergasse in Vienna.

The Vienna Academy refused Hitler admission. This setback, which upset his whole life and made of him a have-not, a rabid social rebel, an outcast and an enemy of his own country, was kept secret from his mother. It would have broken her heart. Klara died of cancer on December 21, 1907, and Hitler returned posthaste from Vienna. His sister Angela had come to attend the funeral ceremony, but did not take part in the procession. She was pregnant. A few weeks later she gave birth to a daughter. This was Geli, the Geli who went to live and to die in Hitler's apartment on the Prinzregentenplatz in Munich.

Hitler returned to his idling in Vienna. His friend Kubizek, who was studying music at the Conservatory, kept him company for a part of the five and a half years of this Viennese stay. They went assiduously to the theater, discussed politics in cafés, went swimming and sometimes skiing. Hitler wrote novels, drew, pontificated, and even composed an unfinished opera, "The Legend of Wieland," which was very involved, very romantic, and very Germanic. Kubizek rarely mentions girls; he admits, however, that Hitler was something of a lady-killer. At the Hofoper, unknown young girls hovered around him like mosquitoes in the Wienerwald. A lodger once tried to seduce him, provoking him with a glimpse of nakedness under her half-open dressing gown. Hitler is said to have blushed. He piloted his friend to the night haunts of the town and showed himself an expert on the social drama of prostitution.

Then Kubizek returned one day from a trip to Linz to find that Hitler had disappeared without leaving an address. The next time he saw him was in 1938 when he,

Kubizek, was among the crowd acclaiming Hitler on his triumphal return to Linz.

This rift in Hitler's relations with "the only childhood friend" is a perplexing one. Having until then lived a life of leisure on a modest income, he had perhaps exhausted his resources and was no longer able to share the rent of the furnished room. But why conceal this state of affairs from his friend, who could certainly have helped him? Why did he never again get in touch with him? Why did Kubizek never try to contact his friend, although he must have been able to follow his activities in the press from 1922 to 1933? It was only when Hitler was appointed chancellor that he wrote him a letter, to which Hitler replied after a long delay of six or seven months. And it was only much later still that Hitler invited his old friend to a performance at the Bayreuth Festival. This was all. Not a single favor, not a single present, not even a personal keepsake, although he never forgot those who had been his companions in hard times. He never even suggested he come to dine at Berchtesgaden, although he liked to invite a stream of guests, even friends of friends.

It must have been a dramatic separation. Kubizek always speaks of Hitler in a particular vein, as though theirs had been a "special friendship." He insists on the fact that women never disrupted their harmony and tells how they used to hold hands. . . . Did he perhaps make advances that Hitler, finally realizing his friend's real intentions, indignantly rejected? It is certain that Hitler's violent aversion for anything connected with homosexuality dates from this period. Hitler was never a homosexual; physically he was absolutely normal, and all the legends on this subject were the invention of his political adversaries.

Another completely unfounded legend is that of Hitler as house painter, unskilled laborer, or among the ranks of the unemployed. It is true that after he had involuntarily ceded his orphan's pension to his sister Paula, his resources were limited. He had to take refuge in an asylum for the homeless and sometimes in 1912 ate in a popular soup kitchen run by charitable nuns. He tried, again unsuccessfully, to gain admission to the Academy. He spent his time mostly in libraries, where his prodigious photographic memory allowed him to assimilate the contents of hundreds of books. Then he found lodging in a *Männerheim* (a men's home), a sort of institution for vagrants where he was able to paint watercolors that a friend then sold for him.

On May 14, 1913, Adolf Hitler left Vienna for Munich, where he earned a scanty living—on an average a thousand marks a year—from his watercolors, which were chiefly urban views. But the girls in Munich were much more accommodating than those in Vienna. They smilingly agreed to pay the bill or buy the tickets.

He was wanted by the Linz police at this time, for he had evaded the Austrian draft and was therefore considered a deserter. Under the threat of extradition, Hitler returned to Linz, where the recruiting board rejected him because of the weakness of his lungs. He returned to Munich and one of his Berlin secretaries affirms that from his association with a woman of rather easy virtue he contracted a venereal disease. Certainly in *Mein Kampf* Hitler devoted a whole chapter to the ravages caused by syphilis. Another rumor, whose only justification lies in the fact that it was told to me by somebody who was in Hitler's circle of intimates, alleges that he was in love with a married woman, an officer's wife, but that she broke off the affair or else the husband had Hitler evicted.

Then came the Sarajevo affair and World War I. Hitler would normally have been mobilizable in Austria-Hungary. Because of this, or out of political enthusiasm or solely as a result of disappointed love, he decided to volunteer in a Bavarian unit.

CHAPTER FOUR

First encounter

Holding the advertisement page of the *Münchner Neueste Nachrichten,* on which certain offers of employment had been carefully boxed in with red ink, Eva Braun stopped in front of 50 Schellingstrasse. Even today few people in Munich realize the historic importance of this street, which has now become too respectable to belong any longer to the bohemian Schwabing district. The young applicant herself, who had left her convent only a few months before, had no inkling that her destiny awaited her in this gray house, whose drabness was relieved only by the leaves of the chestnut tree that by some miracle had grown up in the adjacent garden.

Eva had changed considerably in these few months. True, she was still plump—except for her bosom, which was rather flat for Bavarian tastes—but there was a trace of lipstick on her mouth, a thick coating of powder on her cheeks, and she had discarded her little check coat and schoolgirl's cape. Her braids were no longer hanging down her back as they had when she was waiting for the Munich train at Simbach station; they were now neatly pinned in a flat coil over her ears. A few days later she was to cut them off, thus setting the seal on her emancipation. She was wearing a little brown suit and a beret of the same shade, which, with her youthfulness, gave her a very saucy air. She was not carrying a purse, because she did not possess a brown one that went with her outfit. She always had an obsession for brown and for matching colors. She would rather have gone barefoot than wear a pair of shoes that clashed with her dress.

Her elder sister Ilse was largely responsible for this rapid transformation. The first few days after her return from the convent, Eva watched in wide-eyed astonishment while her sister made up and beautified herself. *"Pfui!"* she exclaimed in disgust. "How can you daub your face like that!" And while she examined Ilse's silk underwear, stroking it with her fingers, she delivered a sermon to her that was probably a word for word repetition of those preached by the nuns in the convent. One day, however, she experimented on the sly in front of the mirror, and then, after their baths, she took her sister's waist and hip measurements. This was when she decided, after much comparison, that it was imperative that she should slim down. Her parents wondered why little Eva had such frequent stomachaches, which prevented her eating during this period.

The girls' room could accommodate only two beds, and so out of sheer logistic necessity, Gretl, the youngest, had been sent prematurely to the convent. This meant that Eva was exclusively under the influence of her older sister. She decided to work for a doctor because Ilse was a receptionist for a Jewish surgeon, Dr. Martin Marx, a position she occupied for eight years until her employer emigrated to the United States, where he still lives, near New York City.

Eva meanwhile found a job with a Dr. Gunther Hoffmann, but she tired of it after a few weeks. She did not like having to sit for long periods in the anteroom in a white nurse's uniform; the patients' questions irritated her, and she could not bear the sight of blood and the other unpleasant aspects of the profession. This did not prevent her in later years from giving herself the airs of a medical expert with Hitler, who took everything in dead earnest.

She looked for another occupation, but her second attempt was even more unfortunate. It involved nonstop typing, and that she hated.

Papa Braun had inherited a tidy sum of money from an aunt, and had put aside a certain amount for his daughters' dowries. He had bought himself a small but solid BMW car, at a time when an auto was still a luxury. It was therefore no longer essential for Eva to try to earn her living, but she persisted in the effort, partly to imitate her sister, but chiefly because she wished to be independent and free to come and go as she pleased. Fritz Braun, who was now a professor, was as strict with his daughters as he was with his pupils. He checked on where they went, what letters and phone calls they received, and he even cut off the electricity in their room after ten o'clock at night. In order to read in bed, his daughters had been obliged to buy a miniature battery lamp that they turned on under the bedclothes.

For all his newly acquired prosperity, Herr Professor Braun had never thought of giving his daughters pocket money. This placed them in an embarrassing situation, as is shown by what was perhaps Eva's first real date. Ilse had found a young man who was prepared to take Eva out dancing. Ilse loved to dance, and she never lacked partners. She would later win the European amateur ballroom dancing championship.

The young man had duly called to fetch Eva, and they had caught a streetcar to the Hotel Regina, where the dance was being held. The door fee was two and a half marks (at the time the mark had a purchasing power equivalent to that of today's dollar), and the organizers had had the idea of making it a ladies' night—the girls were to pay for the tickets. This idea may seem strange to us now, but was quite accepted in those days of full depression. Besides, in Germany, as in the Scandinavian countries and Holland, the girl frequently shares the cost of a meal or an evening's entertainment with her escort.

Eva, however, fresh from Simbach, had not foreseen this eventuality and blushed to the roots of her hair when it transpired that she had not a single pfennig in her pocket. Her companion produced the sum with a painful smile, but Eva was so humiliated that she refused to dance more than once and went home in tears. She resolved to go on working in order to avoid a repetition of this kind of discomfiture.

For this reason, she was now presenting herself, in reply to the advertisement, at the modest house in Schelling-strasse, with its unassuming sign "Heinrich Hoffmann, art photographer." She knew nothing about Hoffmann's connections with the National Socialist Party, which was only one of a multitude of factions harassing the Weimar Republic. A little farther down the street was the printing office of the *Völkischer Beobachter,* the party's official organ. It was natural that an Italian restaurant in this street, with the hybrid title "Osteria Bavaria," should be frequented by the paper's staff members, of which the most famous was Adolf Hitler.

The Hoffmann firm was at that time insignificant. The

boss's affiliations with Hitler and the party made him a
world celebrity and a multimillionaire only after their rise
to power. The country was then in the full throes of economic recession, and photography was an obscure and un-
profitable profession, for it was not until the next decade
that the illustrated press underwent such tremendous ex-
pansion. Yet the jovial, fat, ever-smiling Hoffmann, who
liked to eat and still more to drink, was not a mere nobody. Photography was in his family; he himself had
started as a photographer at the Bavarian court in 1897 and
had made successful portraits of the Kaiser, King Edward
VII of England, and Caruso, not to mention an international incident that one of his photos of the German emperor sparked off at the time.* Along with the tens of
thousands of photographs of Hitler that offered the world
a flamboyant image of the dictator, Hoffmann's other
great feat was that of photographing the childish joy of
Joseph Stalin on the occasion of the signing of the Ger-
man-Soviet pact that made the Soviet leader Hitler's colleague and accomplice.

Hoffmann met Hitler two years after having joined the
Nazi party (with a membership card numbered 427),
when a press service asked him for a photo of the future
dictator. Hitler behaved like Greta Garbo in those days,
refusing to be photographed in the belief that such mystery made him still more interesting. At first Hoffmann did
not succeed in convincing him otherwise, but they became
friends. Hoffmann proved to be an amusing and convivial
character, whom Eva Braun, not entirely jokingly, later
dubbed "the mad drunkard of the Third Reich." He
offered Hitler the possibility of relaxing in a bourgeois
household, far from his daily worries. Moreover, as will
become apparent, Hitler hated to be on terms of intimate
friendship with his political partners. Hoffmann, who always contrived to keep aloof from official activities, ful-
filled a well-defined function, that of discreet confidant.
Everybody around Hitler, even his dog or his mistress, was
there to render some specific service.

After the Nazi debacle, Hoffmann was to complain bitterly of the treatment meted out to him by the Allies and
protested that he was the victim of his friendship. Yet

---

* The photograph was of Wilhelm II when he was insultingly or-
dering about a British general.

thanks to his photos of Hitler, of party members and later of the front, of which he had the monopoly, he managed to amass millions and would have pocketed much more had Martin Bormann not been "breathing down his neck." The ludicrous thing is that after the war he persuaded the Americans to return to him a part of his ill-gotten capital, his photograph collections. The role that he played in Hitler's fabulous rise to power can be considered fundamental. It was he who succeeded in introducing photography as the prime asset in a German political campaign. Thanks to him, Hitler, who had been unknown in 1923, became a hero, a father, a husband, and perhaps even a God to every man and woman in Germany. Hoffmann was one of the chief fabricators of this image of the Führer. The methods he used were known to some extent in America and certainly in Fascist Italy but were completely new in the Reich. For instance, even today in Eastern and Western Germany, and also in Switzerland, the most reputable daily papers rarely publish photographs, and hardly ever on the front page. Hoffmann changed this during the Nazi era.

This decisive technical contribution, as well as the moral comfort that Hitler derived from Hoffmann's company and friendship, justifies the assertion that he played a major role in the history of the Third Reich, all the more so because this irreverent photographer, who was too materialistic to have any ideals, too cunning to believe in promises, too astute not to guess what was going on behind the scenes, too experienced to let himself be bamboozled, had hitched his chariot to Hitler's star simply for love of lucre.

This curious figure engaged Eva Braun almost on the spot for a mere pittance. Hoffmann gave preference to very young girls because in this way he could exploit them economically, the more so since unemployment was rife in Germany at the time. Eva's official title was bookkeeper, a position for which her convent diploma qualified her, but Hoffmann's daughter, no doubt out of jealousy, claims that her only function was to sell prints of their pictures. In reality she was a girl Friday in the modest Hoffmann firm. She sold films, copied out the accounts, dealt with the bills, and worked in the darkroom, an occupation for which she had developed a liking.

Heinrich Hoffmann did not serve Hitler solely in his capacity as cameraman. He also knew his tastes in women

—"pretty, young, innocent girls"—and was careful to choose employees who answered these specifications. He had already tried to contrive a union between his unusual politician friend and his daughter Henriette, who certainly possessed at least two of the qualities required—the first two. She was born on February 3, 1912, just three days before Eva Braun, and was attractive, if rather skinny. Hitler liked them on the plump side. Henriette's mother had started out as a cabaret singer, at least according to data supplied by the Hoffmanns. So Henny, as she was called, had grown up in an "artistic" atmosphere. She acted as a model for her father and had even starred in one or two curious films, which have since fallen into oblivion. In her reminiscences, she alludes to a rather indecorous incident with Hitler:

"He often came to our house for dinner. He gave himself great airs with his dark leather coat, his whip, and his Mercedes, whose driver waited for him in front of the door.

"After dinner, Hitler—at that time he was still Herr Hitler to us—sat down at the piano and played some Wagner followed by some Verdi. 'Do you recognize the leitmotiv of the *Forza del Destino?*' He addressed me as *du,* for I was only seventeen and he was over forty. Then he took his leave and my father accompanied him. I was left alone in the house. The doorbell rang. It was Hitler again. 'I forgot my whip.' This whip was Hitler's fetish. He took it and planted himself on the red carpet of the anteroom, his broad-brimmed felt hat in one hand and his whip in the other. Finally, to my great surprise, he asked me with a very serious air: 'Will you kiss me?' I was chiefly struck by the fact that he had said *Sie* to me this time—the first time in our acquaintance. Yet as he put his face down to mine, I said No. He turned round and went out, closing the door behind him. When my father returned to the house, I told him of the incident. He laughed in my face and declared, 'You're imagining things, you silly goose.' "

It is difficult to guess what really happened. Was Hoffmann right in his suspicion that the whole thing was just the fanciful imagining of a young girl, who later tried to prove to the world that, had she so wished, she could have taken precedence over "the little salesgirl employed by my father for a miserable salary." Or was the affair a much more serious one, with the granting of the kiss and more besides, and did Hitler, a fickle lover, not find Henny to his taste?

Hoffmann nevertheless found an excellent match for his daughter—thanks to Hitler. She married Baldur von Schirach, a young man who walked off the boat from America one fine morning, whistling "Yankee Doodle," and who made the fastidious Henny vicereine of Austria. When she was not sleeping in the bed of the Hapsburgs or wandering in the gardens of Prince Eugene or living on the estate her husband had seized from the Rothschild family, she could take the air in her own castle. For Baldur von Schirach was an aristocrat and a millionaire by birth. His mother was an American by the name of Emma Middleton Lynah-Tillou, and he inherited from his maternal grandmother, well after Nuremberg, a large batch of shares that were high on the Wall Street market. The family's political tendencies are illustrated by the fact that the mother, who was a New Yorker by birth, went to live in Germany during the war. She was burned to death there in 1944 when a plane piloted by a compatriot, an American Air Force pilot, crashed in flames on her house in Wiesbaden.

Baldur von Schirach has written at least one book to explain and justify his role during the war. Yet I must say here that I have vivid memories of Baldur von Schirach's visit to the Mauthausen camp in 1944, when I was interned there. Mauthausen was known as "the murder house," and conditions there were probably more cruel and shameful than in any other camp within the confines of the Third Reich. The poet Baldur von Schirach cannot have been insensible to this Dantesque spectacle. Prison administration in Austrian territory was also far harsher, far more inexorable than in Germany proper. Baldur von Schirach, as viceroy of Austria, prefect and party *Gauleiter,* vested with full powers equivalent to those of the Führer, must have known what was going on in his prisons. He can write books until the end of time to prove the contrary, but he will never succeed in convincing me of his innocence.

Eva Braun did not meet Hitler during the first three weeks of her job. She was a complete ignoramus where politics were concerned, for this subject had never formed part of the convent curriculum, and she preferred to discuss fashions and films with her friends. She paid not the slightest attention to various grotesque characters who

came to the studio to have their photographs taken by the
boss. There was that stiff individual with his tax collector's
pince-nez who said he was a rabbit breeder and whose
name was Heinrich Himmler; or the gray-haired Baltic
gentleman with a voluminous manuscript under his arm
who announced himself as Rosenberg; or the agricultural-
ist with muddy boots, Martin Bormann. Another client,
Rudolf Hess, regularly went to buy a long-life elixir from
the drugstore opposite, while Julius Streicher frightened
the girls with a horrible wax figurine of a rabbi that he
wore around his neck on a string.

Then one Friday evening early in October, Adolf Hitler
appeared on the scene. Here is the account of this first
meeting that Eva Braun gave not long after to her sister:

"I had stayed on after closing time to classify some papers and had climbed up a ladder to reach the files that
were kept on the top shelves of the cupboard. At that moment the boss came in accompanied by a man of a certain
age, with a funny moustache, a light-colored English-style
overcoat and a big felt hat in his hand. They both sat
down on the other side of the room, opposite me. I tried
to squint in their direction without appearing to turn
round and sensed that this character was looking at my
legs. That very day I had shortened my skirt and I felt
slightly embarrassed because I wasn't sure I'd got the hem
even. As you know, I don't like to ask Mother to help me.

"Hoffmann introduced us when I had climbed down.
'Herr Wolf. Our good little Fräulein Eva.' (Hitler always
used the pseudonym Wolf in public.)

"Then: 'Be a good girl, Fräulein Braun, go and fetch us
some beer and sausages from the tavern on the corner.'"

Eva Braun, still imbued with conventional simplicity,
did not realize that this was simply a pretext. Hoffmann
had noticed that Hitler's attention was riveted on the girl,
for he was always fascinated by a pretty pair of legs, and
the round face that went with this pair was distinctly to
his taste. Probably Hoffmann, whose language was often
Rabelaisian, had informed him of the new employee's vir-
ginal state. The business of the sausages and beer was pure
flummery. Hitler, usually a vegetarian, hardly ever touched
a sausage, and he was only a very occasional beer drinker.
Hoffmann simply wanted to get Eva to sit down with them
at the table and so create a more intimate atmosphere, for
at that time class consciousness was still strong, and it was

unusual for the boss and his client to chat with the youngest and newest employee.

"I was starving. I gobbled my sausage and had a sip of beer for politeness' sake. The elderly gentleman was paying me compliments. We talked about music and a play at the Staatstheater, as I remember, with him devouring me with his eyes all the time. Then, as it was getting late, I rushed off. I refused his offer of a lift in his Mercedes. Just think what Papa's reaction would have been! . . . But before I left, Hoffmann pulled me aside and asked me, 'Haven't you guessed who that gentleman is; don't you ever look at our photos?' I answered No, mystified. 'It's Hitler! Adolf Hitler!' he said. 'Oh?' I replied."

Eva Braun hurried home. Pleading an upset stomach, she refused her supper. She had already started her diet, and a sausage or two and a glass of beer were enough for that evening. She merely tasted her chocolate pudding and drank some tea. Only then, interrupting the family conversation, did she ask her father point-blank, "*Vati*, who is that guy, a certain Adolf Hitler?" Her father replied without the slightest hesitation and with a scornful grimace: "Hitler? He's a jack-of-all-trades, an imbecile who thinks himself omniscient and who wants to reform the world. . . ."

It was another two years before the name of Adolf Hitler was mentioned again at the Braun table.

CHAPTER FIVE

"I have a 'chère amie' in Munich . . ."

The day after her chance meeting with Herr Hitler, Eva Braun broke her usual routine and did not go home for lunch. Instead, she took advantage of the break to examine the photograph collection (at that time there was already an enormous mass of pictures of the future dictator in Hoffmann's drawers) and thereby formed a more personal image of the man. The Führer in uniform, surrounded by his "bravos," acclaimed by hundreds of women strewing his path with flowers, surrounded by many-colored banners, this was admittedly a very different image from that of the poorly attired individual of the day before. In Bavaria at this time, a uniform and boots held an irresistible fascination for a woman. It is therefore possible that Eva began to be attracted to this man, although not to the point of mentioning him again to her sister.

The small moustache, the plastered lock of hair on the forehead, the eyes like billiard balls, and the gallows-bird look, how is it conceivable that the Chaplinesque grotesqueness of such a face was not apparent to a girl who lacked neither good taste nor artistic ability? This is a question for the psychiatrists. Was not Chaplin himself, whom Hitler resembled, the great seducer of Hollywood? Hitler's physique must also be compared to that of the other men of his age and milieu. The great majority of Bavarians of over forty, with their beer drinkers' paunches, their bald pates, and their dragoon moustaches, could not have stood such comparison well.

"Hitler? He thinks he imbibed wisdom with his mother's milk. I cross to the other side when I meet him in the street," Papa Braun had said of him at the table. But what teen-age girl will accept such a paternal verdict? Fritz Braun's intransigence only served to arouse Eva's spirit of contradiction. She began to sound out Hoffmann and her working companions, and evidently they revealed to her a quite different aspect of the National Socialist movement and of its leader. Eva was too inexperienced in politics to realize that she was surrounded by fanatics. All her life she was to remain aloof from dogmas and doctrines, forbidding political discussions in her presence (an interdiction with which even Hitler had to comply), and she never became a member of the Nazi party. Nevertheless she was convinced that Hitler was an extremely important man, a great patriot and idealist, and that he was going to "save Germany." It must be said in all objectivity that this last consideration bore little weight for Eva, who was interested basically in the fact that he was going to "save Eva Braun."

At the end of 1929, the Nazi party, after passing through an extremely difficult period, was in a state of resurgence and was gaining the ascendancy that was to lead to its conquest of the Wilhelmstrasse. Some of Hitler's prophecies were beginning to command very serious attention, for he had announced an economic catastrophe, and the Wall Street crash had justified his predictions. The press and radio spoke of this man with increasing frequency, often with admiration, and just as often with apprehension or hostility, but always placing him in the forefront of current affairs. Thus Eva realized that a few months after leaving the convent, she, little Eva, had accomplished the feat of catching the fancy of a "celebrity."

Hitler returned to Hoffmann's studio only on rare occasions; these were the revolutionary years for the Nazi party, and he was constantly on the move. But whenever he came, he asked for "Fräulein Eva Braun; she amuses me." He kissed her hand, bowed to her like an archduke at the Court of Vienna, complimented her on the freshness of her complexion, and before long was calling her "my lovely siren from Hoffmann's." He brought her flowers, sometimes sweets, and Eva religiously kept the first yellow orchid, of which there are still a few dry, crumbling petals in her photograph album. Near this flower is a picture of Hitler in uniform, with a simple signature and the date 1929. This document, Hilter's first gift to Eva (like all kings, presidents, and film stars he felt his autographed portrait was worth a fortune), offers proof of the still quite superficial nature of their relations at this time. Nobody at Hoffmann's attached any great importance to this fancy, for after all Hitler had always shown himself quite gallant with all the girls of the establishment and had freely distributed photos, flowers, and hand kisses.

Moreover, after this Christmas of 1929, his visits to 50 Schellingstrasse grew even rarer. This was because another figure had entered his life, Geli Raubal, now installed with him in the comfortable apartment he had recently rented and which he was to buy a few years later. Geli's presence explains his reluctance to pursue his nocturnal escapades, since he now had a kind of home where he could pass his evenings pleasantly. Besides, Geli often accompanied him to his favorite cafés and restaurants, and she would hardly have brooked the presence of another girl at her table. For some unknown reason—possibly feminine instinct or contempt for the dubious role played by Hoffmann—she always obstinately refused to set foot in the shop. The result was that Geli Raubal and Eva Braun never met.

In 1930, Adolf Hitler was still for Eva Braun merely an older man who paid her sporadic and superficial court. She went dancing, often in the company of Henriette Hoffmann, who had become her girl friend, went out with other men, or ventured to bathe in daring costumes that might have shocked the good sisters of Simbach. She spent her modest salary on clothes and trinkets and devoted hours to her makeup. "When she was expecting a visit from Hitler," Henny Hoffmann relates, "Eva would stuff her brassiere with handkerchiefs in order to give her breasts the fullness they lacked and which seemed to appeal to Hitler. . . ."

She was still a "shopgirl," but she sometimes posed for publicity photographs and assumed vampish attitudes. She adored dressing up. Once, at a small party to which her sister and mother had been invited, a Negro singer started to imitate the voice and mannerisms of Al Jolson to the tune of "Sonny Boy." To the mother's great surprise, the Negro came up to her table and kissed her: It was Eva. The episode deserves to be mentioned, for later Adolf Hitler asked Eva for this photograph of herself disguised as a Jew impersonating a Negro. He, the anti-Semite racist, did not find the incident shocking; on the contrary, he burst out laughing every time Eva mentioned it.

Dancing had become one of Eva's passions, but she was

even more keenly interested in gymnastics. She had joined a national athletic association and before long was taking part in competitions. She excelled on the parallel bars and always retained the habit of doing setting-up exercises, this being the best way of keeping her figure.

It was only at the end of 1930 that Hitler's interest in "the little siren Eva" revived. He would say, "May I take the liberty, *gnädiges Fräulein,* of inviting you to the opera this evening?" Or: "I don't like eating alone; I should so much like to be seen at the Osteria this evening with a pretty woman." They would go to the opera accompanied by Brueckner and sometimes by one or two other body-guards of Hitler. There are witnesses who affirm that at table Hitler held Eva's hand in his and stroked it tenderly. But most of the time it seemed like a father-daughter relationship. He meticulously had her brought home before midnight and banned all off-color talk in her presence.

As far as possible they avoided being seen in public and preferred to go clandestinely to see films, their favorite cinema being the Schauburg in the Schwabing district. Otherwise they drank tea in a discreet corner of the Carlton Café, which was less frequented than the others by the Nazi clique. He invited her out once or twice on picnics —Hitler liked such excursions—but they never rode together in the same car. Nevertheless these Sunday outings in a luxurious Mercedes with a chauffeur and an orderly greatly impressed Eva.

Secrecy was the essential feature of their meetings. Hitler was extremely vulnerable in his capacity as a revolutionary who wished to reform the world and who was the avowed champion of domestic morality. Even his partisans, including Göring and Goebbels, must not suspect that this fair, chubby young girl was anything more than one of the innumerable feminine admirers who were constantly swarming around him. He rarely rang her up, sent her only insignificant messages, and the only witnesses of his meetings were Hoffmann, who was obliging and discreet, and his aides-de-camp, who were and have remained absolutely mute. Eva herself did not wish her escapades to be divulged. Had her father known that she was going out with a man twenty-three years her senior, he would probably have had her sequestered for good in a convent.

Then, above all, there was Geli. Hitler dreaded his niece's wrath even more than Eva feared her father's. The

fact that Hitler's early flirtation with Eva Braun was si-
multaneous with the passion for Geli Raubal attributed to
him by his entourage tends on the one hand to cast doubt
on the absolute nature of this passion and also to invali-
date the historians' conclusions on the character and consequences of this uncle-niece relationship. If there was any
battle between Geli and Eva for Adolf Hitler's affections,
the chronology of events shows that it was Eva Braun who
emerged triumphant.

She had once declared to some friends, "Hitler says he's
a hardened bachelor, but he has his Achilles' heel, and
you'll see, he'll marry me." Nobody took this boast seriously.

He had his own method of prevaricating with women.
First he would affirm that a politician was in an exceptional position. "I have to travel all the time, how can I
allow myself the luxury of a home? And my life is constantly in danger." Then he would continue with the quib-
ble: "Women have a disastrous influence in politics. Look
at Napoleon. And the dancer Lola Montez who was the
ruin of King Ludwig I of Bavaria. Without her he would
have been an excellent monarch. And look at that mad-
woman Mme. Chiang Kai-shek who is filled with hatred
to the point of provoking Japan and so causing her country's downfall."

At first, after each political conversation, Eva ran to
consult encyclopedias and other reference books, but she
soon acquired the habit of listening and forgetting. Hitler
admired her discreet silence, which he interpreted as sub-
mission and approbation. And though she did not like
opera, she docilely attended performances of Wagner's
works with Hitler and assured him that she found them
marvelous.

She listened quietly when Hitler discussed Grillparzer
and praised Shakespeare, spoke for hours and with great
seriousness about the possible existence of sea serpents, or
promised that when he came to power he would encourage the production of space rockets. He even predicted
that, thanks to him, one day man would reach the moon.

Eva tried to read serious books in order to keep up with
her companion. "But studying bored her terribly," affirms
Mitzi Joisten, one of her friends who later became the
daughter-in-law of General Kolle. She preferred the novels
of Pearl Buck, Kathrin Holland and Margaret Mitchell,

and cinema and fashion magazines. (Hitler for his part no longer read fiction.)

"We Braun girls were not very communicative when it came to the details of our private lives," Eva's sister Ilse recalls. "Even among ourselves, in the sanctum of our bedroom, we rarely spoke about our relations with men. There was a very strong barrier of puritanism, perhaps because of our convent education, perhaps because of the Victorian ideas of our parents. I knew that Eva sometimes went out with Hitler, but I knew nothing about the state of her feelings."

Besides, a certain antagonism was beginning to appear between Eva and her older sister, an antagonism that was to endure until the end. To be sure Eva never ceased to respect Ilse, to look after her, and to preserve the solid and rigorous ties of affection that bound the Braun clan, but she no longer wished to let herself be dominated by her big sister and continued to bicker with her increasingly. Gretl, the youngest sister, was still in the convent, and so Eva had nobody else in the house in whom she could really confide.

Eva and Ilse were constantly squabbling over the political situation. Their father refused to be involved, but Eva and her mother had by now become champions of National Socialism, whereas Ilse obstinately defended the opposite point of view. She was more or less in love with her Jewish laryngologist, Dr. Marx, and came home every evening imbued with the countertheses of her own mentor. Thus a sort of debate by intermediary developed every night between the spokeswoman for the famous Hitler and that for the obscure doctor.

Was it her sister's attachment to this older man that perhaps encouraged Eva to take an interest in another comparatively elderly gentleman? She teased Ilse but also imitated her in everything. The Braun girls certainly had a "father complex"; Ilse married twice, each time a man much older than she, and Gretl was to show the same taste for maturity. Eva's best friend has assured me that Eva was terrified of her father, and that for her, life at home was very unhappy.

In addition, Eva had unshakable faith in the prediction of a fortune-teller who had told her that one day the whole world would talk about her and her great love. Did she see in Hitler the man of her destiny? We must not forget the force of the magnetism Hitler possessed, which exercised an irresistible influence over many women. From 1931 on, few young German girls would have dared, wished, or wanted to say No to Adolf Hitler.

However, in all probability, the decisive factor that transformed Eva Braun's infatuation into sincere love was the suicide of Geli Raubal. The prolonged absence of Hitler, who went into sentimental mourning for his niece, the revelation that there had been another woman in his life, a woman who because of him had decided to kill herself, the reports that reached Eva indirectly about her friend's protracted state of nervous depression, all this must have helped to create in the young girl a profound impression. At this point, evidently, she began to love this man who she felt was alone, suffering, and who was therefore capable in her eyes of the noblest emotions. She was now sure that he was not the lout that her sister and her father affirmed him to be.

She saw Hitler again early in 1932. In order to distract his mourning friend, Hoffmann had seen fit to arrange a number of intimate dinners to which he invited Eva Braun. She listened to Hitler expatiating on his grief and lamenting that "we are all responsible for the death of my dear Geli," and she decided the time had come for her to replace this marvelous Geli. Once, speaking to her sister, she commented, "Geli's death was a real catastrophe, she must have been an exceptional woman." Yet gradually, with tact and ingenuity, she began to replace Geli in Hitler's affection.

Eva Braun was still a virgin. She was not a girl to give herself to one man while going with another. It is not easy to determine the exact date of the seduction, but it is reasonably certain that it took place after Geli's death. Hitler would never have dared to bring another girl into his house while his niece was still there. The Haus Wachenfeld at Berchtesgaden (it was only later that the house was enlarged into what was to become the Berghof) was hardly suitable either: His sister Angela was there most of the time; and besides, it would have been difficult for Eva to stay late and then catch a train back to Munich. Hitler had not yet built the autobahns, and the car journey from Berchtesgaden to Munich was prohibitively long. Eva would never have dared to absent herself a whole night. Hitler for his part would never have dreamed of taking the risk of seeing her in a hotel room, thereby exposing himself to possible blackmail.

It was therefore only after Geli's suicide that Eva came to visit Hitler in his apartment at 16 Prinzregentenplatz. "Eva Braun was there often when Hitler was in Munich. She was always running after him, insisting on being alone with him. She was a most demanding woman," Annie Winter, Hitler's housekeeper, assured me.

I have already said that Annie Winter's judgments about people tend to be unreliable, but her factual memories make it possible to establish that Eva Braun became Hitler's mistress in the first months of 1932. Dictators and presidents, and for that matter most ordinary citizens, do not make a public spectacle of their lovemaking, and it is therefore evident that any detail about the event can only be the product of the highest fantasy. Eva herself, as I have already said, was extremely reticent about such subjects and what girl is willing to talk publicly about her first night of love? But there is an enigmatic remark she later made to her best friend. They were looking at the photographs of the Munich conference, which showed Chamberlain, Daladier, and Mussolini sitting together on the big central sofa of the living room in Hitler's private apartment at 16 Prinzregentenplatz. It was a red plush sofa, quite long, with a lace-covered back. Eva, with a roguish wink, allegedly said to her friend Herta, "If Chamberlain only knew the history of that sofa. . . ."

It is probable that it was not the case of a girl of twenty being seduced by a man of forty-three, but rather it was Eva Braun who, to subjugate him, had decided to give herself to Adolf Hitler. Hitler, though the contrary has been erroneously claimed, did not lack sexual initiative. He could long before have overcome any resistance she might have shown, but, despite his Napoleonic airs, he remained incorrigibly bourgeois and he did not want the responsibility of corrupting such an innocent girl. She gave herself to him because this was the only proof of love that she could offer him. It is doubtful that she asked anything in return. A woman in love does not bargain. She must, however, have believed that the tender words Hitler said to her were just as sincere as hers.

Eva's photograph albums bearing the date 1932 at first contain the usual amateur snapshots of family gatherings, outdoor parties, childhood friends. Then, on turning the pages, one suddenly sees nothing but photographs of Hitler, the first pictures that Eva took of her lover. There is also a photo of Eva shaking Hitler's hand, taken at Hoffmann's, with Eva's comment underneath: "If people realized *how well* he knows me!" Then there is the first snapshot of Eva taken at the Obersalzberg, which makes it possible to place this first visit in the early spring of 1932.

But her lover remained fickle. For him Eva was still perhaps only a *Liebelei,* a flirt, and in any case he was too taken up with politics. He no longer had time to come to Munich, and he wanted to avoid hanging a millstone around his neck. He merely sent Eva brief messages that became more and more infrequent. Henriette Hoffmann, who had meanwhile realized that Eva Braun had succeeded where she had failed, took a malicious pleasure in showing her photographs of Hitler taken in Berlin, Hamburg, Weimar, and other places in which he was always pictured in the company of pretty women. Ilse Braun suspects that a certain number of letters or communications from Hitler to her sister were diverted as a result of personal or party intrigues. Hitler's chief aide at this time, Wilhelm Brueckner, who was the intermediary between the couple, was a vulgar character who ill concealed his hostility toward Eva. This Brueckner was subsequently compromised in a curious scandal. He had been unfaithful to his wife, and when she heard that he had a mistress, she tried to kill herself. Brueckner then married his mistress, who was the daughter of Quandt, Frau Goebbels' first husband. Hitler, enraged by all this, considered dismissing Brueckner, but finally merely refused his second wife access to Berchtesgaden.

Eva, weary of waiting for Hitler's return or for the slightest sign from him (possibly she thought she was pregnant), decided on the irreparable. A little after midnight, on the first of November, All Saints' Day, 1932, only a little more than a year after the suicide of Hitler's beloved niece, Eva in her turn aimed a pistol at her heart and fired.

She was alone in the house that evening. Her parents were placing flowers in the family vault in Geijelhoering (Oberpfalz), one of her sisters was still in the convent, and the other on night duty at her doctor's. Because her parents' bedroom was more comfortable, Eva spent the night there in the absence of her father and mother.

Ilse Braun recalls returning home: "My sister was lying on the right side of the bed, but she had regained consciousness. There was blood everywhere, on the sheets with embroidered hems, on the pink cushion—I still remember the color—and on the floor in little pools. Eva, like Geli, had tried to shoot herself in the heart but had aimed very badly! The bullet had lodged just near the neck artery, and the doctor had no difficulty in extracting it. Eva had taken my father's 6.35 mm. caliber pistol, which he normally kept in the drawer of the bedside table beside him."

Ilse remembers a curious detail. "It was cold that night, and in my parents' absence the house was unheated. A glass of water on the bedside table was broken and there were pieces of glass, some of them bloodstained, on the cushion. We thought that another bullet had smashed the glass and, on discovering that the pistol still contained five other bullets, we started wondering if, in the confusion of the moment, Eva had not been attacked and had perhaps fired in self-defense. Finally I realized that the cold had frozen the water in the glass, which had been shattered by the forming of the ice."

Eva had telephoned to the doctor herself, and so must have had enough strength to get up from the bed. But she had not had recourse to Dr. Marx, at whose house her sister was and whose discretion she could trust. Instead, she telephoned Dr. Plate, Hoffmann's brother-in-law. No doubt she wanted Hitler to be informed as soon as possible of her suicide or attempted suicide. It was unlikely that her family would connect her rash action with Hitler and even less likely that they would want to get in touch with him if they did realize the connection.

Hitler, who was in Munich and who had received an explanatory farewell letter from Eva, hastened to the private clinic next morning, a bunch of flowers in his hand. He requested that the incident be kept secret and inquired from the doctor whether the young girl had really wanted to kill herself. Since Geli's tragic end, he took suicide attempts seriously, and he was visibly shocked.

"She aimed at her heart and we saved her just in time," the doctor assured him dramatically.

"She did it for love of me. Now I must look after her; it

mustn't happen again," Hitler is supposed to have confided
to Hoffmann. He was obviously flattered by this great
proof of love—he who was always so immensely skeptical
about women, those heartless creatures who had humiliated him so often when he was a penniless painter and
who now wanted to marry the position and not the man.
Eva had persuaded him by her gesture that this was not so
in her case. He had already noticed her disinterestedness
on several occasions: she had never asked the slightest
favor of him, insisted on paying for her taxis herself, and
sent him a modest present whenever she received one
from him. He also admired her discretion, which he considered an essential quality in a woman. She no longer
spoke of their relations to anybody, never retailed conversations, and Hitler appreciated the fact that she had telephoned Hoffmann's brother-in-law rather than her sister
Ilse and the Jewish doctor. This choice he interpreted as
the laudable desire to avoid a scandal. Dr. Marx might
well have gossiped and exploited the incident. Then Eva
was so young; she had offered him the youth that he, Hitler, had never really known.

Eva stayed only a few days in the clinic; she managed
to convince her parents, who were perhaps only too glad
to be convinced, that she had merely wanted to examine
the pistol in the drawer and that the shot had gone off by
itself. The wound healed, leaving almost no trace of a scar.

In this way the liaison between Adolf Hitler and Eva
Braun acquired a permanent nature. Fritz Wiedemann, the
officer under whom Hitler served in the First World War,
remembers that at this time he asked Hitler if he did not
find a bachelor existence too hard. "It has its points," Hitler blithely replied, then, lapsing into students' slang, "and
for the payoff, I have a *chère amie* in Munich. . . ."

CHAPTER SIX

Hitler and women

Two suicide attempts within 14 months. Two women in their first youth who wished to kill themselves for this man or because of this man. And these were not the only ones so deeply affected by Hitler. The famous surgeon Prof. Ferdinand Sauerbruch described how some of his women patients invoked Hitler's name before submitting to an operation. I have heard that mothers breathed "Heil Hitler" immediately after giving birth and insisted that the baby be shown a portrait of the Führer. Other women are said to have murmured "Heil Hitler" at the peak of sexual satisfaction, and this I can well believe. Did not Balzac tell of the wife who used to cross herself before yielding to her husband's embraces? In my student days, I knew a girl who used to hide a photograph of Hitler under the sheets while she made love, and I remember another who had a swastika tattooed on her navel.

Hitler's chauffeur Maurice told me that very often girls in their teens threw themselves under his car in the hope of getting injured and being subsequently comforted by him. Others presented themselves at Berchtesgaden, often almost naked under their light coats or their BDM (young Nazi girls) uniforms, bent on offering their virginity to the Führer. Others tore open the front of their blouses when he passed. Some women seriously proposed reestablishing the *droit du seigneur* at the time of their marriage. And then, of course, there were the mountains of love letters that Hitler received constantly, the erotic gifts, some of which were in extremely bad taste, and above all, the embroidered cushions that were continually arriving at the Berghof.

How can such fascination for this man be explained, especially since Hitler had not yet acquired the exalted position of Chancellor of the Reich and was being ridiculed, insulted, and vilified in the German press, and at times even tracked down as a criminal by the government police? Physically he was not attractive. He was no John F. Kennedy in looks. He was often badly dressed and it seems strange that a woman should let herself be addressed by a man who brandished a whip made of hippopotamus skin (or was it the tail?) and who was always accompanied by a bodyguard of two armed bullies when he invited a lady to his table in the Grössenwahn in Schwabing. However, in private Hitler did not have the manners of a *Räuberhauptmann* or gang leader, as his enemies affirmed and as Bertold Brecht characterized him in a widely diffused satire.

He was in fact extremely gallant with women, always gave them precedence, never sat down in their presence, bowed to them with nineteenth-century deference, and kissed their hands on the slightest pretext. His voice changed in their presence, its gutturalness being replaced by a mellifluous quality. He spoke to them with the warmth that characterizes Austrians, with the faint accent and vocabulary of a *bon vivant* that impress the Prussians so much. Every woman to whom he spoke was convinced that he placed her, and her alone, on a pedestal and that the Führer's exclusive aim was to please her. Many women, on finding themselves confronted by this charmer instead of by the churlish character they had expected, were filled at first with speechless amazement and then with intense delight. Undoubtedly he had a mysterious hypnotic power which acted upon all those who approached him, whether generals, diplomats, politicians, children encountered in the street, or servants. "I felt myself melt in his presence," Ilse Braun says. "I would have done anything for him," affirms his secretary Traudl Junge. Yet today, both find him grotesque.

All his secretaries declare that he never reproved them, was always patient and readily dictated a phrase again if they had not understood it immediately. He always called them "my child" or "my beauty" and never started the day without complimenting them on their dresses or hairstyles. He took a kindly interest in their private lives and often spoke to them like a father.

He claimed to be uninfluenced by women. "No woman has ever ventured to give me political advice," he boasted.

He also said on one occasion, "A woman's strategy consists in being very good at first, in order to capture the man's confidence, then in pulling on the reins, and finally in grasping these reins so firmly that the man has to dance according to her desires."

He affected a timidity that women attributed to his inexperience or rather to his periods of inactivity in the field of love. In reality "Hitler was not timid in sex," according to Eva's sister Gretl Braun, who must have good grounds for saying this and for adding, "Still waters run deep. . . ."

The idea that Hitler was afraid of women dates from the First World War. As a foreign-born volunteer, he was assigned to an *Ersatz* regiment which was formed at the last moment and took the name of its commander, Colonel List. Fritz Wiedemann, the officer in command of the unit in which Hitler was serving, came of an excellent family, rich in military tradition. It was he who gave me invaluable assistance with my research. A noncommissioned officer called Max Amman was the historian of the regiment. Much later, Hitler made him a *Reichsleiter* of the party, in other words a minister, his proxy and the head of all Nazi publishing enterprises. He made Wiedemann his adjutant, in other words, his subordinate.

"Hitler did not receive any letters; he had no girl friends. I even proposed to various girls that they become his pen pals. Because he received no parcels at Christmas, his comrades wanted to offer him ten gold marks, the proceeds of a collection, but Hitler refused. He never complained about his solitary state. He once wrote: 'The regiment is my home.' "

Men from his unit maintain that Hitler sometimes visited the soldiers' brothel in Brussels (he fought in France and Belgium), but Wiedemann cannot confirm this. It is not an officer's duty to keep a check on his men's activities in this area. It is said that there is a photograph that shows Hitler going into one of these institutions.

Hitler showed great courage during World War I. He was a dispatch rider and was often exposed to enemy fire while delivering his messages. He is known to have been wounded and he was twice proposed for the Iron Cross, first class, which is one of the highest decorations to which a German private can aspire. When he received the decoration—and this detail is less well known—his sponsor was Captain Gutman, a Jew.

When the regiment was at Fournes, in France, Wiedemann, who told me this anecdote, did not like the decor of the officers' mess. "Is there nobody who could paint this wall?" he asked Sergeant Amman. The latter, springing to attention, suggested "Private Hitler." The private duly arrived, saluted, and casually remarked that a softer pastel color was needed, a light green. He went off in search of a ladder and brushes and proceeded to spend a few days redecorating the walls. This is the only absolutely authentic example we have of Adolf Hitler's activity as a house painter.

When he returned to Munich and embarked on politics, Hitler immediately found allies: women, all rich, all of a certain age and all more or less in love with him. Helene, alias Lotte Bechstein, the wife of the rich piano manufacturer Carl Bechstein, introduced him into society and championed him on several occasions, also offering him hospitality for long periods at a time. Viktoria von Dirksen* gave him similar patronage, to the point of earning for herself the nickname "the mother of the revolution." Frau Bechstein, according to Hitler's intimates, was extremely possessive, and if he so much as ventured to have a few minutes of private conversation with a pretty woman during a reception, Lotte would throw a fit of jealousy. There was also Elsa, the wife of the millionaire publisher Hugo Bruckmann. Another affluent lady, Carola Hoffmann, who was ugly but aristocratic, the widow of a professor at Munich University, frequently invited him to her villa on the outskirts of Munich and was always languishingly singing the praises of Herr Wolf (Hitler used this sobriquet at the time). There was also talk about the Finnish Frau von Seydlitz and it was rumored that he was courting Frau Ludendorff, who may have contributed to the establishment of relations between the universally famous general and the obscure politician. These women and others besides helped Hitler and his movement financially, for at the outset the big German business concerns had shown him a certain aloofness. It would appear that only the American industrialist Henry Ford subsidized the newly founded National Socialist movement. The intermediary between Ford and Hitler was in this case Ernst alias Putzi Hanfstängl, whose mother was American, and who

* Born Princess Cantacuzène from Rumania.

was a graduate of Harvard University. This association between Hitler and various auto magnates, Ford first of all,
then the Daimler-Benz owners, and finally those of Volkswagen, is a singular one.

Ernst had a sister, Erna. "Once at the Bayerischer Hof
Hotel," Hitler related, "there was a crowd of women, all
stunning and all covered with diamonds. Then there appeared a woman whose beauty made all the others pale by
comparison. She wore no jewels. It was Erna Hanfstängl."

Hitler had a long and serious affair with her; it was
thought that he was going to marry her. But Erna dabbled
too much in politics; her brother, who had become the
head of the foreign press, fell out of favor, and it would
even appear that Hitler (the gratitude of the great is unaccountable) wanted to have him thrown out of an airborne
plane.

Another lady who aspired to the role of political muse
was Princess Stephanie of Hohenlohe, who had divorced
Prince Friedrich Franz zu Hohenlohe-Waldenburg-Schil-
lingfuerst. She was something of an intriguer. She had
Lord Rothermere invited to Berchtesgaden and encouraged a meeting between Fritz Wiedemann, who was then
Hitler's aide-de-camp, and Lord Halifax, but Hitler did
not respond to her blandishments, perhaps because she
was of Jewish descent.

When he was not immersed in politics, Hitler received
pretty Munich girls in his modest apartment, then on the
Tiechstrasse. His friend and chauffeur Emil Maurice rem-
inisces: "He always offered flowers, even when he was
penniless. And we used to go and admire the ballet dancers." Hitler did not like male dancers, but he had a predilection for ballerinas and later he even wished to introduce
a sort of social security scheme for them with a guaran-
teed minimum salary and unemployment benefits. He had
the greatest admiration for an American dancer called
Myrian Verne, whom he even invited to the Berghof. His
preference was for waltzes, in which, according to his description, "Myrian Verne floated through the air like a
goddess," and disliked everything that was modern and
smacked of jazz. The chauffeur remembers that they
sometimes went to the art academy to admire models posing in the nude. Hitler circulated quite at his ease in the
midst of all this nudity. He had often frequented artists'
studios in Vienna.

There were certain rumors for which it has been impossible to find any documented confirmation. But an unconfirmed rumor is not necessarily false. After all, for a long time a mere whisper of a rumor, ignored by almost everybody, was the only indication of Eva Braun's existence.

Jenny Haug, his chauffeur's sister, was allegedly Hitler's mistress around the year 1923. This is an assertion made by the biographer Heiden, whom William Shirer copies faithfully. I give little weight to these stories of servants and chauffeur's sisters. Many men sleep with their secretaries or maids. A Viennese lady, Suzi Liptauer, who lived in Munich, seemingly tried to hang herself in a hotel room in 1921 because Hitler had broken with her. I found this information in the highly respectable British Museum Library in London. The photographer Hoffmann confirmed the episode and added that the lady subsequently married and enjoyed Hitler's protection. But Hoffmann is not a very reliable witness. There is also talk about Professor Troost's widow, and about Frau Bouhler, and about the actress Pola Negri—the names are too numerous to be all listed.

I cannot, however, dismiss the excommunicated nun Sister Pia, Eleonora Bauer. She was a modern Amazon who took part in the punitive expeditions of the party, and in November, 1923, participated in the Putsch in front of the Feldherrenhalle. It even seems that she was fired at. It is claimed that she had an affair with Hitler and that she had a child who was brought up at the expense of the party and was then employed, through party leader Christian Weber's influence, on the editorial staff of the *Völkischer Beobachter*. One thing is reasonably certain: This gutter heroine slept with everybody and would have had great difficulty in establishing the paternity of any child she may have had.

The story of Maria Reiter Kubish does not belong to the realm of fantasy. She is alive and protests its authenticity. Her sister, Anni Steger Hehl, is more circumspect and in the course of a conversation admitted that perhaps only half the story is true. Emil Maurice for his part remembers the episode clearly, and many people at Berchtesgaden confirm the account, but I suspect that this may be the result of autosuggestion through press accounts.

Maria Reiter, commonly known as Mitzi, was born on

December 23, 1909, the youngest of four girls. She was sent to a convent school and then went to work in her sister Anni's fashion boutique in Berchtesgaden. In 1925, Hitler was living there in the Deutscher Hof while waiting to return to the Obersalzberg, and the hotel was just opposite the shop. There was a large garden, the Kurpark, where Hitler walked his Alsatian, Prinz. Evidently Prinz became friends with Mitzi's police dog Marko, while his owner flirted with the girl. They went to the sister's shop, where Hitler proposed that little Mitzi should come with him to a concert. "But you are thirty-six," protested Anni, "and my sister is only sixteen."

Hitler went off in high dudgeon, brandishing the inevitable whip. But he came back and finally took the two sisters to a party meeting. After his speech he started to flirt boldly with the younger sister, fondly calling her Mitzerl, to the extreme jealousy of the two daughters of the hotel proprietor, Metke, who were both in love with Hitler. Hitler is supposed to have compared Mitzi's beautiful eyes to those of his mother.

Another evening Hitler apparently asked to kiss her and the girl refused. Then Hitler's face hardened and he decreed, "We must not see each other anymore."

But Mitzi met him again, and they went for a walk around the lake. Hitler put his hands on her shoulders and then kissed her on the lips. Mitzi scarcely resisted.

"He held me tight and said, 'I want to crush you.' He was full of wild passion."

Hitler left on a journey, but came back toward Christmas and they exchanged presents; she had embroidered some cushions with swastikas (what a passion German girls have for cushions!), and he gave her an autographed copy of *Mein Kampf*, which was later stolen by American GI's.

Maria Reiter then visited Hitler in Munich, they made love, Hitler talked of renting an apartment and living with her, and Maria dreamed of marriage. Time passed, and in July, 1927, Maria, who had returned to her sister's, learned that Hitler was in Berchtesgaden but was courting another girl. Driven by jealousy to the verge of blind despair, she took a clothesline from the courtyard, secured it to a door, and wound the other end around her neck. She fainted. When Gottfried Hehl, her brother-in-law, found her, she was at death's door.

For a long time she had no further news of Hitler; finally a party official, Max Amman, asked her to sign a paper before a notary declaring that there had never been anything between her and Hitler. On May 10, 1930, she married an innkeeper in Innsbruck. But she was not happy and left him.

Hitler saw her again in 1932. He made her sit down on the famous couch of the apartment in the Prinzregentenplatz. "Stay with me tonight," he supposedly asked her, and Maria readily agreed.

The years passed. Maria obtained a divorce and married the SS Hauptsturmführer Kubish, who was a member of Goebbels' personal bodyguard. In 1936, Maria saw Hitler again and asked for her husband's transfer to Vienna, where she wished to live. Hitler promised her this promotion, but during the French campaign, Kubish was killed and Hitler sent the widow a hundred red roses. This was the last contact between the former lovers.

I have considerably shortened the account given by Maria Reiter Kubish, who now lives near Hamburg. One gets the impression that she is merely repeating a story concocted for her by the editor of a popular magazine—the journalistic tricks of the trade are evident. But there is certainly an element of truth in all this. They knew each other and they probably flirted together. For Hitler it must have been an insignificant episode. All the evidence—books, letters, keepsakes—has disappeared, having been destroyed, according to Maria Reiter, during the pillage of Berchtesgaden. For many years after the fall of the Third Reich, Maria Reiter Kubish lived with Hitler's sister Paula, who under the pseudonym of Frau Wolf had rented a cottage in the vicinity of Berchtesgaden, on the Waldsee. This association lends considerable weight to the affair; but, as I have already mentioned, Paula Hitler was never in full possession of her faculties and was apt to display excessive credulity mingled with a desire to exploit the story financially when she insisted on the veracity of this relationship. She cannot even have known about it at the time, since she very rarely visited her brother.

Inge Ley, a ravishing blonde, had always greatly excited Hitler's admiration. One day he had said of Ley, her husband: "How can such a man not be in the seventh heaven living with such a woman?" Inge, a ballerina by profession, was very unhappy with her drunkard husband, who was the head of the *Arbeiterfront;* once she had even taken refuge in the Obersalzberg. Eva Braun's sisters, and also Hitler's secretaries, unanimously affirm that there was never anything between the Führer and the scintillating Inge Ley. She jumped out of the window in Berlin in 1943. She had previously written Hitler a letter that left him visibly depressed.

Another suicide attempt was that of Martha Dodd. Not the slightest detail of it has survived, but as the protagonist was the United States ambassador's daughter, it is possible that the affair was immediately hushed up, with diplomatic solidarity. Martha's father, Prof. William Dodd, dean of the history faculty at Chicago University and a disciple of Wilson, was a surprising choice as ambassador in Berlin. He remained very much in the background. His German was scanty, although he had studied a year in Leipzig. His daughter, however, was extremely pretty, typically American, with a degree from one of the best American colleges; flirtatious and dynamic, she scandalized the salons with the shortness of her dresses and the audacity of her Charleston. The gossip columnists listed the names of all the men with whom she was reported to have flirted. Hitler had noticed her at Bayreuth at a gala performance of *Parsifal.* She apparently looked like Geli. But Hitler was apt to claim that any woman he found attractive looked like Geli. He invited Martha to the Kaiserhof for tea and met her on various other occasions. There was at the time speculation about a German-American *rapprochement,* and Putzi Hanfstängl was a constant visitor at the American Embassy. Martha declared that she was madly in love, her only dream was to meet her Führer again, and she talked about engineering a triumphal tour of the United States for him. It seems that this affair did not meet with the approval of Göring, who, through his Gestapo chief, Rudolf Diels (at the time Göring still had complete control of this organization) went fishing in troubled waters. He presented Hitler with an alarming dossier on the young American girl: "She was apparently arrested in Chicago for drunkenness, divorced after only a few months of marriage . . ." But Hitler paid no heed to such idle rumors; what horrified him was a hint that Martha Dodd was an agent of the Soviets.

He refused to see her again and even banned her from

big diplomatic receptions. The report then circulated that she had tried to slash her wrists. But nobody believed it.

And her career as a spy? After the war Martha Dodd married a millionaire. She and her husband were accused in the McCarthy era of being Communist agents, and her passport was withdrawn. She went to live in Mexico, and later in Prague and Moscow. Her name has been connected many times with mysterious activities from behind the Iron Curtain.

Hitler, who as a young boy in Linz did not even dare speak to the Dulcinea of his dreams, content to admire her from afar, and who did not receive so much as a Christmas card from a girl friend while he was a soldier at the front, now found all this sentimental idolizing absolutely natural.

"Women adore heroes," he explained modestly. "Without a man a woman is absolutely lost. The hero gives a woman the sensation of being totally protected. Her nature demands a heroic man. . . ."

His bachelor freedom—or at least apparent freedom—was essential in Hitler's estimation because of his political greatness. If the women of Germany were to discover that he had a permanent attachment, or, worse still, if his marriage were to be announced, he would immediately have lost their favor, or so he thought, and his prestige would be severely undermined. "In politics," Hitler is said to have declared, "feminine support is essential; the men follow automatically." Perhaps for this reason, when asked in public or in society if he ever intended to marry, he always replied, "I am already married—my wife is Germany."

CHAPTER SEVEN

Private diary

Ilse and Eva Braun had inherited from their father a typically German mania for order. They instinctively put everything away in its proper place, never threw anything out, even old streetcar tickets, discussed their Christmas plans at Easter, and naturally kept a diary. Gretl, who was very easygoing, did just the opposite; she saw no need to order either her possessions or her thoughts. She found life complicated enough as it was.

The two girls, however, did not fill their diaries with intimate confessions. They merely used them to classify events and to note down various expenses, memoranda, a commentary on a visit to the theater, the address of a good dancing partner. Eva never made the slightest allusion to Hitler in her diary. She did not wish to run the risk of its being read by her father, who might conceivably have done so despite his usual probity.

Much later, at Berchtesgaden, Eva kept a diary that was more personal and therefore very secret. The notebook was bound in green leather and contained not so much revelations and sentimental writings as copies of documents, bills and bank statements, a list of important dates, and above all rough drafts of all the letters that Eva sent to Hitler, including the personal messages that she placed on his desk on special occasions, such as anniversaries of meetings, military victories, and so forth. This green diary was locked in the safe when Eva had to abandon the Berghof, and its fate remains shrouded in mystery.*

In 1947, the Tyrolean actor Luis Trenker offered to the

---

* Part of it, for the year 1938, is in the possession of a Londoner. It is not yet authenticated, and its contents are without interest—just some routine notations.

public a volume of private memoirs that he attributed to
Eva Braun. This Trenker, who declared himself by turns
German, Austrian, Italian, and even Swiss, depending on
the fortunes of war, was chiefly noted in the movie world
as the star of several films glorifying the Hitler myth. He
was for a time in high favor with the Führer and Goebbels. He claimed to be the possessor of the original of Eva
Braun's memoirs and to have received them from Eva herself, but he was never able to produce any documents.
This apocryphal composition caused an immense stir (in
1947 the public was extremely gullible) and unfortunately
misled not only the readers of the sentimental press but
also a number of well-intentioned historians.

Although the book in question has since been withdrawn
from the catalog of all the serious libraries, it helped to
create a completely fictitious popular image of Eva Braun
as a Nazi Mme. de Pompadour, living in an erotic atmosphere, bathing naked in the moonlight and sleeping between
sheets embroidered with swastikas. For a long time the
existence of this audacious fake silenced witnesses who
knew the truth. I use the term "fake," for, on the lodging
of a complaint by the Braun family, the civil tribunal of
Munich in a decree dated September 10, 1948, condemned
the publisher of the apocryphal diary to a large fine and
six months' imprisonment. It ordered the withdrawal of the
volumes already published and established the nonexistence
of the documents in question. The tribunal, because of the
Allied occupation, declared itself powerless to institute
measures against the French publisher, for at that time the
Germans had no remedy at law against nationals of the
victorious states.

In the course of the lawsuit and the violent controversy
that followed in the German press, it was amply proved
that almost all the details revealed in this so-called private
diary were totally contrary to the facts. It was inconceivable that Eva Braun should have confused dates so utterly,
ignored the exact address of her own house, mixed up
events and people and affirmed that she had met Hitler
five years after the actual date of the first meeting. But
even discounting this controversy and the evidence of relatives and friends, merely by reading Eva Braun's letters
(some of which have come into my possession), visiting
the places where she lived, consulting address books, municipal archives, and telephone directories, one finds over-

whelming proof of the absolute spuriousness of the book. Its authors possessed not a vestige of the talents that a successful literary imposter requires. They also lacked imagination. A woman who had been present at the hearing and had been intrigued by the case made a hilarious discovery in the course of subsequent research. She found that the greater part of the apocryphal "memoirs" had been lifted from an old book by Countess Larisch-Wallersee. This book dealt with the tragic love of Rudolf of Hapsburg and Marie Vetsera. The fakers had copied the historical account word for word, comma for comma, chapter for chapter, and had simply changed the names. Marie Vetsera naturally became Eva Braun, and Archduke Rudolf, Hitler, Archduke Otto was transposed into Streicher and Metternich into Ribbentrop.

After this discovery, the last shadow of doubt was dispelled and everybody gloated over the affair. But Papa Braun could not but remember that on the night when Eva was born, he had thought for a moment of calling the baby Marie, in honor of Rudolf's secret love.

Yet all this time there existed a very private and wholly authentic diary. It consisted of twenty-two pages written by hand between February 6, 1935, and May 28 of the same year. For a long time, made wary by Trenker's fake, I was skeptical about its value. With such a precedent, it could logically only be another fraudulent attempt in equally bad taste. I had only examined a few samples of Eva Braun's handwriting, but these were far from conforming with the calligraphy of the diary pages. And why did the text stop in May, 1935, at a time when Eva's great affair was only just beginning?

The authenticity of the document, however, is now absolutely beyond dispute. Eva's sister Ilse has confirmed before a notary that the writing is her sister's, that she knew of this diary as early as 1935, and that she vividly remembers reading it at that time. Nothing has been changed, there is not a single deletion or addition. The details, it will be seen, coincide with the facts. Finally, the family put at my disposal what remains of Eva's correspondence and so enabled me to compare the two handwritings again. For Germans write in two ways: in Latin and in Gothic characters, *Altdeutsch* or *Fraktur,* as they call them. The two styles of calligraphy are so different that it is impossible even for a graphologist to decide whether a person who has written something in Latin characters is also the author of a piece written in *Altdeutsch*.

In those days Eva Braun was extremely unhappy. She had never been prepared for a back-street existence such as she was leading in Munich. She found it extremely difficult to adapt herself to Hitler's unpredictable visits and absences and was still perplexed by his sudden changes of behavior, all charm and tenderness one day, indifference the next, and brusqueness the third day. In typically feminine fashion, she was no longer satisfied with the proofs of affection that Hitler had given her after her attempted suicide and after his nomination to the post of Chancellor. She was obsessed by the fear of losing him, and this terror was to dog her until the day of her death.

The perusal of her diary confirms this state of mind. It also gives a direct insight into the kind of life Eva led in Munich, and is a measure of the intensity of her love, this young girl's first love.

The translation of the text respects Eva's style. She always spoke the Bavarian dialect, as her mother and sister still do, and she wrote as she spoke except for an occasional attempt at a more literary turn of phrase. For, despite her credits at the secondary school and her aristocratic education at the Simbach convent, Eva Braun had no talent for writing. She massacred syntax and had a complete disregard for spelling.

6 February 1935

Today seems to me the appropriate day for inaugurating this "marvel." I have just happily reached the age of twenty-three, but whether this is really a cause for happiness is another matter. At the moment I am very far from feeling that way.

I probably expect too much from a day that should be so "important."

If only I had a "little dog" I would be less lonely. But that would be asking too much.

Mrs. Schaub came as "ambassadress" with flowers and a telegram.

[Mrs. Julius Schaub was the wife of Hitler's chief aide-de-camp. The flowers and the telegram were therefore from Hitler.]

My office looks like a flower shop and smells like a mortuary chapel.

[It is obvious that Eva made no great secret of her

situation at Hoffmann's, or else how could she have explained to her colleagues the arrival of so many flowers? Far from hiding them, she displayed them with a certain vanity.]

All things considered, I am ungrateful. But I did so want a basset puppy, and still no sign of one. Perhaps next year, or even later, it will go better with somebody who is approaching spinsterhood.

[Eva's sister Ilse, who helped me to annotate this diary, remarked that Hitler was not so much mean as perfunctory in the matter of presents. She also commented that her sister, without admitting it to herself, was hoping not so much for a basset hound as for a marriage proposal. . . .]

Above all, I must not despair. It's time I learned to be patient.

I bought two lottery tickets because I was convinced that it was a question of today or never, but they were *Nieten*.

[The lottery tickets that are on sale for ten cents in the streets of Munich indicate, as soon as the envelope is torn open, the sum won or else the word *niete*, nothing.]

So I'll never be rich. There's nothing to do about it.

I would have gone today with Herta, Gretl, Ilse and Mutti [Herta Schneider, Eva's best friend, her two sisters, and her mother] to the Zugspitze [the peak at Garmisch-Partenkirchen], and we would have been surrounded by warmth and light, for the great joys are those one feels when others are also rejoicing.

But it's No on the trip. This evening I am going to dine with Herta. What else can a very simple woman of twenty-three do? And so my birthday will end with guzzling and boozing.

I think this will be acting according to his wishes [Hitler's wishes].

11 February 1935

He was here just now. But no little dog, no cupboards stuffed with dresses. He didn't even ask me if I wanted anything for my birthday.

But I bought some jewelry on my own. A necklace, earrings, and a ring for fifty marks—very pretty. Let's hope he likes them.

If not, he can find me something himself.

15 February 1935

It looks as though the Berlin idea is going to come off. But I shan't believe it until I am in the Chancellery of the Reich. Let's hope that it will be a pleasant occasion.

It's a pity that Herta isn't coming instead of Charly [another friend, Charlotte]. Her company would guarantee a couple of gay days. Probably there will be a big hullabaloo, because I don't suppose Brueckner will show his agreeable side to Charly for a change.

I don't yet dare to be really happy about it, but if everything goes well, it could be marvelous. Let's hope so.

18 February 1935

Yesterday he arrived quite unexpectedly and we spent a delightful evening. But the best thing is that he is considering the idea of taking me away from the shop—but I prefer not to rejoice too soon—and presenting me with a little house. I daren't think of it, it would be just too wonderful. I would no longer have to open the door for so many "honorable clients" and be obliged to play the part of a shopgirl.

[Eva's sister made the comment here that life at Hoffmann's had gradually become intolerable for Eva, who in any case was never overfond of work.]

Dear God, please let this come true and let it happen in the near future. Poor Charly is ill and can't come to Berlin. She has no luck. But perhaps it's better this way.

There are times when He behaves in a vulgar fashion [the "He" is written with a capital by Eva Braun] and that would make her unhappier still.

I am infinitely happy that he loves me so much and I pray that it may always remain so. I never want it to be my fault if one day he should cease to love me.

4 March 1935

I am mortally unhappy again. And since I haven't permission to write to Him, this book must record my lamentations.

He came on Saturday. Saturday evening there was the Nocturnal Ball.

Frau Schwarz [the wife of the treasurer of the Nazi party] had given me an invitation for a box. I therefore had to go, especially as I had promised to do so.

I spent two marvelously beautiful hours with him

until midnight and then, with his permission, I went to the ball for another couple of hours.

[Hitler's dual role should be noted: He is both Eva's lover, spending two hours with her on the sofa of the big drawing room in Prinzregentenplatz, and a father figure, who authorizes the young girl to go and amuse herself at the ball with people of her own age and milieu.]

He had promised that I would see him on Sunday. But although I telephoned and asked for him at the Osteria [Hitler's favorite restaurant where, as the text shows, Eva also met him] and left a message that I was waiting for news of him, he took the plane to Feldafing and even refused the Hoffmanns' invitation to coffee and supper. There are two sides to everything. Perhaps he wanted to be alone with Dr. G. who was here, but he could at least have let me know. I was waiting at Hoffmann's like a cat on hot bricks. I imagined every moment that he was about to arrive.

We went to the train, because, on his return to Munich, he decided to go off again, and we reached the station just in time to see the rear lights of the last coach.

Hoffmann left the house late as usual, and I wasn't even able to say good-bye.

Perhaps I still take too gloomy a view of things. Let's hope this is the case, but he won't be back for a fortnight and until then I shall be miserable. I have lost my peace of mind.

I don't know why he's angry with me. Perhaps because of the ball. But he himself gave me permission to go.

I'm racking my brains to discover the reason why he left without saying good-bye to me.

The Hoffmanns have invited me to *The Venetian Night* but I shan't go. I'm too sad for that.

11 March 1935

I only want one thing, to fall very ill and to hear nothing of him for at least a week. Why has nothing arrived for me, why do I have to bear all this? Oh, if only I had never met him. I'm desperate. Now I'm buying sleeping tablets again; then I fall into a state of semi-imbecility and no longer have to think so much about all this. Why doesn't the devil carry me off? Hell must be infinitely preferable to this.

[Ilse remarked that this solitude weighed enormously

on Eva, for she was forced to kick her heels waiting for Hitler, who more often than not arrived unannounced. Her sister Gretl went out with her friends every evening and Ilse was working or taking part in her dancing competitions. This state of affairs explains why Eva was taking ever larger doses of narcotics.]

I waited for three hours outside the Carlton [a hotel in Munich, not far from the district where Eva lived] and I had to watch him buying flowers for Anny Ondra [an actress married to the former world boxing champion Max Schmeling] and inviting them to dinner.

(A lunatic vision, written the sixteenth of March.)

[This note was inserted in the diary later. Eva must have reread the entry and then added the comment and the date.]

He needs me for special reasons. It can't be otherwise (nonsense).

[Again, Eva is annotating her own diary.]

When he says he loves me, he thinks it is only for the time being. The same with his promises, which he never keeps.

[Little Eva, in her political ignorance and at the age of twenty-three, had here discovered a fact that most of the statesmen of Europe only realized much later and at what a price. . . .]

Why doesn't he have done with me instead of tormenting me?

16 March 1935

He's in Berlin again. If only I weren't all at sea when I can't see him so often. Of course, it's normal that he shouldn't take a great interest in me at the moment with all that's going on in politics.

[March 16 was the date of the rearmament of Germany, Hitler's first fateful decision, his first triumph.]

Today I'm going up to the Zugspitze with Gretl and I imagine that my madness will calm down. Everything has ended well and this time too, all will be fine. I simply must wait patiently. . . .

1 April 1935

Yesterday, he invited us to dinner at the Vierjahreszeiten [the most elegant hotel in Munich]. I had to sit beside him for three hours without being able to say a single word to him. As a farewell gesture, he gave me an envelope with some money inside, as he has already done once before. How lovely it would have been if he had also written a line of greeting or a kind word. But he never thinks of such things.

Why doesn't he go and dine at Hoffmann's? There at least I could have him to myself for a few minutes. I hope he won't come back until his apartment is ready.

[Hitler was having his apartment fixed up and in the meanwhile was living in a hotel, where it was impossible for Eva to visit him. At the Hoffmanns', on the other hand, the master of the house left the "two lovers" alone together.]

29 April 1935

I feel apathetic. About everything. I spend my time singing *"Tout ira très bien, Madame la Marquise,"* but it doesn't help much. The apartment is ready, but I can't visit him. Love has been struck off his schedule. Now that he's back in Berlin, I'm coming back to life a little. But there were days last week when I cried every night as I accepted my "duty." I had a bilious attack when I stayed at home alone on Easter Day.

I've made desperate efforts to economize. I'm getting on everybody's nerves with my attempts to sell them everything. Starting with my suit, then my camera, and down to theater tickets.

But everything will work out all right. The debts are not so terrible.

10 May 1935

Mr. Hoffmann lovingly and as tactlessly informs me that he has found a replacement for me. She is known as the Walküre and looks the part. Including her legs. But these are the dimensions he prefers. If this is true, though, he will soon make her lose thirty pounds, through worry, unless she has a gift for growing fat in adversity like Charly.

[The Walküre in question is very probably Unity Mitford, the British Walkyrie, as she was nicknamed in Munich. This ephemeral rival of Eva will be mentioned again later. Ilse, however, thinks that the reference might also be to Winifred Wagner. The fact is that Eva's sisters as well as such girl friends as knew about her liaison used sometimes to tease her about large Winifried, of whom Hitler had once said, "The only person whom I can fittingly marry as Führer is the lady Wagner. Then it would be a national undertaking." And so

Eva's sisters, to the tune of a Tino Rossi song that was then extremely popular, *"Veni, veni, veni, o canta a me,"* provoked her with the version "Winnie, Winnie, Winnie, Winifried Wagner, I'll marry you." Eva pretended to be amused, but then went sniveling to Hitler, who, in his vexation, reacted with that unpredictability that was fast becoming legendary. He prohibited the sale of the record and the continuation of a triumphal tour that Tino Rossi was at that time making in Germany. I remember taking the crooner to the station at the Berlin Zoo. He attributed this decision to some colossal diplomatic friction and probably still believes that this was the reason. . . .]

If what Mrs. Hoffmann says is true, I find it monstrous of him not to have informed me.

He really ought to know me well enough by now to realize that I wouldn't try to stop him if he suddenly lost his heart to somebody else. What happens to me must be a matter of indifference to him.

I shall wait until June 3, in other words a quarter of a year since our last meeting, and then demand an explanation. Let nobody say I'm not patient.

The weather is magnificent and I, the mistress of the greatest man in Germany and in the whole world, I sit here waiting while the sun mocks me through the windowpanes.

That he should have so little understanding and allow me to be humiliated in front of strangers. . . . But men's pleasure . . . etc. etc., or again, "As one makes one's bed . . ." All things considered, it's my fault, but one always tries to accuse others. . . . This Lenten fast will end one day and then everything will taste better.

But it's a pity that just now is spring.

[Eva Braun is trying to imitate the sentimental philosophizing of popular novels and even quotes a few proverbs, all this in Bavarian dialect, to heighten the confusion. But her passionate love and childish jealousy are clearly discernible between the lines.]

28 May 1935

I have just sent him a decisive letter. Will he take it seriously?

Well, we'll see.

If I don't receive a reply before ten o'clock tonight, I'll simply take my twenty-five tablets and fall asleep very gently. Is this the mad love he promised me, when he doesn't send me a single comforting line in three months? It's true that recently his head has been full of political problems, but there must be moments of relaxation. And what about last year? He had a lot of trouble with Röhm and Italy. But in spite of this he found time for me.

[The lovelorn Eva evaluates international events from her personal point of view. The execution of Ernst Röhm, the head of the SA, the murder of Dollfus, the meeting between Hitler and Mussolini in Venice had only one common denominator for her: They were all pretexts for Hitler to leave her.]

It is hard for me to judge if the present situation is as difficult for him, but a few kind words sent to Hoffmann's or elsewhere would not have distracted him unduly.

I'm afraid there's something else behind it all.

I've done nothing wrong. Absolutely nothing.

Perhaps another woman, not the Walküre girl, that would be really rather unlikely, but there are so many others.

What other reasons could there be? I can't think of any.

28 May 1935

Oh God, I'm afraid there won't be a reply today. If only somebody would help me. Everything is so horribly bleak. Perhaps my letter arrived at an inopportune moment. Perhaps I shouldn't have written to him.

However that may be, this uncertainty is more difficult to bear than a sudden end.

Dear God, help me. I must speak to him today, tomorrow will be too late.

I have decided on thirty-five tablets. This time I must make "dead sure."

If only he got somebody to telephone to me.

Late at night on May 28, or more exactly in the early hours of May 29, Ilse Braun found her sister in a state of coma. Availing herself of her experience as a doctor's assistant, she administered first-aid-treatment and then summoned her employer, Dr. Marx, whose discretion she could trust.

While the doctor was attending to her sister, she found

the notebook where Eva had kept her diary. She tore out the pages.

She had decided not to say anything about this new suicide attempt. Their parents, especially their father, were already extremely distressed at their two daughters' plans to move out and would have found this fresh blow hard to bear. Fritz Braun might have committed some foolish indiscretion that would seriously have compromised Eva's reputation. People would have started to think of her as crazy, and Hitler himself might have had doubts about his mistress's mental stability. Moreover, Isle Braun suspected that her sister had to some extent staged this suicide, for she had carefully left her diary in full view and had taken only twenty tablets of vanodorm, a narcotic that Ilse, with her medical experience, knew to be milder than Veronal. Above all, Eva had known that Ilse would very probably return home that night, not to mention her other sister Gretl, who was also due back at any moment.

There was yet another reason for Ilse's desire for secrecy. She did not wish to implicate Dr. Marx in the affair, for he was Jewish and therefore particularly vulnerable. True, the Nuremberg Laws had not yet been promulgated and the persecutions were only just starting, but there was no predicting how Hitler might react if he learned of the matter.

It was therefore decided to attribute the incident to excessive fatigue, which had led Eva to take an overdose of narcotics. After a few days of rest, her recovery was complete.

Much later, Ilse returned the pages of the diary to Eva, who kept them carefully. Shortly before her death, she asked that they be destroyed. But her sister Gretl saw fit to put them in safekeeping in the Austrian mountains, in the hands of the mother of an SS officer in Hitler's personal bodyguard, Franz Conrad.

Although Eva's sisters do not know of this, it is likely that Hitler was aware of the existence of the diary. He apparently accepted the story of his mistress' indisposition quite calmly. But Ilse Braun thinks that he had guessed the truth. For the suicide attempt, whether genuine or not, had the desired effect. A few months later Hitler kept his promise for once and rented Eva an apartment and the next spring bought her a villa—both in Bogenhausen, a pleasant district on the edge of town. She no longer had to work at Hoffmann's. And from then on, even in the most intensely dramatic moments of the Russian campaign, there was rarely a night when Hitler did not try to telephone or convey a message of endearment to his mistress.

CHAPTER EIGHT

Papa Braun writes to Adolf Hitler

One afternoon a little sister of the poor, with a wicker basket on her arm, came knocking at the door of the Brauns' apartment in Hohenzollernstrasse, as she always did at the end of the month, asking for alms in the shape of food and a few small coins. But this time the nun did not merely offer prayers in exchange. She announced, "What a blessing that nice Herr Hitler has come to power; the Lord be praised."

Franziska Braun, in a great state of delight, went to wake up Eva, who, this afternoon of January 30, 1933, was resting from the exertions of the previous night. Not that she had been celebrating, but she had been obliged to work late because Hoffmann had received enormous orders for photographs. Eva herself heard the incredible news from the mouth of the nun, who repeated it for her benefit. Her lover, the man whom her father had called an Austrian tramp, had become Bismarck's successor.

Her first reaction was: "I've won my bet." She had in fact made a wager of twenty marks with her sister Ilse that there would some day be a Hitler government—a sum that Ilse, chronically short of money, never paid her, under the pretext that the sweetheart of the Chancellor of the Reich could afford the luxury of renouncing any gambling debts owed her.

This was Eva's great hour. Her mother rejoiced with her and extolled the wisdom of a daughter who had managed to frequent the "right people,", while Ilse, mortified, was forced to admit that she had lost the battle and that her younger sister had scored a point for once. Eva's father of course muttered, "We've had so many chancellors, one more won't change anything." At the same time, how-

ever, as an ex-officer faithful to military tradition and to
the monarchy (immediately after his demobilization in
1918 he had volunteered for service in the "Oberland"
partisan brigade that liberated Munich from the Bolshevist
Communists and subsequently became a member of the
"Stahlhelm" paramilitary organization, the famous steel
helmets), he was dazzled by the fact that the great, the
venerated, the heroic old veteran, Feldmarschall Paul von
Hindenburg, had shaken hands with Herr Hitler.

During the next few days at Hoffmann's, Eva conscientiously collected innumerable photographs of the monster
procession of a hundred thousand Berliners who, torch in
hand, had moved through the night like a sea of flames
down the avenue called Unter den Linden. It was a spectacle without precedent. Even Queen Victoria, even the Kaiser had never aroused such mass enthusiasm. "Look, Papa,
whole Berlin is in the streets—Berlin, the capital of the
Reich, not a provincial village like Munich."

Eva's parents interpreted this exultation as the satisfaction of a little girl who has just seen the football team of
her school win the championship. They now knew indirectly—for Eva had not yet mentioned the fact to them—
that their daughter was acquainted with Hitler and received invitations from him on certain occasions, but they
imagined, or liked to imagine, that these relations were of
a purely professional nature. Eva had in fact taken charge
of Hitler's photographic file at Hoffmann's and claimed to
be a sort of "account executive" for the politician.

Yet her mother and sister recall that after the first brief
elation, she fell into a long spell of melancholy. Her sister
affirms that she even caught her in tears—and Eva Braun
hated expressing her feelings in this way. This reaction
was caused by the realization that her friend's new position of eminence would impede their private meetings still
further. First, there was the obstacle of distance, for Hitler
would live permanently in Berlin, first at the Kaiserhof
Hotel and later at the Chancellery, and from now on he
would be merely an occasional visitor in Munich. Then
the duties of his office would absorb nearly all his time.

Hitler, however, in his new position as Chancellor had
not severed his contacts. He had promised to speak to Eva
on the telephone on the evening of his nomination, and
the mere fact that she was able to get through when there
were thousands of congratulatory calls and telegrams from

the Reich and abroad (from the United States alone there
were eighty-seven requests for a line that night) proved
that for Hitler Eva was no longer just a girl like any other
girl. He returned to Munich as soon as possible and invited Eva to his apartment. He went with her to the Osteria and the Carlton as usual, and invitations to Berchtesgaden arrived with increasing frequency. Eva would pretend
to her family that she had some mission to accomplish for
Hoffmann, and, carrying her small green suitcase, would
take a seat in the black-and-silver Mercedes. (The big
manufacturers had put an even larger number of their cars
at the disposal of the new Chancellor. Hitler, for his part,
was not only to contribute greatly to the prosperity of this
firm but even worked on perfecting the designs of several
models. The managing director of the enterprise was a frequent guest at Berchtesgaden; in fact, he could be said to
have become a member of the inner clique.) The car,
however, never stopped in front of the Brauns' apartment
—this would have excited the curiosity and gossip of the
neighbors—but on the corner of the Turkenstrasse nearby.

Contrary to Eva's apprehensions, Hitler as Chancellor
had relatively more leisure, or rather, more occasions, to
concern himself with his personal problems, than he had
had as a simple politician. The active struggle was over,
and he no longer had to expend so much energy himself,
for he now had hundreds of thousands of people at his orders and the whole state machinery at his disposal. The
police, secret or otherwise, was there to preserve the in-
violability of his private life and not, as formerly, to inter-
fere with it. He could now dispose of special trains for his
journeys; in fact he sometimes demanded thirteen or four-
teen coaches to accommodate his suite and his guests.
This soon became his chief method of transport, for he
disliked motoring. He also had a private airplane that he
occasionally used, although he had to surmount an innate
aversion for flying whenever he went on board. Later he
forbade Eva to fly, but she disregarded this ukase as she
disobeyed many of Hitler's other interdictions.

On February 6, 1933, less than a week after Hitler's
accession to power, Eva celebrated her twenty-first birthday. On this occasion she received her first jewels from
Hitler: a matching ring, earrings, and bracelet of tourmalines. The semiprecious stones were mediocre and rather
small, for Hitler was far from generous, but the setting

was finely worked and gave the impression of being old. When Eva went home, she had to hide this finery in her purse. It always remained her favorite jewelry.

To foil Eva's matrimonial plans, Hitler first of all explained to her that his new position made it even more impossible for him to think of getting married. He still needed the feminine vote, for his regime could only be consolidated by fresh elections. Then he was no ordinary statesman. He had a vocation, his activity was a priesthood. He had to continue to convince the German people that he had devoted himself day and night exclusively to their service, that there was nothing that could distract him, divert him from his task—neither amusements, holidays, love affairs, or a home, and children. He was like the Pope, like Catholic priests. They did not marry, could not marry.

Of all the pretexts advanced by Hitler to justify his secret liaison, this was perhaps the only one in which he seriously believed. It was a relic of his Catholic education, of the days when he admired the mystical devotion of the monks who were his teachers—to such a point that apparently, according to *Mein Kampf*, he thought for a brief moment of taking orders.

Eva was in fact, then, not so greatly tormented by the idea of marrying, but was solely concerned with the immediate present. This entailed preserving Hitler's affections, consolidating her victory, continuing to see him and enjoying the opportunity of being near him for as long as possible. For until January 30, 1933, Hitler, despite his English-style raincoats, his boots and his whips, his henchmen and his cars, his political extravagance and his oracular speeches, still belonged to her own world. He frequented the cafés in her neighborhood, and lived in an apartment that was admittedly larger than that of her parents, but nonetheless an ordinary apartment. Now, however, he was living in a palace, with people bowing low to him and murmuring "Your Excellency" and soldiers presenting arms to him. He had become one of the "princes of this world." It must be remembered that Eva, in spite of her family's social status, her convent education, and her father's inheritance, knew nothing of the world. She had set foot outside Munich only to go to various villages, she had never bought herself an elegant dress (she made all her clothes herself), had never penetrated into high society, possessed no jewelry, had never had a car door opened for her by a liveried footman. She was like the beggar girl in the fairy tale who strikes up a friendship with a passer-by and later discovers that he is the king or the sultan.

The newspapers and also her boss spoke of the Berlin receptions where Hitler was to be seen in evening dress, surrounded by dazzling women. He hated this attire, but wished to prove that he, the parvenu, could be every whit as elegant as a *Junker*. There were many theater and cinema stars, for whom Hitler had a predilection; he even suggested that on great state occasions, the wives of ministers and ambassadors, who were often old and gawky, should be replaced by such alluring actresses as Olga Tschechowa or Lil Dagover. . . . He wished to create an eclectic atmosphere that would put his guests at their ease and possibly facilitate their political seduction.

At the time of his Italian journey, Hitler complained bitterly of having been stuck at table next to the deaf Queen Elena of Italy, who seemed to him more ferocious than the cuirassiers of the royal guard and who bored him dreadfully. How different things were at his Berlin receptions, when he offered his arm to Olga Tschechowa, the most famous star of the moment and one of the most scintillating women in Europe. She sat down on his right at table while another beauty was on his left. He ate sparingly, but the meal was one long flirtation: He paid compliments to the ladies, held Olga Tschechowa's hand, kissed it, and then raised his other neighbor's hand to his lips.

So it was that the foreign papers, and even more, Hoffmann's office were full of gossip about the Führer's loves: Hilde Krahl, Olga Tschechowa, Paula Wessely, Henny Porten, and later Leni Riefenstahl.

Hitler encouraged these idle rumors: They increased his prestige, satisfied his ego, and at the same time enabled him to conceal his real feminine interests from the world press. The tattlers were so convinced that the new Lola Montez could only be an exotic *femme fatale* from the films or high society that they paid no attention to the simple little shop assistant who was there all the time under their very noses.

Thus the legend of Hitler's love affair with Leni Riefenstahl is completely unfounded. She herself, after exploiting it to the full, had finally to destroy it. She was only received once or twice at Berchtesgaden, and then on the occasion of an official audience. There is not the slightest proof, not a shred of serious evidence to suggest the possibility of a private encounter, even a chance one, of a personal correspondence or of any form of direct contact. Eva Braun, who was so jealous of all women, even of her own shadow, was not even aware of Leni Riefenstahl as a rival.

Hitler's extreme gallantry toward Olga Tschechowa may have reflected something more than passing admiration. She was too wise and too independent a woman to let herself be caught in the Hitlerian toils, but I am convinced that she had a certain influence on him. When, as the result of an article on the monstrous treatment of the Jews in the Warsaw ghetto, I had the misfortune—or perhaps the good fortune—to incur Hitler's disfavor, she interceded for me, and it may be thanks to her that I escaped immediate deportation.

Eva too had dreamed of becoming a film star. She was always boasting about her successes in amateur theatricals and had at one time thought of taking singing and elocution lessons. But her father had thrown up his hands in horror. Where was she going to find the money for this crazy undertaking? He was certainly not going to encourage any daughter of his to abandon her legitimate occupation in order to become an entertainer. How could she contemplate dragging the old, the honorable name of Braun in the mud, and what would his colleagues in the teaching profession think of him?

For once, unknown to him, he had an ally. Hitler abhorred the idea of Eva's becoming a ballerina, singer, or a stage actress. He was too selfish to be prepared to share "his" Eva with anybody else, and he did not wish her to appear in public. Her role was the exact opposite: to remain as unobtrusive as possible.

Eva did not completely renounce this dream, however. She harked back to it from time to time, and once in Berchtesgaden she announced, "When the Chief has won the war" (she often called Hitler the "Chief"), "he has promised that I can go to Hollywood and play my own part in the film of our life story."

She consoled herself meanwhile by exercising, in her lover's name, a sort of supreme censorship on the plays and films produced in Germany. She wrote synopses for Hitler, who did not have time to see everything and who besides tended to like only farces and adventure films. Eva was chiefly interested in American movies and organized private screenings even when, for political or economic reasons, the distribution of films from the United States was prohibited. She found nearly all of them to her taste, but seldom tried to persuade Hitler to lift the interdiction imposed by Goebbels. On the contrary, she derived a certain pleasure from the realization that she was in a privileged position and that the rest of Germany was debarred from sharing her enjoyment. Besides, her rare interventions had just the opposite effect. For instance, she was immensely enthusiastic about *Gone with the Wind*. She pictured herself as a Scarlett O'Hara courted by a Rhett Butler-Hitler; once she even dressed up as a Southern belle and mimed a scene from the film, which she had persuaded Hitler to see. No doubt impressed by the scenes of civil war and finding a certain pro-racist element in the film, he decided to allow it to be shown in all German theaters. Then Eva started to talk about nothing but Clark Gable—what a man, what a hero, what style, what a superb actor! She had photographs of him in her room, began to imitate his voice and speak English at table, and expressed a desire to take up riding. She demanded a new screening at least once a week. Finally Hitler, his patience exhausted and his jealousy aroused, gave a counterorder. Under the pretext of a foreign-currency shortage, the film was sent back to Metro-Goldwyn-Mayer, who never understood the real reason for this change of policy.

To return to 1933. Now that she was the mistress of the Chancellor of the Reich, Eva decided that she was entitled to a private phone in order to be able to speak to him in Berlin and also to be informed of his presence in Munich, for he usually arrived without warning. She overcame the objections of her parents, who could not see the need for this installation, with the excuse of her work commitments for Hoffmann. Her father found it hard to understand why the telephone had to be placed near Eva's bed, why nobody was authorized to answer it and why his daughter bolted the door during certain conversations or even hid under the bedclothes. These precautions were necessary, for even if Hitler had used his assumed names, Wolf or Schneider, his voice would have betrayed him, and her parents must be kept in the dark about the real state of his relations with Eva. Hitler, Chancellor though he was, found it difficult to get through. There were too many busy bodies who tapped his line. He therefore had to resign himself to using the public call boxes like any ordinary person, and as he never had enough change on him, this was not always a simple undertaking. The members of his entourage hazarded anxious guesses about the identity of the person at the other end of the line. Was Hitler telephoning to some supersecret service, or was he having a clandestine conversation with Mussolini, Henry Ford, or even the Prince of Wales?

The irregular hours kept by Eva exasperated her parents. Her mother was always lamenting, "But where is your sister; didn't she say with whom she was going out?" Her father would bang his fist on the table: "Always at the cinema, at this hour. A girl ought to be home by ten o'clock. She says she's spending the night with a girl friend. Do you know these people?"

Eva explained her nocturnal absences in various ways, according to the occasion. When she went to Berchtesgaden, Hitler, always mindful of appearances, did not accommodate her in Haus Wachenfeld but in the Hotel Post or the Berchtesgadener Hof, according to the evidence of the manageress of one of these hotels. Later, Eva stayed at the Platterhof, the vast hotel in the immediate vicinity of Hitler's property.

Eva's father, in spite of all the explanations, made great scenes when his daughter returned, especially when she absented herself over the weekend. For, anticlerical and Protestant though he was, he tyrannically insisted that his daughters should attend Sunday Mass.

Gretl, whom Eva had nicknamed Mogerl because she was always sulking, had left the convent, and the three sisters were very cramped for space in their room. Moreover, whenever Eva received her telephone calls from Berlin she turned everybody out. There were many other causes for friction. Finally, one evening at table Eva shocked her family by announcing, "I've decided to have my own apartment. I'm over twenty-one and I have the means. Ilse and Gretl can come and live with me." Ilse, who by now had an inkling of the factors involved, did not want to play chaperone. The adventurous and carefree Gretl, on the other hand, accepted with enthusiasm. The idea of making Eva live with one, if not both, of her sisters came from Hitler, who, with his bourgeois mentality, demanded categorically that the proprieties be respected.

Eva moved into the apartment on August 9, 1935. It was situated in the Wiedermeyerstrasse, a residential street in the Bogenhausen district, in the immediate vicinity of Hitler's lodgings. It had three comfortable rooms, with servant accommodations and central heating, and there was an elevator. Hitler paid the rent indirectly through Hoffmann. With his inveterate avarice, he had bought the furniture at a reduced price. There was not a single picture on the walls and Eva had to borrow linen and cutlery from her mother. A Hungarian maid had been engaged, whose chief occupation, when she was not playing Ping-Pong in the hall was drying the washing of her lover, an army sergeant, on the balcony of the apartment. These articles of masculine clothing floating in the breeze were a strange emblem for a habitation reserved for two young ladies. . . .

Hitler disappointed his young mistress's hopes of frequent visits, and ventured very rarely into this new abode. He could only go there late at night in order to escape observation by the servant or the neighbors. Even then, it was impossible for him to free himself from his police escort, some of whom inevitably mounted guard in front of the house, while others waited on the stairs. Their presence created such confusion that he preferred to stay away. Thus the eternal waiting continued for Eva, even in this new house; she was glued to the telephone day and night, not daring to run the risk of missing a call. It was a monotonous, irritating, depressing wait, a wait which was to last until the end of her life and which was the very essence of her great love.

Although Ilse visited her sister from time to time, she had not happened to meet Hitler; only the other sister had had this opportunity. Eva preferred to keep her elder sister at a distance because she distrusted her impertinence. On the other hand, she greatly wished to introduce her parents to Hitler. Herr Professor Braun, however, like all fathers with marriageable daughters, apparently had no desire to meet an individual, Chancellor and Führer though he might be, whose role as far as his daughter was concerned seemed to him highly dubious. For he was aware that Hitler's behavior was not that of a suitor, though Eva spoke of him in terms that revealed more than a strictly professional interest. But his hand was forced. One afternoon, during a Sunday excursion to Lambach, near the Austrian border, the Brauns were sitting on a café terrace, when they saw Eva coming across the main square of the little town toward them. "What a surprise, Papa and Mama. I'm with the Führer's escort, for the photos. I simply must introduce you. . . ."

An American judge who wrote a book dealing in part with the life of Eva Braun has transformed this incident into a Greek tragedy. According to him, the mother was filled with shame, while the father, after overcoming his consternation, took Hitler aside and presented him with an ultimatum: "Do you or do you not intend to marry my daughter?"

Fritz Braun denied the truth of this story under oath and his wife has assured me in person that it is ridiculous. If Frau Braun was intimidated it was purely out of excessive respect for this "great man" and the fear that the choice of her dress and the state of her hair were not worthy of the occasion. As for Papa Braun, who perhaps pretended not to know that his daughter had a liaison or was very much in love with Hitler would never have put himself in a grotesque situation by broaching such a question. Moreover, Fritz Braun never washed his dirty linen in public, especially in a café, and as a state employee and an officer of the reserve, he would never have dared to show such lack of respect for the Chancellor of the German Reich.

His surprise must only have been relative, because all week their daughter had been telling them that if they went to Lambach on Sunday, she would try to introduce them to Hitler, and she had given them detailed instructions on how to behave. The meeting was brief and pleasant. Hitler talked about the fineness of the weather, paid a compliment to Eva's sweetness, and kissed the hand of Mama Braun, who was too overcome to speak.

Fritz Braun, who was quite as obstinate as his daughter, was far from mollified by this encounter and did not give up the attempt to assert his paternal rights. He considered that this introduction authorized him to write to Hitler, and the resulting letter has a certain historical significance, not because it expresses the state of mind of a father, but because it is one of the rare documents proving that a

German dared at this time to send the Führer a written protest:

Munich

7 September 1935

Your Excellency,

I find myself in the extremely unpleasant position of having to importune you with a problem of a private nature, in other words, of having to express to you my distress as a paterfamilias. You, the Führer of the German Nation, who are confronted by other and certainly much greater cares. But since the family is the smallest but also the most vital of the social cells, a cell that enables an honest and well-organized state to develop, I think that this step is to some extent justified, and I would therefore ask you to help me.

My family is at present divided, for my two daughters Eva and Gretl have moved into an apartment that you have put at their disposal and I, as the head of the family, was presented with an accomplished fact. Naturally, I have always greatly reproached Eva when she came home long after normal office closing hours. For I believe that a young girl who is working intensely for eight hours a day needs to relax in the family circle in the evening in order to remain in good health. I know that I am thereby defending a point of view that, alas, seems old-fashioned. The parents' supervision of the children and the children's obligation to live at home until such time as they get married is nonetheless an inviolable principle. This is my code of honor. Quite apart from this, I miss my daughters enormously.

I should therefore be very grateful, your Excellency, if you would grant me your comprehension and your help, and I conclude this letter with the plea that you will not encourage this thirst for liberty in my daughter Eva, despite the fact that she is over twenty-one. Please advise her to return to the bosom of her family.

Yours very respectfully,

Fritz Braun

Herr Braun was not only an excellent diplomat, as this letter proves, but also a prudent man. He did not send the missive directly to Hitler, thus avoiding the possibility of interception by subalterns or of an overviolent reaction on the part of the Führer, who was beginning to send people to concentration camps for the slightest peccadillo. Instead, he asked Heinrich Hoffmann to give the letter in person to the Chancellor. Hoffmann, who was no less prudent and had no wish to lose his hen that laid the golden eggs, gave the letter to Eva, who, after reading it, tore it into a thousand pieces. She gave her father the impression that his message had been conveyed but had remained unanswered.

This was probably what Fritz Braun had really wished for; nevertheless, as a systematic man, he had kept a copy of the epistle for his pals of the *Stammtish* and later, for the denazification tribunal and for posterity.

Franziska Braun has said to me that she also, without her husband's knowledge, wrote a similar letter to Hitler. She never got a reply.

CHAPTER NINE

The mountain over the salt mine

There is a story that, while still a young boy, Hitler once bought a lottery ticket in Linz and, convinced that he was going to win first prize, made innumerable plans in the weeks before the draw for the luxury villa that he was going to build with the prize money. Naturally his number did not come up, and for weeks Hitler sulked, as was his wont then and as he continued to do later in life when he was told of bad news such as the loss of a battle. The historian of Hitler's youth, Franz Jetzinger—whom I knew in prison, when we shared the same cell on the "Elizabeth promenade" in Vienna—told me of the episode. He was skeptical about its veracity and yet to me it seems plausible. We all build castles in the air at one time or another.

Eventually Hitler did build his dream castle. The relatively small town of Berchtesgaden owed its bygone prosperity to the fact that it served as a hunting lodge for the Bavarian rulers and was conveniently situated near the Austrian border, so that its inhabitants grew rich from smuggling. It should be noted here, however, for the benefit of those who do not know the district, that the town of Berchtesgaden is quite wrongly cited as the place where Hitler established his residence. The town was completely ignored by Hitler and his court; only Eva Braun went there on rare occasions to shop or to accompany her friend Maria Schönemann to Sunday Mass. Hitler never set foot there after his accession to power. His entourage and the SS guards of course frequented the local hotels and beerhouses to alleviate their boredom, and thus the neighborhood grew enormously prosperous thanks to them. Hitler's residence was situated on the northeast slope of a mountain, the Hoher Goll, immediately south of Berchtesgaden. On the other slope of this mountain, about ten kilometers from Berchtesgaden by road, there is a tiny village called Obersalzberg. The name means High Salt Mountain and no doubt referred to the salt mine at Berchtesgaden. During the war inmates of the Dachau concentration camp were sent to suffer a slow death in this mine, a detail that the inhabitants discreetly gloss over, even today. Hitler therefore lived on the verge of Obersalzberg and liked to call his vast house the Berghof. The habitués preferred to say the "Berg." Yet the world continued to call it Berchtesgaden, as I shall.

For many centuries, the mountain had merely afforded refuge to struggling farmers who in winter were forced to work in the salt mine, woodcutters, and especially poachers and later smugglers who had fallen foul of the authorities. Then in 1877, a lady by the name of Maurizia Mayer, who was commonly and graciously known as Moritz, bought a dilapidated farm, the "Steinhauslehnen" for 13,500 marks. She was an energetic woman who proceeded to enlarge her property and open a restaurant called the Platterhof. Tourists heard about the inn and soon civil servants from Munich began putting up cottages in the immediate vicinity. In 1911 Karl Schuster built a hotel there called the Türkenhof, on the spot where a veteran of the wars against the Turks once had a hut.

A few yards from the Türkenhof, on a slope that commands an unrivaled view of Salzburg and the breathtaking Austrian Alps, a certain Winter, a commercial counselor, had a large country house built in 1916 and 1917, which he called Haus Wachenfeld. In 1925 Hitler persuaded the party and his patrons to rent this house for him so that he could make it "his hermitage." He had been liberated from the Landsberg prison, and the interdiction on the National Socialist Party having been recently lifted, he had tried to organize the first meetings in the town of Berchtesgaden.

His familiarity with the place dated from his prewar peregrinations. He sometimes went walking there on Sundays to catch a glimpse of Austria in the distance and chat with the picnickers from Salzburg. Dietrich Eckart, his poet friend, who gave Hitler the name "Führer," often took him there with Anton Drexler, one of the founders of the party, and Hermann Esser, another early disciple. After Hitler's release from prison in 1924, he installed

himself at the Purtscheller Haus (hotel) in order to escape
public notice and finish certain chapters of *Mein Kampf*.
Frau Bechstein, whose husband had a house in the neighborhood, paid for his lodging. In this way she could have
him conveniently close to her.

The royalties of *Mein Kampf*, which averaged a million
marks a year (the book was undeniably a best seller even
when Hitler was still little known and more or less ridiculed), plus the appanages of the party, which was then in
the ascendant, enabled Hitler to buy Haus Wachenfeld.
Later on he made a few temporary modernizations to the
place and carried out a number of interior improvements.
His sister Angela Raubal became the housekeeper at the
villa, and after the death of her daughter Geli, she took up
permanent residence there. Hitler stayed there more and
more frequently and regularly invited his circle of intimates. From time to time Eva Braun was of the company
but not often enough to give rise to gossip. Angela Raubal
hated Eva, for in her opinion Hitler should have been totally faithful to the memory of her daughter, who had
died so tragically. One even wonders if it was not the
mother herself who created the myth of the love affair between Geli and her half brother.

Angela Raubal saw in Eva Braun an upstart who, under
her apparent demureness, was slyly working to ensnare her
poor brother, who, with his simplicity and inexperience,
was such an easy prey for ambitious females. She referred
to Eva Braun as *die blöde Kuh,* the stupid cow, an epithet
she was not the first to coin. Even the Braun sisters were
just as disrespectful in their choice of nicknames for this
girl who was bent on pursuing an inaccessible middle-aged
politician and who created chaos in the family with her
periodical suicides. In fact, an intimate friend of Ilse
Braun's, while talking to me confidentially twenty-two
years after Eva's death, had a *lapsus linguae* and referred
to her as *blöde Kuh.* Eva and Ilse, who were always
squabbling, did not hesitate to call each other all sorts of
names, and naturally this hostility was reflected in their re-
spective circles.

Angela Raubal for her part was forever trying to turn
her half brother against Eva and constantly humiliated her
when she was invited to Haus Wachenfeld. Usually, all the
rooms somehow happened to be occupied, and Eva had to
be lodged at the Platterhof or at another inn some dis-

tance away. For in 1933, the Türkenhof adjacent to Hitler's house had been taken over, and the Gestapo and secret services had moved into the premises.

Angela ostentatiously avoided shaking Eva's hand, greeted her simply as *Fräulein* and not with the more respectful formula *Gnädiges Fräulein,* and ignored her presence most of the time except when she was alone with Hitler, then she would find some pretext for interrupting the tête-à-tête.

Angela seemed less preoccupied with morality whenever her half brother invited some of the young girls who went wandering about the neighborhood to tea. They sampled the pastries that Angela Raubal had ordered, the Führer stroked their hands, and they went home, ecstatically floating in the clouds, as though they had met Saint Michael or Siegfried in person. Every day more than five thousand visiting pilgrims climbed the Obersalzberg in the hope of catching a glimpse of their Führer on this corner of what had become the "holy mountain." They waited patiently for hours on end, under a burning sun or with their feet numbed by snow—depending on the season—with the patience shown by the faithful on Sundays at St. Peter's in Rome hoping for the Pope's benediction. The women were the most obstinate; they stayed until well after nightfall. They all hoped to be invited by Hitler, and more than one was prepared to offer something more than her admiration and the assurance of her ardent Nazi faith. But Hitler merely spoke briefly to the youngest and prettiest, signed a few autographs, and always behaved with perfect decorum toward these afternoon admirers. He could hardly do otherwise, even if his principles of conduct had allowed it, for by then he was living in a glasshouse. But certain aides-de-camp and other male members of his entourage sometimes noted down the names and addresses of the more attractive visitors and apparently a number of adventures resulted.

The good Germans of the time particularly admired the simplicity of their Führer's rustic life. For Haus Wachenfeld was only a modest country house, a big Bavarian chalet which today would be looked at askance by a new-rich shopkeeper. The first floor was built of ashlar, but the second floor was of wood with a balcony all round in the Alpine style. Later, a terrace was built in front of the house. There were large stones on the roof, no doubt to stop the wind from blowing the slates off. The kitchen was in the basement. There was an attic, and a dog kennel behind the house—in other words nothing lavish. But there was the luxury of the mountains. Hitler had chosen this northeast slope because it overlooked the Salzburg plain, a spectacular panorama. This slope was comparatively deserted and a zone of silence encircled the house. From a few paces away there was a view of the Kehlstein peak with eagles and vultures soaring around its precipices. From the Kehlstein it was sometimes possible to see the summits of the Dolomites and the towering ranks of the Bavarian Alps. At the foot of the mountain lay Berchtesgaden on its undulating hills, and on the other side of the mountain stretched the silver expanse of the Königsee with its possibilities for swimming and occasional sailing.

There was one disadvantage: The shadow of the mountain lengthened very fast at dusk, and at night it was bitterly cold in the house. The ladies liked to huddle around the blazing fires. "We're forever roasting our *derrières*," remarked Eva Braun.

Hitler, who declared himself a nature worshipper, had vetoed the cutting down of trees, even for important constructional purposes, and he also had a number of houses demolished because they obstructed his view. In order to protect the surrounding fauna he later made Bormann issue a regulation forbidding the inhabitants of the vicinity to keep cats or dogs. He even changed the local appellations: A mountain whose outline reminded him of Field Marshal von Moltke's profile became Moltkeberg. He named a mountain face opposite the Kehlstein the Mausoleum because it was there that he wished to be buried. Eva Braun called a certain hill *Schokoladehügel* simply because on walks Hitler was in the habit of resting there and distributing chocolate to the ladies during the halt. This Berchtesgaden language has to be treated with great circumspection. For example, for years I let my imagination wander over a photograph in Eva's album showing a room in the residence full of softly padded furniture, the *Türkenzimmer*. I pictured harem nights with odalisques dancing in this room, all wreathed in the smoke of incense. To my great disillusionment, I was then informed that the *Türkenzimmer* was so called simply because it overlooked the Türkenhof inn.

At the beginning of 1936, Hitler decided to transform

this modest property. He now had vast financial resources at his disposal, and he realized that as a head of state conducting diplomatic negotiations of a highly personal nature, he needed a more imposing residence. Moreover he wished to offer his guests—such was his fear of solitude —the greatest comfort in order to be sure of their visits. These were the explanations he gave to Hess and Bormann. In reality he was simply realizing a youthful ambition. His would be no dream castle like Ludwig II's Neuschwanstein, no exquisite residence like Frederick the Great's Sans Souci, but the material embodiment of the aspirations he had had as a completely destitute member of the lower middle class.

In times gone by, in Linz, he had wanted to own a domain in order to have Stephanie, the girl he admired as a youth, preside there. In 1936 he had another woman at hand, more submissive but quite as attractive: Eva Braun. Therefore he abruptly dismissed his sister Angela from Berchtesgaden without even allowing her a period of grace. She had to leave by train with only a few trunks, and be satisfied with a modest pension. She protested that she was the victim of treacherous intrigues. In actual fact, her brother had never forgotten the humiliations inflicted on him by this half sister and her husband during his dark days in Linz and Vienna, and was merely casting off a dead weight. Angela Raubal later married a Dresden architect, Professor Hamitsch, who was subsequently killed during a Russian offensive. She very rarely went back to visit her half brother and lived the rest of her life in Vienna.

Having thus got rid of an embarrassing witness, Hitler himself prepared the plans for a bedroom, a boudoir, and a bathroom in the immediate vicinity of his own room and studio. When everything was ready, he officially made Eva Braun his mistress by inviting her to become mistress of the new Obersalzberg.

Admittedly Eva did not carry the keys, rarely supervised the kitchen operations, and never interfered with the servants, for she hated any form of household responsibility. There was a housekeeper, Margaret Mittelstrasse, who dealt with everything and was completely devoted to Eva. A certain Doering and his wife were in charge of the administrative machinery. One of the cooks, Lilly, came from the Osteria, Hitler having engaged her on the strength of a dish of cheese noodles that he had savored one day. The other cook, Mrs. Schaflitz, was expert at concocting strange dietetic mixtures on her electric stove, and Eva was careful not to intervene in this department.

Although Eva, in spite of her position as mistress of the house, was forced to disappear on the occasion of visits by important personalities and had also to keep out of sight when Hitler was holding a council of war or presiding at a meeting of his party lieutenants, she was highly respected, and even Bormann did not dare to displease her. Between 1936 and 1945, she spent over two thirds of her time at the Berghof and arranged for her close friend Herta to have an apartment permanently at her disposal. Her sister Gretl also spent considerable time at the Berghof, and Eva invited almost all her friends and acquaintances in turn.

Instead of demolishing Haus Wachenfeld, Hitler built all around it, as one builds a cathedral around a chapel. A Munich architect, Professor Roderich Fick, directed the work. Additions were made, a floor was added, the monumental steps that were to feature so often in newsreels were constructed. The most valuable materials were used, marble imported from Carrara, Bohemian stone, and precious wood that cost a fortune in foreign currency.

More or less detailed descriptions of the exterior and official parts of the Berghof are to be found in many books and memoirs of famous personages, and the image of the two helmeted SS mounting guard like statues at the foot of the steps is still a vivid one. But what was a woman's impression of the Berghof? Hitler's personal secretary, Traudl Junge, who was Eva's contemporary and her rival in charm, gave me this account of her impressions on her first visit to the Berghof. "From my room under the eaves of the old Haus Wachenfeld I went down by a spiral staircase to the antechamber, predominantly of glass, that opened onto the courtyard on one side and onto an enormous drawing room with a magnificent fireplace of green faience. Then I crossed the immense lounge, as shown on the postcards, distributed by millions, with its gigantic window looking onto the Untersberg peak. Then I entered the long, spacious dining room where there was a table for twenty-four with real armchairs, instead of upright chairs, all round. The walls were paneled with pine and the furniture was of the same wood. There were imitation medieval lamps of wrought iron, a large cupboard set in the wall and a few precious vases to lend a touch of color to these rather heavy surroundings.

"The main hall was impressive. I admired the tapestries on the walls, and Eva Braun, whose great aim was to appear cultured, said that they were genuine 'Aubusson-Gobelins.' They could be automatically raised when a film was to be shown, a screen being lowered in their place and the walls at the other end opening to reveal apertures for the projector. The hall was Gothic in style, and I was struck by the mosaic tables and the fireplace, which, according to Eva, was a gift from Mussolini.

"There were other rooms on this floor, including a kitchen cum pantry, a foyer, and a guardroom, but I was eager to go up to the floor above, by a velvet-covered staircase, to the Führer's apartments. There was a huge corridor, quite as imposing as the great hall on the first floor, with enormous pictures on the walls in lieu of windows. Vases, curios, statuettes everywhere, an extremely valuable but motley collection that obviously consisted of presents from a great variety of sources.

"There was a tomblike silence in the corridor. I had been asked to take off my shoes. In front of a door, two Scottish terriers mounted guard in stony immobility and did not even raise their muzzles when they heard us. They were Stasi and Negus, and the room was that of their mistress Eva Braun. Close by was Hitler's bedroom. Between the two rooms was an immense bathroom with a bath of marble from the Dolomites and gilded taps. But the bathroom did not have access onto the corridor. Then came Hitler's big studio. On the other side of the corridor was a small two-room apartment with a bath that was occupied by Hitler's manservant and chauffeur. A little room for Eva's maid was right beside the staircase leading to the floor above."

There are photos of Eva's room, which was heavily furnished with a sofa below a picture of a nude for which she is said to have posed. The walls were hung with silk and the whole thing was reminiscent of one of those *chambres separées* in Franz Lehár's operettas. There was a portrait of Hitler hanging opposite the nude which would have given nightmares to most women. Another detail: The number of the ivory telephone on the bedside table was 417, while that of Hitler's bedroom was 600.

This bedroom, to which access was so restricted, was

extremely simple: a Bavarian-style cupboard, pedestal tables, books scattered here and there, and an ordinary camp bed. Hitler wished to give the impression that, like all the famous *condottieri,* he slept in conditions of martial austerity. His room opened onto a vast balcony which was forbidden territory for everybody except Eva. Apparently he liked to contemplate the stars late into the night.

Traudl Junge affirms that she never became acclimated to the Berghof. "The place had a strange, undefinable quality that put you on your guard and filled you with odd apprehensions. The only comfortable room was the library on the first floor, which in the old house had been Hitler's private sitting room. It was rustically furnished, with beer mugs placed here and there for decoration. The books at everybody's disposal were of no great interest: world classics that nobody seemed to have read, travel atlases, a large dictionary, albums and drawings, and of course copies of *Mein Kampf* bound in gold and morocco leather. I also liked the little winter garden with its greenhouse full of orchids, but the finest feature of the Berghof was the terrace, which was immense, full of color, pleasant, with the whole world for a backcloth."

It would take too much space to describe the Berghof in detail, with its underground passages, its chancellery offices, the quarters for the aides-de-camp, the surgery of the dentists Dr. Blaschke and his assistant Dr. Richter, who came especially from Munich to give Hitler and Eva Braun dental treatment (a detail that will later prove significant), its carved cupboards stuffed with parchments proclaiming Hitler an honorary citizen of more than five thousand German and foreign towns, the attics with their accumulation of presents from the four corners of the globe, including fifty or so cushions with *Ich liebe Sie* embroidered on them, and many other gifts of which undoubtedly the most mystifying was the sword of the Landshut public executioner.

Hitler owned only the land surrounding the Berghof, a small park adjoining it and the "Teahouse," of which further mention will be made. To protect his privacy, he asked Rudolph Hess to ensure that the immediate vicinity was not invaded by importunate visitors. Hess bought the adjacent real estate with party funds. But when his assistant Martin Bormann took the matter in hand, he indulged in an interesting form of speculation. He had originally obtained the land at a low price because for a good number of landowners Hitler was a rather embarrassing neighbor. When he became Chancellor, however, the situation changed. The prices soared, and then Bormann forced the sale of the land and properties under threat of legal seizure. He now had the law on his side, but he rarely had recourse to judges and bailiffs. The SS merely harassed the recalcitrant owners so much (clients were debarred from the inn, electric wires were mysteriously cut) that they finally capitulated. Bormann then sold this land at a high price to important government personalities. Like the courtiers of Louis XIV, who offered a fortune to occupy lodgings as near as possible to the royal apartments, the Görings, Speers, Ribbentrops, and naturally Bormann himself built or modified houses close to that of Hitler. Göring's estate was impressive, but he rarely went there. Goebbels, on the other hand, who played at being a poor relation, made shift with the Bechstein house, which Bormann had appropriated in apparent ignorance of the friendship that Helene Bechstein had once cultivated with the then unknown Hitler. The Bechsteins had to content themselves with a lodge in the neighborhood, while the main dwelling was refurbished and put at the disposal of important guests. Mussolini, for instance, stayed there when he was at Berchtesgaden. Bormann had chosen for himself a chalet which had a modest exterior but was furnished in exquisite taste and provided with all modern comforts. He had also acquired a farm, the only building that still exists today, which theoretically supplied the Berghof with milk, butter, and vegetables. There was a greenhouse for mushrooms that had cost a small fortune. The pretext for its installation had been that Professor Morell had suggested a mushroom diet to Hitler, but the Führer refused to touch them, such was his dread of being poisoned. One can imagine the profits that Bormann made from the sale of land and above all from the construction of new buildings, which was also his domain.

Hitler, although he had begun to isolate the Berghof hermetically from the rest of the world, had decided that the admirers who came to see him must be able to spend the night in a comfortable hotel room at a cost of one mark. He therefore had the Platterhof rebuilt. Bormann supervised this gigantic work, which continued well into the war. He had priorities and could find the most unobtainable construction materials. This hotel destined for the people finally served only to accommodate a few party high priests and Eva Braun's friends. Toward the end of the war, it was transformed into a military hospital. It was not destroyed, and the Americans turned it into a holiday hotel for the army. Needless to say, they built a huge golf course just under Hitler's old windows. They too prefer to admit only officers or visiting politicians.

On the eve of the Second World War, it was practically impossible to gain access to the Obersalzberg without a special pass. A barbed-wire entanglement three feet high had been placed around Hitler's residence and the adjoining buildings. This was the *Hoheitsgebiet*, the seignorial compound. Another barbed-wire barricade surrounded the entire zone, which was under the supervision of the local police. Internal protection was entrusted to officers of the criminal police and to Reichssicherheitsdienst (security service) brigades under the direction of superintendent Rattenhuber. Later, spacious barracks were built for the SS. The troops came from Berlin in regular relays to serve as a guard of honor, although the possibility of a parachute attempt by Anglo-American troops, or else, in the event of a putsch, a surprise attack by the German Army were probably also envisaged. The members of the guard were recruited among the SS on the basis of seniority and well-tested fanaticism. They had the inscription *Adolf Hitler* embroidered on the left sleeves of their uniforms. They were divided into three squads: first, the door guards and the operators of the telephone exchange, secondly the car-park guards commanded by Kempka, Hitler's personal chauffeur, and finally the domestic personnel, who were called the *Schatten*, or shadows, and included the men-servants Linge, Krause, Schneider, and Junge. At night the neighborhood was patrolled by soldiers armed with machine guns who were under orders to fire first and ask questions afterward. "A minister's uniform is no justification for being there," was the injunction given by Bormann. Passes had to be in order. Eva Braun's was permanent and gave her the status of a secretary. Those of her friends and sisters stated that they were "guests of the Führer."

These precautionary measures grew more drastic as the military situation deteriorated. A year before the famous plot of July 20, 1944, there had been an attempt on Hitler's life in the vicinity of Berchtesgaden, at Klessheim Castle. A bomb had been found in a soldier's knapsack during a maneuver in the Führer's presence. The soldier had intended to throw it at Hitler.*

In order to complete the enormous task he had undertaken, Bormann had practically transformed the Obersalzberg into a vast building site and had been forced to take on foreign labor, voluntary or otherwise. At one time there had been five thousand men working there, most of the time in revolting conditions and for a miserable pittance. They were Czechs, Poles, later Ukrainians, and toward the end predominantly Italians. These workmen could not leave the zone but were free to circulate after working hours. They were forbidden to approach Hitler's house, for the Führer did not wish to see strange faces outside his windows.

I have been assured that there were never any prisoners from concentration camps among these workmen. By chance, while escaping from a locality close to Berchtesgaden where I had sheltered after a bombing raid during my transportation from Vienna to Dachau, I struck up acquaintance with a lady on the train. Together we had to cross Munich while the town was ablaze, its streets littered with corpses. Under these conditions the lady became loquacious and confided that she was the wife of one of the Obersalzberg SS. Yes she said, there were *KZ Haftlinge* (concentration camp prisoners) who were employed "for dynamiting the rock and laying the foundations." But they were chiefly there to impress the foreign workers, for the SS brooked no delay, absence, or slovenliness in the work. For the slightest lapse, the foreigners were thrown into prison and tortured. At night in their quarters the SS would boast of these brutal feats of discipline. There was a brisk sale of objects confiscated from the aliens. Every wife of an SS was entitled to have a woman from the East as a servant, without any obligation to pay her wages.

My traveling companion told me she had often met Eva Braun. "She was dressed like a stage lady, which looked a little ridiculous up there on the mountain. She smiled at

---

* In a conversation reported by Dr. Henry Picker in *Hitlers Tischgespräche* Hitler related how a Swiss was on the watch for three months in Berchtesgaden for the opportunity of assassinating him under the pretext of presenting him with a petition.

the children and always pretended to photograph them. She had a supercilious air. We used to call her 'the merry widow.' "

Life at the Obersalzberg was very pleasant for the SS, who in any event preferred it to being at the front. They lived there in great comfort; there were assembly rooms, sports grounds, and even a day nursery. Moreover, the SS had an irresistible attraction for the local country girls. A few they married, as in the case of my lady traveler, but most of the time they merely contributed vigorously to the improvement of the Aryan race. Apparently this activity was encouraged, and special vitamin pills were even distributed. Picturesque spicy stories were sometimes told about affairs with ladies living at or visiting the Berghof.

Something that seemed to me incredible then, in December, 1944, and which I later discovered to be absolutely true, was the traveler's revelation that there had never been a cell of the National Socialist Party at the Obersalzberg. Hitler had provided for everything except that.

CHAPTER TEN

A day at the "Grand Hotel!"

Ilse Braun describes her first meeting with Hitler in a page of her diary written in 1939, as follows:

" 'Wait for us in the library, I'm going to introduce you to the Führer,' Eva had said to me. Embarrassed by the shortness of my cyclamen-colored lace evening dress, not knowing what to do with my hands, desperately longing for a cigarette, but under strict orders from Eva not to smoke, I stayed there kicking my heels. . . ."

It was New Year's Eve, the one day of the year which was officially celebrated at the Berghof and which therefore gave the ladies a chance to dress up and Eva the opportunity to triumph once a year in her extravagant evening gown, which had cost so much in anxieties, fittings, and money. Neither Ilse nor Eva suspected that this would be the last peacetime New Year's Eve. Hitler never celebrated Christmas; he usually spent it traveling, with political colleagues or in seclusion in his Munich apartment.

"Hitler was wearing tails in honor of the occasion. My sister had been at great pains to persuade him to dress with a minimum of good taste. 'Look at Mussolini,' she would say, 'he has a new uniform. And you, with those postman's caps.' She asked him to give up his eternal dark ties and his black shoes. She insisted that his valets should press his clothes every day. At the Obersalzberg, until the outbreak of war, Hitler nearly always wore civilian dress. Eva was constantly chiding him because his hair was badly combed, the lock on his forehead did not meet with her approval, or he had cut himself while shaving. Hitler would reply: 'There is more blood shed as a result of razor-blade gashes than on the battlefields of all the wars ever waged.'

"Hitler came toward me, took my hand, and raised it to his lips. His eyes were sky-blue, intense in their gaze, striking but always fixed, immobile. I was slightly disappointed, for I had imagined a more imposing man, more like the portraits that were displayed everywhere. He was always gesticulating dramatically with his hand. I examined his hands. They were very white, sensitive like those of a musician, not very masculine, but attractive. He complimented me: 'But the Braun sisters are all beauties.' He apologized for the fact that the room he had put at my disposal was not of the best—'We have too many people here, there's a shortage of space'—and insisted that I must consider myself at home in his house. When he looked at me, beads of sweat formed between my breasts, and I did not even have the courage to say *Danke schön* (thank you), though I had promised myself to make a great speech.

"The guests that evening, with a few exceptions, belonged to Hitler's favorite group and were about thirty in number. The only people known to the general public, apart from Hitler, were the Schmelling couple, the former world boxing champion and his wife, the Czech film star Anny Ondra. Otherwise the guests included Dr. Morell and Dr. Brandt with their ladies, the press chief Dietrich, his aide Lorenz, von Hasselbach, another of Hitler's doctors', the dentists Dr. Blaschke and Dr. Richter, Martin Bormann and his brother Albert." Little has been said about Albert Bormann, who was one of Hitler's aides, but did not get on with his brother. Martin, in fact, treated him in public with the contempt that he might have shown a servant. Hitler, however, faithful to his policy of "Divide and rule," kept him in his entourage. "There were other aides-de-camp—Brückner, Schaub, von Puttkammer, Albrecht, Engel, von Below, Schmundt, the photographer Hoffmann, Gerda Bormann, and the wives of some of the other gentlemen, the secretaries Wolff, Schroeder, and Gerda Daranowsky, Eva's friends Marion Theissen and Herta Ostermeyr, the managing director of the Daimler-Benz company, Werlin, and my sister Gretl.

"I noticed an abundance of caviar on the table. Hitler was very partial to it. But the champagne was a German brand. The dishes bore the gilded initials A.H., and so did the solid gold cutlery. I remember the fireworks show at the end of the meal. The quartermaster Willy Kannenberg had been specially imported from Berlin to organize the festivities. He revealed to me that the whole display had cost only 94.50 marks, which still seemed to me excessive, for there were only a few paltry rockets that staggered painfully up over the terrace. There was no dancing. Hitler detested and consequently banned this form of amusement (despite Eva's cajolery, he would not so much as dance a waltz with her when they were alone). Then Hitler went into the anteroom and took up his stand between two candelabra to receive the congratulations of the guests and then those of the staff. He took part in the lead-pouring ceremony, a Teutonic tradition dating from time immemorial. It consists in pouring some molten lead into a small basin of water and interpreting the future according to the shapes it assumes. Hitler did not seem satisfied with his results, for afterward he sat down in an armchair, gazing dejectedly at the fire, and hardly spoke for the rest of the evening. Eva was extremely worried about him."

Another mountain tradition was a fusillade in honor of the guests, for which the reservists and guides of Berchtesgaden presented themselves armed with carbines and antique shotguns (Hitler had financed them with 300 marks). On the Austrian side of the border, we could see the New Year torches and bonfires burning. Then, in the morning, the municipal band played Hitler's favorite marches and Franz Lehár melodies.

"When Hitler and Eva had taken their leave," Ilse Braun continues, "the atmosphere relaxed slightly, still more champagne and brandy were served, Kannenberg played the accordion (there was never a dance band even for New Year's Eve at the Obersalzberg), and I went down into the cellar, where a bowling alley had been set up. My sister was mad about the game, but Hitler, after trying once and missing every shot, refused ever to touch it again."

On normal days, however, life was not so spectacular at the "Grand Hotel," as Eva liked to call the Berghof. She had of course been inspired in this choice of a name by one of her favorite American films, based on the novel by the exiled writer Vicki Baum, of which she had organized a showing in spite of Goebbels' express interdiction.

An attempt will be made here to describe an ordinary day at the Berghof, using only the descriptions given to me by Eva's sisters, Ilse and Gretl, and by Hitler's two private secretaries, Gerda Daranowsky, known as "The Daran" or "Dara," and Traudl Junge. Gerda Daranowsky later married General Christian, who subsequently became the liaison officer between the Luftwaffe and the Führer. Her beauty was exceptional. "As soon as I have a pretty girl working for me and she has begun to know the routine," Hitler used to complain, "she is immediately snatched away from me. If I want to keep a secretary for any length of time, I have to make do with some fat horror." In reality, Hitler encouraged such marriages and in this case had granted Christian his promotion to the rank of general.

In the morning, the Berghof was wrapped in silence. In fact, the place seemed deserted. Ilse recalls that her sister asked her not to take a bath in the morning because the house was built of concrete and the noise of the water running in the bathroom disturbed Hitler's sleep. The inmates came down to breakfast according to their pleasure or the demands of the service. There was orange juice, coffee, tea or cocoa, a large assortment of brown bread, jam, and butter. During the war, butter was rationed in theory, but one could ask for more; white bread was reserved for Hitler, allegedly because of his stomach complaints. He rarely came down to breakfast. When he did, Eva was never far away. He took two cups of milk, some Leibniz biscuits, and some bitter cocoa. Eva asked for strong coffee and a generous portion of butter.

It was only toward midday, when the sun was high over the Kehlstein, that Eva Braun's Grand Hotel awoke from its torpor, like a stage set at rehearsal time. The Mercedes cars, black as locomotives, stopped with a sound of screeching brakes and arrogant boots on the asphalt sweep in front of the imposing flight of steps. The SS, looking like operetta soldiers, presented arms. Later, during the war, the visitors were chiefly generals of all arms and ranks. They preferred to go onto the veranda to smoke a last cigarette while waiting for the conference.

No member of Hitler's immediate entourage, least of all Eva Braun, could be present in the great hall or the drawing room during these political or military confabulations. They lasted indefinitely. Punctuality may be the courtesy of kings, but it was certainly not one of the qualities of Adolf Hitler. "That man was never hungry," remarks

Traudl Junge. It was often four o'clock in the afternoon
before lunch was served.

Finally a growling is heard: It is Negus and Stasi, Eva's
two black dogs, followed by their mistress. This is a sign
that Hitler is in the vicinity. Presently he approaches her
and kisses her hand ceremoniously like a reigning prince.
Then he kisses the hands of the other ladies, greets the
newcomers, and everybody chats. But not a single *apéritif*
is served. Eva talks to her friend Herta, to Dr. Brandt's
wife Anni, and to Frau von Below. The men address her
with a slight bow and call her *Gnädiges Fräulein*. The ladies, even her very close friend Herta, say Fräulein Braun.

Hitler comes over to tease her and make fun of her
dogs (which Eva is allowed to take with her to the table),
comparing them to a movie star's fans. "Your dog Blondie," retorts Eva, who did not like being mocked in public,
even affectionately, "is a calf." She is referring to Hitler's
favorite German shepherd. (Eva's Scottish terriers did in
fact look ridiculous—Hitler vetoed all photographs showing him with these dogs—but they were vicious and could
never abide Blondie's presence. Thus the Alsatian is
banned from the drawing room and confined to Hitler's
bedroom or the kennels.) Sometimes in the evening, when
the atmosphere is particularly *gemütlich* and Hitler has
managed to cajole Eva with the gift of a piece of jewelry
or the promise of another trip to Italy, he ventures to ask,
"Effie, will you allow poor Blondie to join us for half an
hour?" And Eva graciously smiles and gestures to the servant, who takes the redoubtable Stasi and Negus and shuts
them in their mistress's room. He comes down again with
Blondie, who can at last lie down at her master's
feet. . . .

The idea of a dictator with the whole of Europe temporarily under his sway asking a young girl for leave to have
his dog beside him, perhaps at a time when he has just issued orders for the subjugation of a whole province or the
camp deportation of a few thousand people, may seem absurd. But absurdity was one of the dominant characteris-
tics of the "Grand Hotel."

Heinz Linge, who was both Hitler's majordomo and his
personal valet, now approaches one of the lady guests and
informs her that the Führer is about to offer her his arm to
go to table. Another orderly advises the rest of the com-

pany of the order of precedence at table, and finally Linge announces: "The Führer is served."

Hitler was extremely particular about the service. He inspected the slightest details of the table, and woe betide the servants if a fork was out of place. Hand-painted Rosenthal china and silver with the Hitler monogram were customarily used. Eva supervised the flower arrangements. The napkins were folded in paper envelopes bearing the guests' names (soap was in short supply). At either end of the huge table there were saltcellars and oil and vinegar cruets of Bohemian glass.

Hitler insisted that the soup should be served very hot and could not stand any delay. The dishes were so scalding that once the Crown Princess of Italy, Maria-José, burned her tongue while tasting her soup.

The guests were required to finish their helpings and the servants could not remove a plate until it was empty. At first, it is said, the guests' manners were deplorable, but they grew more elegant as time went by. Hitler even sent an emissary to study table etiquette at the court of England, and his findings were passed on to the court of Berchtesgaden.

Martin Bormann always gave his arm to Eva Braun. This observance underlined Eva's position as mistress of the house. She sat on Hitler's right, while he took his place in the center of the big table, facing the window. The guest of honor was seated opposite him. The servants immediately brought in the salad, which was considered an hors d'oeuvre, and then the succession of dishes. An orderly inquired what drinks were desired. Hitler, with a frown of disapproval, allowed his guests to drink beer or Rhine wine, but both he and Eva Braun took only mineral water or cider. Occasionally he asked for a special beer which was brewed expressly for him at Holzkirch and which had an alcohol content of only 2 percent. He was not totally opposed to alcoholic drinks, however. Sometimes when he had a cold, he laced his tea with brandy, and after meals he frequently took a Fernet Branca or a Boonenkamp bitters.

At Hitler's request, the menus were written in German and in the simplest of terms. The dishes were often execrable. One could eat better in the most humble eating house on the Alexanderplatz. At the Berghof, however, quantities were unlimited, and the quality of the raw materials was unexceptionable. The vegetables, for instance, were grown in a special kitchen garden where the water was brought in from pure mountain springs. There was a special menu for vegetarians, but usually the only vegetarian was Hitler, who had a real obsession about meat. He maintained that carnivorous human beings were quite as cruel and pitiless as wild beasts. He ate meat only in *Leberknödel* (liver dumplings), his favorite Bavarian dish.

True, the other members of the company could eat beefsteaks ad libitum, except that at table, especially to newcomers, Hitler would deliver a sermon about the "carrion" they were eating, or would relate how he had visited a slaughterhouse in Poland, where cows were being massacred, calves were howling, blood was flowing . . . until nobody had any appetite left for sausages or steaks.

Except for the delicious Viennese pastries, most of the dishes set in front of Hitler's guests were inedible. Eva would tease him about his fads. He had dietetic specialties prepared by a cook from the clinic of Dr. Zabel, whose methods were inspired by those of the Swiss dietitian Bicher-Benner. A dish which Hitler relished and which can give some idea of the nature of these concoctions consisted of baked potatoes flavored with cream cheese and then liberally doused with linseed oil. . . .

Eva also followed a diet, but this was to keep her figure. Hitler joked with her: "When I first met you, you were plump, and now you're as straight as a ramrod. Women always say they want to make themselves beautiful for a man and then do everything that is contrary to this man's tastes. They do their utmost to conquer him, but then become slaves of fashion and think only of making their little friends jealous."

Politics were never discussed at table. The conversation was innocuous. Hitler complimented the ladies, recalled amusing episodes of his youth, chaffed Ambassador Hewel, whom he wanted to marry at all costs to Eva's sister and later to Ilsebill Todt. "Ilsebill is as pretty as a sunrise," he would say. Pretty women were his favorite topic of conversation. He would tell Eva that the Duchess of Windsor was only very slightly made up (he disliked makeup, which he described as "war paint," but Eva paid no heed and wore thick lipstick and powder), that her jewelry was simple, and he would describe her dress or her way of shaking hands. He marveled at the actress Zarah

Leander's plunging neckline, went into raptures over Anny Ondra's legs, made remarks about the Queen of Bulgaria or some minister's wife. Eva diverted the conversation to films or a fashionable play.

Hitler, as is well known, did not like contradiction, but he tolerated it when it came from a pretty guest. Ilse Braun and sometimes Gretl tried to prove to him that tobacco was quite harmless, but it was chiefly Eva's Viennese friend, Marion Schönemann, née Theissen, who showed incredible audacity.

It was Sunday, and she had just got back from Mass. "Was there a crowd there to admire your hat?" Hitler teased her. "Yes," she replied, "it was crammed. The crowd has got bigger and bigger since the party has been telling people not to go to church."

On another occasion: "People are grumbling; there's nothing in the shops these days. . . . Why are you chasing the poor nuns out of their convents? . . . But Herr Bormann, when you've finished trampling on my foot, you're hurting me. . . . Yes, Your Excellency," Marion continued with her irresistible Viennese accent, "those poor nuns, they already have to do without men and now the party is taking the rest away from them. . . . But Herr Bormann, have you finished? I've got my new shoes on, and you're demolishing them with your boot. . . ."

Hitler laughed, and Marion was repeatedly invited to the Grand Hotel.

The meal normally lasted sixty minutes and then everybody got ready for a walk. Hitler put on a gray oilskin lumber jacket and his peculiar felt hat, took his cane, and called for Blondie, whom he kept on the leash. He walked slowly and Blondie was on tenterhooks, for the fields were full of rabbits and squirrels basking quite fearlessly in the sun.

The destination of the walk was the Tea house, which must not be confused with the imposing pavilion which Bormann built at the top of the Kehlstein and which the United States division that liberated Berchtesgaden christened "The Eagle's Nest."

The Tea house was a small pavilion built on a hill called the Mosslahnerkopf, just opposite the Berghof. It had only three rooms, a lounge, a hall, and a boudoir. But from the windows at the back of the house there was a magnificent view of the Ach Torrent roaring down between houses that seemed no larger than matchboxes, with the baroque towers of Salzburg in the background. The guests lay down in the meadows when the weather was fine, and Eva would often take one photograph after another. She would ask Hitler to take off his hat, which he refused to do because of the sun, or else to remove his dark glasses or sit in a more becoming position.

In winter, they gathered around the fire. The pavilion was an architectural horror, but the furniture was comfortable and the staff served coffee, cakes, and liqueurs. Hitler drank tea made of apple peel, or so he claimed. The conversation was not general. Eva had noticed some peasant coverlets stowed in a corner and proposed to the ladies that they should take them away and make ski jackets of them. Bormann was talking about his beekeeper's worries. He wanted to produce honey for all of Berchtesgaden, but the queen bees were always decamping. Then Hitler would talk about his future plans, often using saucers, cups, and spoons to illustrate his speeches. When he was telling a story and forgot an important passage or detail, Eva would prompt him with a key word and Hitler, remembering, would continue to demonstrate with another cup. Then, although he claimed that he fell asleep with difficulty and only in conditions of absolute calm, he sometimes dozed off in his chair. Eva would pursue the conversation in a hushed voice and everybody else, out of tact and to please her, pretended not to notice that Hitler was napping.

It was during one of these very bourgeois siestas at the Tea house that an aide-de-camp burst in with the news of Rudolf Hess's flight to England. Hitler was beside himself with rage, summoned Hess's aide, Karl Heinz Pintsch, who was at the Obersalzberg to present his report, and threatened to have him shot on the spot. He wanted to arrest Hess's wife Ilse and their son Wolf-Rüdiger and have them deported to a concentration camp. Eva, however, intervened and pleaded with emotion for the young woman, although she admitted that Hess had made "a strange impression on her." She saw to it that Frau Hess was always treated with consideration.

Eva Braun's relations with the wives of other high-ranking commanders were not so personal. Anneliese von Ribbentrop, the heiress of the champagne king, ignored her royally. Elsa Himmler hardly ever came to Berghof.

"There's a woman born to be unhappy," Eva Braun said of her. Emmy Göring, who laid claim to the title "First Lady of the Third Reich," was at least the president of an association of the parvenu ladies of the Nazi regime whose slogan was "Away with Eva Braun." In her memories Frau Göring affirms that all her attempts at a social *rapprochement* were repulsed by Hitler's orders. She juggles with the truth just like her husband, the inimitable "Marshal of the Reich" who promised to call himself Meier if a single enemy plane flew over a square meter of German soil. Here is the true version of the story: Hitler had pleaded with Göring that Eva be treated with more respect by her companions. "I am the chief. But Eva is too young and too inexperienced to be a First Lady. But she is the only woman of my life, and after the war, when I go into retirement in Linz, she will become my wife."

Emmy Göring was deaf to such arguments. One day at Berchtesgaden, she invited the ladies of the Berghof to come and take tea in her villa. She invited everybody—secretaries, assistants, and even the hairdresser, Milli Schellmoser. The list of invitations had been draw up in alphabetical order, and Fräulein Braun appeared under the letter B. It was a flagrant affront. Hitler reacted vigorously. He telephoned to Göring and requested him to forbid his wife to concern herself any further with Fräulein Braun. Emmy Göring was no longer invited to the Berghof, and it is small wonder that Eva looked black every time there was a mention of Emmy in her presence.

With Magda Goebbels, it was more a question of rivalry in love. Magda was pretty, and Hitler was always attracted by her charm and when she visited the Berghof, Magda flirted outrageously with him.

Eva had never forgiven her the fact that she was kept away from the Obersalzberg during the period when Magda Goebbels, revolted by the scandal provoked by her husband's liaison with the Czech actress Lida Baarova, took refuge in Hitler's house, vociferously demanding a divorce. Hitler managed to calm her, and probably out of discretion, had kept his usual "clan" at a distance. But Magda often tried to snub Eva. Once, for example, she was boasting about having learned certain French expressions "in the smart boarding school where I was educated . . ." "But in my convent, dear madam," Eva interrupted her, "we spoke French fluently. . . ." She proceeded to spout French for a quarter of an hour, to the great vexation of Frau Geobbels, while the Führer, amused and very proud of his Eva, listened complacently, although he did not understand much of the speech either.

Eva writes in a letter: "Frau Goebbels has thanked me for the flowers through her secretary. I find this discourteous of her."

This document lends significance to an incident reported by Ilse Braun: "One evening before dinner Eva was chatting with Magda Goebbels in the latter's room. Magda was in an interesting condition, and very visibly so. At one point she turned to Eva and said to her, 'Fräulein Eva, could you please do up my shoelaces? I can't bend over.' Eva, without replying, went to the bell. A maid, Liesl, appeared. 'Would you be so kind as to tie Madam's shoelaces,' Eva suavely ordered the servant, and then left the room."

Eva's relations with Speer's wife were very amicable, and she also had a great liking for Bormann's spouse, whom she considered a good friend. Unfortunately Gerda Bormann was almost always pregnant (she had ten children) and had little free time. Eva found it very difficult to find a moment when she could photograph her friend with a normal figure. She accused Bormann of treating his wife and children brutally, and once went to Hitler in a high state of indignation because Bormann was publicly thrashing one of his boys. His chief offense in her eyes, however, was that of running after every petticoat in Berchtesgaden and even farther afield. Bormann thought of himself as a second Casanova and respected nobody, except Eva, whom everybody considered "untouchable." Eva's sisters and friends assured me that she loathed Bormann and that a secret rivalry characterized their relations. These ladies, however, all hated this miniature monster, and they may well be attributing their own aversions to Eva. Nobody liked Bormann, and Eva was probably no exception, but she was too intelligent not to realize that Bormann was Hitler's *deus ex machina* and that he could create serious difficulties for her and even, by dint of intrigues, ruin her. Until the end, Eva's sole objective was the conquest of Adolf Hitler, and she would certainly not have risked an open conflict with Bormann, yet "if she had wanted, she could have eliminated him," the Braun sisters still maintain.*

Hitler went back by car from the Tea house. There was a Volkswagen waiting, into which Blondie also climbed. Eva preferred to walk home with the rest of the party.

While Hitler was resting in his room, Eva organized card sessions, but the only game she played was a sort of tombola called Bimbo, for Hitler disapproved of games of chance. Sometimes she showed her photograph albums or amateur films that she had shot. Most people, however, took advantage of these free hours to write private letters or simply to go and smoke outside.

The evening meal was announced by telephone. The company assembled in the lounge around eight o'clock. The men were in mufti, but the ladies had made themselves beautiful in creations that came from the best dressmakers. Eva was the most elegant; she changed outfits six or seven times a day and frequently summoned the hairdresser for a setting. She always wore matching jewelry—a necklace, brooch and bracelet, and a diamond watch. She ordered her shoes from Ferragamo, of Florence. Hitler did not like these metamorphoses. "I don't recognize you with that new hairstyle," he would complain, or, "As soon as you have a pretty dress, instead of putting it on every night, you hide it away. . . ."

He noticed every detail of feminine dress or appearance: a new purse, a novel hairdo, extra-sheer stockings. He spent a good quarter of an hour every evening paying compliments and kissing hands.

The procedure at table was the same as at the midday meal, except that cold meat was the chief item on the menu. Traudl Junge remembers a dish that was one of Hitler's favorites, *Hoppelpoppel* (fried potatoes with eggs), another dish he relished was noodles with tomatoes. In all seasons there was fruit from Bormann's glasshouses.

The conversation was just as innocuous as at lunchtime. "Your napkin is stained with lipstick," Hitler would say to Eva. "What are you painting yourself with?" "But my lipstick comes from Paris," Eva protested. "Ah, if you ladies

---

* Martin Bormann in a letter to his wife warned her that if something should happen to him, Eva Braun would surely have Gerda Bormann evicted from their Berchtesgaden villa. "Please, my treasure," he wrote, "do not be conspicuous in the presence of Eva!"

only knew that French lipstick is made with the grease of kitchen slops. . . ." But the ladies merely laughed and continued to come to table with painted lips. All except Frau Bormann. Her husband had forbidden her to use makeup.

After dinner, Hitler had a political and subsequently a military conference. He left the company with the promise that it would not last long. As he crossed the threshold, a complete transformation came over him. A few minutes before, he had been a jovial country squire. Now he was a fierce and indomitable warlord.

Before the outbreak of war, a film was shown after he returned. Eva Braun chose the programs, and liked romantic pictures, although Hitler was always clamoring for cowboy or adventure films. He sat in the front row, with Eva beside him in another chair and the other spectators behind. Everybody was invited, even the house and kitchen staff. When an American picture banned elsewhere was being shown, the room was packed. In the case of a German propaganda film, many people found a pretext for doing something else.

Toward midnight, Hitler, accompanied by the Braun sisters, goes to sit in front of the fire in the great hall. The electric lights are switched off and only a few candles are left on the tables. The flames dancing in the fireplace competed with the rays of the moon glancing off the snow on the mountains outside. Hitler drinks tea, but Eva demands champagne, and brandy and schnapps are also served. Later there are apple cakes for the Führer and rolls for the other guests.

There is subdued conversation between neighbors, but sometimes Hitler, overhearing a word or a phrase, launches into one of his interminable monologues that could well last until the morning. Then Eva tugs him by the arm and tries to distract his attention.

Eva often had discussions with her friend Herta and the photographer Walter Fratz, who was a permanent resident at the Berghof. One evening quite suddenly Hitler started to whistle the "Donkey Serenade." "That's wrong," Eva declared. "It's not," protested Hitler. Finally, to settle the discussion, Eva asked for the record, which was duly played. "You see, you're wrong," Eva exclaimed triumphantly. "You witch, it's the composer who has made a mistake," Hitler insisted. Everybody laughed except the Führer.

Music was often played on the phonograph. The records, which Hitler had numbered himself, were kept in a black box. It was Bormann's function to choose them and work the machine. The repertoire was monotonous: Johann Strauss, Franz Lehár, Richard Wagner, and Hugo Wolf. From time to time Eva shook the company out of its torpor by putting on a modern American tune. "That's a nice record you've got there," Hitler remarked. "Yes," Eva Braun exulted, "and your friend Goebbels has just banned it throughout the Reich. . . ."

The night is drawing on. The guests drink enormous quantities of coffee; it all has a rather spectral air. At last Hitler gets up, wishes his followers good night, and goes up to the first floor. A few minutes later, Eva Braun retires in her turn. She goes to her room and locks the door behind her. Hitler also bolts the door of his studio as usual. The lights go out one after another, Hitler's window being one of the last to melt into the darkness. Silence, unbroken until the following noon, descends once more on the Berghof. . . .

CHAPTER ELEVEN

The love nest in the Wasserburgerstrasse

The dossiers of the Munich police reveal that on March 30, 1936, in other words at the time when the Berghof was being rebuilt, Fräulein Eva Braun and her sister Gretl moved into a little villa at 12 Wasserburgerstrasse, in the Bogenhausen district. The villa still exists. Its external appearance has hardly been modified, except that a garage has been added and the bushes planted by Eva have grown into big trees, some of which bear fruit. Only the name of the street has changed: it is now the Delphstrasse.* A postman, Georg Otter, is the only person who remembers those times. Other neighbors have gone away, disappeared, or died.

"They were charming young ladies who gave me generous tips and sometimes a cigar. No, I didn't deliver any official mail with an eagle and swastika stamp, but piles of letters, from Berlin too. The younger one often came to wait for me at the gate, for the young ladies had devilish little dogs who barked all the time. Sometimes the elder sister looked at the letters from Berlin and sighed, "Always bills." And she often gave me mail to post; I remember the blue of the envelopes and the initials E.B. on the flaps."

This house, built in 1925, had been advertised for sale in the newspaper. Bauer, Hoffmann's business manager, visited it and returned the following day with his boss and Eva Braun. She was delighted with it. It was quiet and isolated. The Wasserburgerstrasse was at that time on the edge of the town; it was almost a suburb but ranked nonetheless as an elegant street. Since the war, it has been described as having cafés and even a night club. This is

---

* In honor of a Jesuit priest executed by the Nazis.

pure invention. Even today, one has to walk a considerable distance to find so much as a newspaper stand.

The villa was situated in the same district as Hitler's apartment, on the opposite bank of the Isar. This proximity was only relative, however, and it took half an hour to walk from one dwelling to the other. It is true that with the villa, Hitler had put a Mercedes-Benz, with the registration number II A 52500, at Eva's disposal, but it was garaged in the Dachauerstrasse.

It was Hoffmann who signed the contract and paid with a check for 30,000 reichsmarks drawn on his private account. This is roughly the equivalent today of 30,000 dollars. It was only in 1937 that the property was transferred before a notary to the name of Fräulein Eva Braun. The telephone directory indicated her profession as that of secretary.

Eva's salary, which remained unchanged until the end of the war, was 450 reichsmarks a month. This would not even have covered the real-estate taxes.

The Brauns claim that their photographs—which were much more lifelike than Hoffmann's or those of the professional photographer in permanent residence at the Berghof, because Hitler posed more accommodatingly for the Braun sisters—were and still are exploited by the Hoffmann firm and that the purchase of the house was merely a repayment for services rendered. This is partially true. Hitler would often admire a photo taken by his mistress and show it to Hoffmann with the innuendo: "That's great; it's worth 20,000 marks." For Hoffmann who made millions, thanks to his friend, such an insinuation was tantamount to an order.

Nevertheless, had Hitler wanted to buy his beloved a nest, he would not have done so through Hoffmann, but through the party treasurer Schwarz, or through Bormann, whose discretion was equally to be trusted. He did not anticipate that the party dossiers would one day be confiscated by the victorious Allies. But, it must be repeated, Hitler liked to be generous with other people's money.

At all events, the love nest that he was offering to his young siren was no Trianon, large or small. It was only a paltry suburban villa that no American business tycoon would dare to offer to his secretary. It was and still is hard to believe that this little two-storied house, insignificant or even ugly in its architecture, was once the romantic dwelling place of the woman loved by the most powerful man in Europe.

"The one-family house," specifies the deed drawn up by a notary at the time of purchase, "is in the center of a garden of 798 square meters, with 20 meters on the street; the dimensions of the building are 8 meters 20 by 10, and its capacity is 697 cubic meters."

I have visited the place a number of times. A fairly high wall ensures complete privacy. The entrance is on the side and leads into a simple hall with a coat closet, then a lounge connecting with a kitchen on the left, with a door opening into the garden. The kitchen is minute, with barely room for two people to turn around, and the gas stove has only two burners. To the right of the staircase there are two rooms, the first a sitting room with a fireplace and a door leading onto a little terrace. It was curtained off from the second room, which served as a dining room provided the number of guests was strictly limited. On the first floor, at the top of the stairs, there was Eva's room, with Gretl's opposite and a blue-tiled bathroom between the two. There is a little maid's room off the kitchen and a slitlike attic which could barely accommodate a bed. This was used as a spare room. It was known as the smoking room because, during Hitler's rare visits, the sisters had to hide there to smoke their cigarettes.

Hitler's visits could be counted on the fingers. He took endless precautions, and the neighbors were never aware of his presence. He sometimes brought a picture or some knickknack, and Eva would prepare tea for him. Gretl left them discreetly alone, but he never stayed late into the night. Thus the villa cannot properly be called a love nest.

Eva had wanted this house chiefly to assert her independence from her family, to have her own place, to feel really at home. She would say with loving pride, "My dear little Braunhouse."

The testimony of Eva's best friend Herta can relevantly be cited here. She voluntarily revealed to me that Eva was unhappy at home from the time she left the convent. Her family apparently nagged her continually because of her association with Hitler and also made her life difficult in other ways. Her father threatened to lock her in her room and showed her nothing but indifference. He never gave her presents or a holiday trip and he contradicted her constantly. Her sister Ilse, so Herta alleges, was malicious toward her and was forever mocking her contemptuously. This perhaps explains why Ilse's friends called Eva *die blöde Kuh*—the stupid cow. Her mother badgered her endlessly: "What does that man want with you? He treats you like a slut. . . . When is he going to marry you? . . . You look pregnant." Eva supposedly warned her more than once: "Mother, if you don't stop tormenting me, we're going to part company."

Her friend Herta was so upset by all this that she invited Eva to spend a large part of her time at her house. It was in these opulent surroundings—for Herta's family was extremely wealthy—that Eva often had telephone conversations with Hitler, as well as receiving his messages and letters. For although Eva had a phone in her room at her parents' house, they eavesdropped and also censored her mail.

Herta Ostermeyr, who married a regular army officer, Erwin Schneider, in 1936, was herself very worried about this liaison between her friend and a man old enough to be her father—a liaison that offered so little likelihood of ultimate marriage. She therefore tried to distract Eva by introducing her to hosts of young men, her husband's brother officers, by taking her to dances and on trips, or by organizing small parties. But all to no avail. Eva preferred to mope alone, in endless expectation of a note from Hitler.

Only once, Herta reveals (and I have since checked the accuracy of this), did Eva take an interest in another man. It was after the second suicide attempt, when she went with her mother and her younger sister to Bad Schachen, a charming hotel castle on Lake Constance, near Lindau. A certain Peter Schilling, a businessman, younger than Hitler but nonetheless over thirty, started to court Eva. "He was really smitten," Herta relates. "They immediately became inseparable friends and they made a fine couple." Eva apparently confided to her friend that she liked Schilling very much, that she found him perfect, and that in other circumstances she might have been able to love him. "But there's already a man in my life, and there will never be another. It's too late." So she refused to see him again and would not even speak to him on the telephone. There is no way of knowing whether she told Hitler of this incident.

Once established in her own house, Eva underwent a

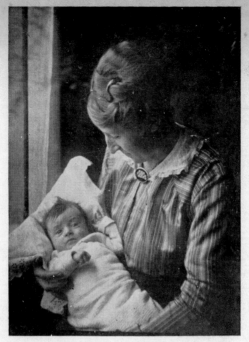

Eva and her mother, 1912

Announcement of Eva's birth

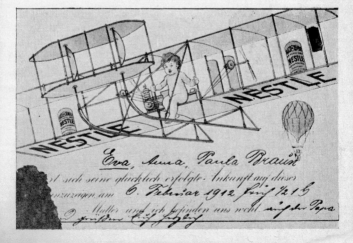

NESTLE

NESTLE

Eva, Anna, Paula Braun

t sich seine glücklich erfolgte Ankunft auf diser

inzuzagen am 6. *Februar* 1912 *fünf ½ 1 ½*

Mutter und ich befinden uns wohl auch der Papa

grüßen

Eva (right) and her sister Ilse

The Braun family: about 1920: Fritz Braun, Franziska Braun. In front the three sisters: Gretl, Ilse, and Eva (from left to right).

Eva and her "first flirt," from her album

Eva (left) with her friends Herta Ostermayr and Inge Schropp

Eva at Simbach Convent

Eva at nineteen—Hitler's favorite photo

"Gigolette" at a Munich ball

Eva as Al Jolson

Eva posing for Hoffman

Eva Braun meets Hitler; Munich, 1929

Hitler and Eva at Castle Herrenchiemsee: about 1932

Eva flies to Berchtesgaden; in front cockpit (left).

Geli Raubel, Hitler's niece

Hitler's favorite photograph of 1938

Dem lieben Holgerl herzlichst
Eva.

26. 11. 38

The Braun family, about 1942. From left to right:
Ilse, Fritz Braun, Franziska Braun, Gretl, and Eva

Carnival in Munich; 1939

Eva in Venice

Eva in Rome with Frau Dreesen

Eva wearing her grandmother's wedding dress

At Garda

Unity Mitford and Hitler in the English Gardens, Munich

At the Nuremburg party celebrations, 1937 (Unity Mitford behind; Eva next to Anny Brandt, Frau Morell, and Eva's mother)

House on Prinzregentenplatz where Hitler lived on second floor

Villa of Eva Braun on Wasserburgerstrasse, given to her by Hitler

Eva at picnic Obersalzberg

Arriving at Berghof in the super Mercedes

Wedding of Marion Schönemann

While Hitler is away, Eva amuses herself with Bormann and friends

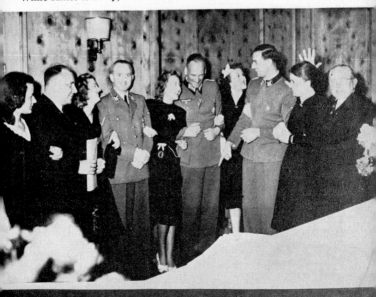

Reichsleiter Bormann   Dr. Dietrich   Prof. v. Hasselbach   Prof. Brandt   Prof. Hoffm

Nickerchen im Teehaus

A good lunch and a nap in the teahouse

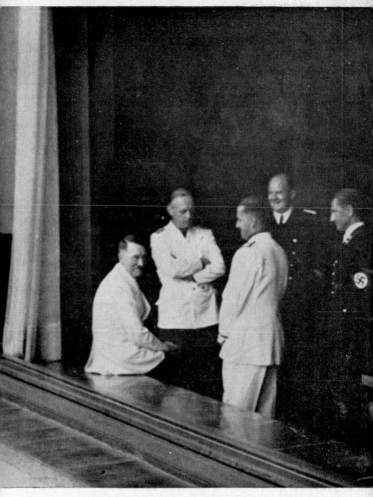

Hitler with Ciano and Ribbentrop,
photographed from Eva's room in the Berghof.

Eva and Hitler with their dogs (Blondi at right)

Hitler and Eva leaving the Berghof. (Note camera.)

Berghof hospitality. Hitler inspects the table.

Menus from 1937 and 1943, equally frugal

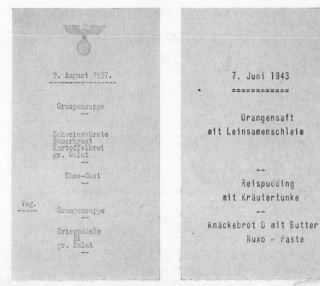

9. August 1937.

Graupensuppe
--

Schweinswürste
Sauerkraut
Kartoffelbrei
gr. Salat
--

Käse-Obst
--

Veg.

Graupensuppe
--

Griesnudeln
Ei
gr. Salat
--

7. Juni 1943
============

Orangensaft
mit Leinsamenschleim

--

Reispudding
mit Kräutertunke
--

Knäckebrot D mit Butter
Nuxo - Paste

Entry to Eva's dressing room at the Berghof

Eva's bedroom at the Berghof

Hitler reading, Berchtesgaden. (Note glasses.)

Hitler's study at the Berghof

Eva with Uschi, daughter of Herta Ostermayr

Hitler with Goebbels' children

Eva's birthday, 1944, Berchtesgaden

Gretl marries Fegelein

Eva and Albert Speer

Eva and Magda Goebbels at lunch with Hitler

. . . . und dann fuhr Ribbentrop nach Moskau

And then Ribbentrop goes to Moscow . . .

aber trotzdem, Polen will nicht verhandeln.....

but Poland will not negotiate . . .

und der Führer hört den Bericht am Radio!

and the Führer hears the news on the radio.

Happy New Year at Berghof, 1938

A subdued New Year at the Berghof, 1944

Eva and the Speers before the fireplace in the teahouse.

The teahouse as a souvenir shop after the war

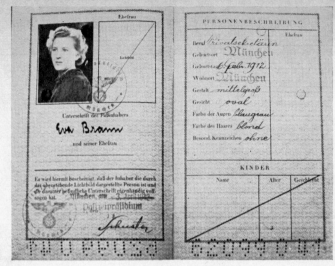

Eva Braun's passport

Part of Eva's will

The Berghof . . .

. . . and what happened to it.

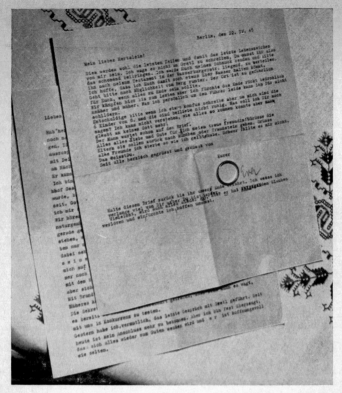

Last letter of Eva Braun and her wedding ring

Blondi and puppies

Wedding certificate of Eva and Adolf Hitler dated May 29, 1945

complete transformation. Her nest was not only a love gift from the Führer, but also a consolidation of her new position. Like the Berghof for Hitler, it was the realization of her youthful dreams. She often received her friends there, with dancing and laughter late into the night. "I spend nearly all my time with Liserl, George, Pepo, Toni, and Roeschen," she writes in a letter dating from the spring of 1937. In another, she talks of the many professors whom she has invited to her house. Later, when she had made peace with her parents, she organized gay family parties.

Hitler had found her a constant companion. This was Basko, a German shepherd of the same lineage as his own dogs. Previously, when she was in the Wiedermeyerstrasse apartment, he had given her a little dog "with bear's fur." These two animals barked incessantly because the children of the neighborhood were always teasing them. For the sake of peace, Eva had the wooden fence that surrounded the house replaced by the present brick wall. Later, Hitler presented her with Stasi and Negus as birthday gifts, and they barked even behind the wall. Negus was killed in Berlin by a Russian grenade. Stasi, who was at the Obersalzberg at the time of the debacle, escaped in the confusion and by some mysterious instinct managed to cover the sixty-odd miles (and certainly more, for he cannot have run in a straight line) that separated the Berghof from the house on the Wasserburgerstrasse in Munich. The place was deserted except for American soldiers or other intruders who were intent on pillaging and chased the dog away with stones. . . . A kindly neighbor threw him a bone and gave him water. . . . Then Stasi disappeared into the night.

Although the outside of the house was simple, the inside was very adequately and tastefully furnished. All the silver and linen bore the initials E.B., and I remember that immediately after the war, when I visited the place, I still found a few books in the sitting-room bookcase, carefully marked "Eva Braun." The family must still possess some of the furniture, which included a number of extremely valuable pieces. The dining-room furniture, for example, in mahogany, was specially designed by Professor Trost, at Hitler's order. Eva Braun's will contains an imposing list of pictures by reputable German artists of the time. There were landscapes by Fischbach, Rickelt, Baskon, Midgard; one by Wax, a large painting by Gradl, a canvas by Gallegos, another by Franke, portraits by Rosl, Popp, Hugo Kauffmann, and Gallegos. Eva's favorites were a watercolor by Hitler, "The Asam Church," a portrait of Hitler by Bohnenberger, a north Italian landscape by Bamberger and also a head of a young girl that Martin Bormann had given her for her birthday. There was a valuable painting attributed to the school of Titian, which was a gift from Mussolini to Hitler, another portrait of the Führer by Knirr, and a Reinhardt. Several other Bohnenbergers, including a portrait of Eva, a landscape of Rimini, some old watercolors of Venice and canvases by Tiedgen, Hoberg, Krauss, and Hengeler Hilbakt completed the collection. To this inventory—which may seem tedious but is nonetheless necessary if an exact idea of this house is to be given—should be added several valuable rugs, including a Samarkand and a Gobelin (these may well have been imitations, however).

Sometimes, but very rarely, strangers who in some way had managed to pierce the incognito of this house at 12 Wasserburgerstrasse presented themselves at the gate and, braving the barking of the dogs, slipped petitions into the letter box. They were requests for help, for a job, or sometimes a more dramatic plea.

The Reverend Father Barnabas Liebisch, O.S.B., from Kitzingen in Bavaria, testifies that in December, 1943, a little before Christmas, he presented himself at the door of the little villa. Gretl Braun answered when he rang the bell. The reverend father had come to ask for Eva Braun's help at the suggestion of Mother Palmeria of the Third Order of St. Francis, who was the principal of the Dillinger Institute in Maria-Medingen, where Gretl Braun had gone to school. A relative of this good lady, a certain Dr. Hans Woelfel of Bamberg, had been arrested by the Gestapo for defeatism and was in a very unenviable situation. It seems that Gretl answered coldly that she would "try to do something . . ."

On May 10, 1944, Dr. Hans Woelfel was nevertheless condemned to death and on the following July 3 he was beheaded in the courtyard of the prison in Brandenburg.

Gretl confirms this sad episode, but declares that she conveyed the plea for a reprieve to Bormann with the recommendation of her sister Eva.

The villa had only two exceptional features. One was the large television set, which was one of the first in use in

Germany, no doubt a gift from the Telefunken firm and a great source of pride to Eva. The other feature was the cellar, where the most up-to-date air-raid shelter had been installed. Hitler had designed it himself, and even today one is impressed by its solidity. There was a ventilator and an air pump, an armored door leading to an underground passage of reinforced concrete that insured an exit even if the house was totally destroyed (and also a means of escape from police or army attempts to arrest the occupants), a radio and a telephone as well as an electric generator. There was also a miniature bunker that afforded complete protection. Several large cupboards were crammed with provisions and medical supplies.

The significant thing is that the construction of this shelter was started in the summer of 1938. This was a time when the Führer had convinced the German people of his pacific intentions, when he was assuring the world that the Sudeten region was his last territorial demand, and when he was no doubt promising his beloved Effie eternally happy and peaceful days in this little nest that he had offered her.

CHAPTER TWELVE

Attempt in Naples?

Although she was not belligerent by nature, Eva felt that she had a private score to settle with Czechoslovakia at the time of the Munich crisis.

Here is the reason: One September evening, her father appeared unexpectedly on her doorstep. So far he had paid only one or two visits to the little house in the Wasserburgerstrasse. He was in a towering rage. His *Stammtisch* friends, to provoke him, had shown him a Czech weekly, published in Prague but bought by one of the company in Vienna, on the occasion of a business trip. The magazine had printed a photograph of Eva, taken at Berchtesgaden, with the caption "Hitler's Pompadour." Fritz Braun reproached his daughter hotly.

Eva for her part was in a sulky mood. She had just returned from the Nuremberg Parteitag, where she had vainly waited for a visit from her parents. She had wanted to win them over to her cause by showing them the grandiose spectacle of the demonstrations. A postcard has survived indicating that she had great difficulty in procuring invitations for them. But the curious thing is that on the other side of the card there is a portrait of Hitler in martial dress. A girl who writes to her parents on the back of a photograph of her lover, and sends it unsealed by post! This detail shows how far Eva, and all her compatriots with her, had lost their sense of proportion. They were living in a phantasmagoric atmosphere, where it was impossible to draw a boundary between the ridiculous and the sublime.

There was a violent exchange of reproaches. From Papa Braun: How could she flout the honor of the family in this way? A Braun daughter the mistress of an elderly man, living with him without being married to him, what a disgrace! From Eva: Was he incapable of understanding that the Führer was a man apart, with responsibilities toward the nation, that patience was necessary, that the sacred duty of every patriot and every German was to accept certain sacrifices? Eva not only did not deny anything but proclaimed: "Nothing but death can separate me from him."

Fritz Braun stormed out, slamming the door behind him. He had ordered his daughter never to set foot in his house again, and for many months this banishment was strictly enforced.

Fritz Braun had so far obstinately refused to join the Nazi party. His career had suffered as a result, and Eva in one of her letters notes her father's bitter disappointment at having been passed over on the occasion of an annual promotion. After the scene in Eva's villa, Fritz Braun went to the headmaster of his school and, after informing him of the article in the Czech weekly, offered him his resignation, on the grounds that "a man cannot educate pupils when he has lost his authority over his own children." The headmaster duly registered the incident in an official document and consulted the higher authorities, who apparently reassured Herr Braun. They declared that his professional integrity had been in no way impaired. The whole incident seems childish, for even Papa Braun must have realized that in Nazi Germany nobody would have dared dismiss a schoolmaster because his daughter was the Führer's mistress. But the episode proves that there were nonetheless some people who knew about the Braun affair as early as 1937.

Hitler, informed by telephone of these developments, advised Eva to show herself conciliatory with her father and reprimanded Hoffmann severely. "From now on, I don't want a single photo of Fräulein Braun put on the market." He gave more stringent orders to his subalterns, forbidding them still more expressly to divulge the details of his domestic life. The slightest indiscretion would be punished with drastic severity.

The scandalmongering in the Czech periodical passed unnoticed in the rest of the country. Indeed until the end Eva Braun's name was never featured in any diplomatic reports or press correspondents' cables. This professional blindness—and I am among the first to confess it—perhaps explains why certain journalists later turned historians, in order indirectly to justify their earlier inadequacy, and tried to present Eva Braun as a sadly insignificant character. Yet her existence was not completely unknown to the outside world. In the British Museum, for example, there is a document that cites Eva Braun among those suspected of being Hitler's concubines. This document was probably based on an indiscretion of the Intelligence Service. I have been told that the French Deuxième Bureau knew about Eva Braun and that later the OSS had a dossier on her with photographs. It has even been affirmed that in the course of hostilities this organization had devised a plan to kidnap her. Since the public is not allowed access to many of the OSS files, it is impossible for the present to check this affirmation. Allen W. Dulles, who was the OSS representative in Europe during the Second World War, replied with an evasive smile when I questioned him on the subject. There is also a report that Moscow once assigned an operative in Berlin to make inquiries about a certain woman named Braun.

On the other hand, although one would expect the Austrians to be among the best informed about the private life of their former fellow citizen, the Chancellor Kurt von Schuschnigg assured me that he never received the slightest indication of Eva Braun's existence at the Ballhausplatz, the Chancellor's residence in Vienna. But Eva nonetheless played a small part in his own life. At the time of his last sad conversation with Hitler at Berchtesgaden, the Führer, in order better to intimidate him, had given instructions that he should be served neither food nor drinks. Eva, who was at the Berghof but as usual had been instructed to keep away from the guests, had disregarded the order and insisted that the majordomos should arrange for the serving of a dish of hors d'oeuvres of which she had supervised the preparation herself. "The Führer must eat, and a visitor, whoever he may be, must be politely treated." Thus from time to time Eva ventured to give her terrible lover lessons in good manners.

Later, much later, when Schuschnigg, condemned to life imprisonment, had asked his jailers for permission to marry the Countess Vera Czernin, Eva, who heard Göring talk about the matter, pleaded with Hitler that the request should be granted. "I would follow you to prison, deportation, or death. . . . You can't refuse that."

Hitler gave his authorization, and Schuschnigg has probably wondered whether it was to the Pope or to his friend Mussolini that he owed this concession.

The *Anschluss* had been a great occasion for Eva, that of her first journey with Hitler. Perhaps indirectly she was grateful to the Austrian chancellor for this. But she detested the people in Prague who had allowed the publication of a newspaper that had caused such severe friction between herself and her father.

Hitler had gone in some trepidation to Austria—had he not threatened Schuschnigg that he would annihilate the Austrian army and reduce Vienna to a heap of ashes?—and he was pleasantly surprised by his frenzied reception in Linz, the town of his youth. According to Hitler's aide Fritz Wiedemann, the Führer had not yet decided on the annexation of Austria but was thinking of creating a form of federal union with the Reich.* But the Austrians' exuberant joy made him change his mind, for it convinced him that he had the people behind him. Nevertheless his triumph would have been incomplete without the presence of the woman he loved.

He telephoned to Eva from Linz, asking her to join him in Vienna. There exists a totally incorrect account of this journey, which affirms that Eva left without permission and without luggage and went to importune Hitler. This was not her line of behavior, and besides it was impossible for a private citizen to cross the frontier without special authorization, for it must be remembered that Austria was in a state of siege.

In reality, the journey was carefully organized. Eva had two chaperones to accompany her—her mother and her friend Herta—and she was lodged at the Imperial Hotel. The party was considered as part of the official escort, and in the confusion of the moment, nobody paid great attention to it. "You can't imagine what a fantastic spectacle it was," Frau Braun wrote to her daughter Ilse. The postcard has survived, with all the comments of the group on the historic event, and three words from Eva: *"Ich bin verrückt."* (I'm crazy.)

Crazy with joy, crazy with pride, crazy with satisfaction, crazy because it was a crazy world, her lover's world.

---

* Von Ribbentrop confirms this in his memoirs written in the Nuremberg prison.

The town where he had suffered such humiliation, where he had known hunger, was giving him a triumphal welcome such as no emperor had ever received. The hundreds of thousands of Viennese who sang all night long in front of the hotel had not come there because they had been ordered to do so. People cannot be forced to sing and laugh. Of course, the Nazis had only just arrived, and the Gestapo had not yet had time to organize itself there. Eva's father and her sister Ilse had said that the Germans regretted having brought Hitler to power, that the muzzling of the press prevented people from expressing their real opinions, that the anti-Jewish persecutions and the concentration camps were reprehensible, that Hitler was hated abroad . . . and yet at his victorious entry into a foreign country, a country that logically should be hostile to him and where the press had been free, a country that had no reason to treat him kindly since he had deserted it and had imprisoned its chancellor, here this first foreign country was receiving him like a god. . . .

Eva was surrounded by chaperones in Vienna, but she was lodged in a room separate from those of her mother and her friend. Only a corridor divided this room and that of Hitler. The Führer lingered a long time on the balcony raising his hand in greeting to the crowd that chanted over and over again, "We shan't go home as long as the Führer is there. . . ." But finally he retired for the night. And it is probable that he spent it with Eva, in the big rococo bed in the princely suite of the Imperial Hotel.

Yet even if Hitler and Eva had only met furtively at night thanks to underground passages, it seems inconceivable that in our day and age a head of state should be able to frequent a mistress for sixteen years unknown to his people and the rest of the world. Was Eva Braun a myth?

The total ignorance of the average German is readily explained. In a system where the press and the radio were strictly controlled, where all information regarding the Führer's private life had to be censored before release, where any speculation on this subject was severely punished, and where the country was submerged by propaganda destined to create an archangelic vision of a Hitler living only for the Reich, this ignorance was inevitable. Besides, it was not a matter that at that time greatly preoccupied the German in the street.

Keeping the secret was physically facilitated by Hitler's

growing isolation, which was only broken by direct contact with the public on rare and carefully organized state occasions, by the fact that his residence at Berchtesgaden, lost as it was in the Bavarian Alps, was practically inaccessible, and by the war, which made this separation still more complete and during which Hitler's liaison with Eva assumed a more intense and permanent nature.

True, there were rumors, which, inevitable in any totalitarian regime, abounded in the Third Reich. There was a flood of idle talk, of hints, of stories big and little, of conjectures, of confidences, of revelations, but this *vox populi*, far from satisfying the general curiosity, blunted it still further. How could one choose among so many pseudoversions? Even if the name of Eva Braun had been suggested to me at the time, I would have eliminated it as I had to eliminate hundreds of other names.

It should also be remembered that those who might have given currency to a version closer to the true state of affairs were probably discreetly shipped off to a concentration camp, an extremely effective way of scotching a rumor.

It is also possible that a considerable element of feminine pique was involved. All those society women, actresses, wives of industrialists, generals and academicians, princesses even, who aspired to the position of first lady of the regime could hardly have stomached the idea of being eclipsed by a little secretary, sprung from who knows where, who was as insignificant and as slight as an autumn leaf. Their vanity could ill have borne this blow, and it is therefore possible that those of them who had got wind of the role played by Eva Braun preferred to ignore it and to suggest the name of some more brilliant rival. . . .

The love life of a head of state, when he is extremely popular and has unusual means at his disposal, such as SS brigades or millions of dollars, is a highly delicate subject. This is illustrated by the fact that although for years the entire Washington society assiduously cultivated innumerable rumors about the love life of various U.S. Presidents, including recently Franklin Delano Roosevelt and John F. Kennedy, whose supposed affairs and infidelities have been the source of much gossip. Yet the general public in America, despite radio, television, satellite communications, and the greatest freedom of the press in its whole history, often remains ignorant of these rumors, true or false. Only a few columnists or opposition writers have made hidden allusions to these matters, designed to be read between the lines and comprehensible only to a few insiders.

Hitler had established a strict point of policy that people in Germany should not be informed about anything they did not need to know. He himself, for example, never revealed his destination to Eva when he left her to go on some journey. It was from the newspapers that she learned that he had gone north, at the time of the attack on Norway. She only knew of his presence at his headquarters near the Russian frontier from a radio announcement. It was hard for a woman to receive in this indirect way the news that the man she loved had gone off to war, without even a word of farewell.

Eva was in contact with only a minimal number of the members of Hitler's entourage. Hitler did not like new faces and insisted that his immediate entourage should always remain a closed circle. There were Dr. Morell, Dr. Brandt, Bormann, the aides-de-camp, Hoffmann, various other friends, and of course Eva, her sisters, and her friends. An extreme solidarity characterized this clique, for its members realized that the slightest indiscretion would result in immediate expulsion from the "court," and there is no worse punishment for a courtier than to be banished from the presence of his "sovereign." As for Hitler's subalterns, they had been carefully selected, and many of them were incorporated in the SS formations. Moreover, they were fanatics who had no intention of gossiping about their beloved Führer.

In spite of everything that has been written about the history of the Third Reich, it is not yet sufficiently realized that the great men of the regime—Göring, Himmler, Goebbels, Keitel—rarely penetrated into Hitler's intimate circle. When they went to Berchtesgaden, their visits were of a more or less official nature. Göring, it is true, had a villa in the immediate vicinity of Hitler's residence, but his visits were subject to the same ceremonial as those of others. Emmy Göring, his wife, says now that she never met Eva Braun. She assured her interrogators at Nuremberg that she had been debarred from all contact. Himmler was hardly ever invited to the Berghof. "He sends shivers down my spine when I see him," Eva Braun said of him. Hess made himself very scarce, and Rosenberg, Streicher,

Todt, Ribbentrop, von Neurath, von Papen, the *Gauleiters* and the rest of the Nazi hierarchy were practically excluded from the intimate gatherings—one might almost call them family reunions—at the Berghof. Hitler wished to immerse himself in a feminine atmosphere during his periods of respite. "How good it is to relax," he would say. "All day long I hear nothing but heavy, irksome, noisy masculine voices around me."

It would have been difficult to reduce his flock to silence. Goebbels and Göring could not abide each other. When Goebbels entered a room, Göring immediately left it. This was hardly surprising, for the little doctor had described big Hermann as "a soldier with the heart of a child." Göring for his part professed a royal contempt for Ribbentrop and on several occasions had accused him of incompetence to his face. Himmler was generally feared and disliked. Hitler, far from smoothing out these differences, seemed to take pleasure in aggravating them. This was his personal method of preserving equilibrium and explains how he contrived to dominate his commanders until the last. Göring, Goebbels, and company certainly knew about their leader's liaison, but they also knew how to hold their peace. Besides, Goebbels, who ran after every little movie extra, and Göring, who collected, confiscated, and stole works of art, were hardly qualified to reproach others. Himmler probably had his dossier on Eva, for his representative at the Berghof kept him informed of the slightest detail, but he was biding his time. Curiously enough, Hitler did not entrust him with the task of investigating Eva's Aryan origins. It was Bormann who very discreetly took this matter in hand. For on this subject Hitler was adamant. Eva, her sisters, her parents, her friends had to be thoroughly scrutinized. He did not wish to run the risk of having a mistress, and still less children, tainted with Jewish blood.

Himmler, to requite this intrusion upon his prerogatives, established his own dossier to prove that Eva's older sister Ilse was involved in a shady espionage scheme.

Ilse gave the following account of the incident: "At the time when I was taking part in the European dancing championships, I traveled through Italy, Austria, and Yugoslavia. This was in 1935. I happened to meet an Italian naval officer at La Spezia. I've always had a weakness for Italian officers. It was a light-hearted affair, but I realized on my return to Munich that my mail was arriving with undue delay. I learned later that my letters were being photocopied. I complained to Eva, who assured me, 'You're crazy, my dear.' But then that brute Brückner summoned me and insidiously embarked on a long interrogation. Satisfied at last, he explained the mystery to me. Himmler had apparently accused me of spying for the Italians. And when Himmler had been reassured, he apologized with the remark, 'If you had kept me informed about Fräulein Braun's position, this misunderstanding would never have risen. . . .' "

Hitler, always acting through Bormann, who at that time was almost totally unknown to the general public, had given instructions that no official document should betray Eva's special position. The identity card that allowed her to penetrate the barriers of the Chancellery of the Reich and of Berchtesgaden simply indicated that she was a "secretary," and this was how she was presented when circumstances demanded an introduction. She had a pass that entitled her to free travel on the railways, but there were thousands of party members who enjoyed the same privilege.

I have in front of me her passport dated 1942, a private passport that could have been issued to any citizen, except that in 1942, not every citizen could obtain a passport. The money at her disposal she received directly from Hoffmann or from some party pay office. Privileges, favors, invitations, exceptions to the rule, such as the purchase of cameras, which were extremely rare during the war, were always the result of efforts by aides-de-camp, of concessions by persons of influence, of interventions by the party, but invariably under some pretext or other.

Wiedemann, for instance, told me how he personally procured perfumes in Paris that he then offered to Eva. He obtained for her in Hungary, thanks to his friendship with Princess Stephanie of Hohenlohe, some white fox furs that she treasured until the dark days in the bunker. In those times it was impossible to trace such favors back to their source.

Hitler and Eva put on a permanent act in order to convince the staff that they were merely good friends. Even when they had just spent the night together, they greeted each other next morning like two strangers meeting in the restaurant car of a train. They never allowed themselves the slightest expression of physical affection in public. There was to be only one tragic exception to this rule. Eva addressed Hitler as "My Führer" like everybody else; formerly she had called him "Chief" or "Herr Hitler," but her lover had specifically insisted on this new appellation. In order to avoid the risk of making a mistake in public, she acquired the habit of referring to her lover by this official title even in the most familiar conversations.

Heinz Linge, Hitler's servant, affirms in his memoirs that he surprised his master and Eva Braun in an embrace that would have delighted an avant-garde writer, and this in Hitler's bed. There is nothing incredible in this, in fact the wonder is that he only saw such a scene once. This valet's testimony, which might seem inadequate by itself, can be supplemented by Captain Fritz Wiedemann's memories of another episode. "I had to knock that morning for service reasons—an extremely urgent cable—at Hitler's door, without going in. Imagine my surprise when I saw outside this door, as though in a hotel, Eva Braun's little Viennese shoes beside Hitler's cumbersome boots. They went through all that playacting and then left their shoes outside the door. . . . I couldn't help thinking of La Fontaine's fable and I burst out laughing as I went downstairs. . . ."

When a visitor of note was expected at the Berghof, Eva was confined to her room just as the convent boarders were shut up when there were male guests in the parlor. Only once in Berlin did she have the opportunity of meeting Charles Lindbergh and his wife Anne, whom she found adorable. She suffered acutely from being denied the excitement of being present during the visits of former President Hoover, of Admiral Horthy, the regent of Hungary, of Chamberlain, of the King of Bulgaria, of Sir Anthony Eden, of Lord Rothermere, of the Aga Khan, of Cardinal Pacelli, who was to become Pope in 1939, of Lloyd George, of King Carol of Rumania, of Prince Paul of Yugoslavia, of the King of Sweden, and of innumerable other notabilities who were received at Berchtesgaden before 1939. Yet for Eva, these visits were personal triumphs, for she had been told that her lover was nothing but a usurper, boycotted by foreign nations. And those who today may be inclined to condemn Eva's political blindness must admit that any woman in the world would

have been greatly impressed by the arrival of such a
stream of celebrities at the "court" of Berchtesgaden.

Eva begged Hitler to let her be introduced to the Duchess of Windsor on the occasion of the famous couple's
visit to Berchtesgaden. This wish was understandable. Eva
had subjected her lover to endless eulogies of the ex-mon-
arch who "had renounced an empire for love of a
woman . . ." Eva never attacked a problem directly but
proceeded by innuendo. According to some, she hinted
that Mrs. Simpson had something in common with Eva
Braun, and that a sincere lover could accept a small sacrifice—not the loss of a crown like Edward, but the risk of
a slight blow to his prestige, by marrying the woman that
he declared he loved. Hitler pretended not to understand
and in order not to aggravate the situation, claimed that
the demands of protocol prohibited the meeting.

He was just as inexorable with regard to Galeazzo
Ciano's visits, partly because of the Italian diplomat's lack
of discretion but also because he was jealous of Mussolini's brilliant son-in-law. Eva did not hesitate to proclaim
that she found Ciano most attractive. She collected photographs of him, blushed as she expatiated on his charm, his
youth, his style, and reproached Hitler for not dressing
with his elegance. Moreover, Eva considered Italy her second homeland. She had come back full of enthusiasm
from a trip there. Her mother and her friend Herta had
accompanied her, and the journey had been financed as a
birthday present by Hitler, who had put one of his own
Mercedes cars at the travelers' disposal.

In protest, Eva stayed at her window to photograph
with her telephoto lens all the phases of Ciano's Berches-
gaden visit. She even managed to take a very fine picture
of the statesmen at the window of the big drawing room.
Ciano noticed the figure of the young girl and had the impertinence to ask Ribbentrop her name. His colleague's
reply was justifiably evasive, and Hitler immediately dis-
patched an SS with orders to Eva to close her window.
She gave a graphic description of the episode in her
album.

Ciano was successfully deluded, for in his famous diary,
he makes no allusion to Eva Braun, but mentions a
Fräulein Siegrid von Lessert (actually Laffert). This omis-
sion makes it difficult to evaluate the events that follow.

Adolf Hitler officially returned Mussolini's visit in

May, 1938. This was his only journey abroad in his capacity of head of state, and as the stenographic report of his conversations at the front shows, this Italian trip left him full of wonderment, although he was considerably bored by the royal family of Savoy and greatly irritated by certain peculiarities of protocol. He was particularly struck by the huge Mappamondo room in Palazzo Venezia, which served as Mussolini's study, and on his return he gave orders for the building of his own study with the same proportions. He also wished to adopt the training methods of the Italian assault battalions, who during maneuvers used real ammunition and not blanks, as had so far been the practice in Germany.

Eva had demanded to be of the party. After all, was she not an "expert" on Italy, and how could anybody dare to exclude her from the *trionfo* of her man? Hitler, flattered, granted this request provided that Eva was duly chaperoned. Since Papa Braun objected to his wife's undertaking another journey, a certain Frau Dreesen was chosen. She was the proprietor of the big Rhein Hotel at Godesberg, and Hitler was grateful to her for the help that the Dreesen family had given him early in his career. Thus Eva Braun, Frau Dreesen, and her son Fritz formed a group with Dr. Morell and Dr. Brandt, who was then Hitler's personal physician, and their wives. Under various pretexts this group became part of Hitler's official suite. During this journey, however, Eva's personal contacts with Hitler were extremely rare; she did not attend any of the official receptions and had to be content with surveying the scene from a distance.

The day before the grand parade of the Italian fleet, a spectacle after Hitler's heart, Eva Braun apparently received a visit from an official of the Italian secret police. The incident was reported to me by Fritz Dreesen, although he was not present at the interview that took place in Eva's room at the Hotel Excelsior in Rome. His source of information was his mother. According to her account, the official asked Eva and her group not to attend the parade and not to go to Naples because the police had been informed that certain elements, either dissident Italians or foreign agents, were bent on disrupting the Italo-German entente, and since they could not pierce Hitler's heavy guard, were planning an attempt against the members of his entourage. Eva Braun's life was therefore in danger.

The young woman shrugged her shoulders. She had no desire to give up the pleasure of a visit to Naples and wanted to know why she should have been selected as the target for such an attempt. The official apparently replied that the warning was a general one, and asked that the Führer should not be informed of it, to avoid arousing his anxiety.

The following day, Eva and her friends went on board a sloop to watch the parade. Hitler was naturally with the king and Mussolini on the flagship. In order to reach the gangplank, Eva and her group had to pass through a milling throng. Neapolitans love such spectacles and had gathered en masse. Suddenly, in the midst of the hubbub of this eddying crowd, Frau Dreesen gave a terrified scream. She was taken on board the ship, Dr. Brandt examined her and discovered that she had been injured in the shoulder. In order not to raise the alarm, the company decided to remain on board during the parade, while Dr. Brandt dressed the injury with the help of an Italian doctor. On their return to the Excelsior, Hitler was informed of the incident by Dr. Brandt and, visibly concerned, apparently came to visit the patient and make sure that nothing had happened to Eva. The episode had no diplomatic repercussions.

Is this story authentic? Gretl Braun, who at that moment was flirting with an Italian navy officer and too busy to notice anything is of the opinion that it was mostly the product of the imagination of a young man who misinterpreted the unruly exuberance of the Italian crowds. There was certainly a melee, and Frau Dreesen was jostled and bruised on the shoulder. The business of the attempt on her life she may have invented later.

A postcard from Eva to her parents states that "we were present at the parade of the fleet, which was very fine. Unfortunately I have caught a cold and my throat is sore. We leave tomorrow for Taormina and not for Capri. . . ."

Why did she not return with the official suite, and above all, why did Brandt and Morell stay with her? Did they simply want to continue their holiday, or was medical attention needed for Frau Dreesen?

In another postcard, one of those publicity cards offered by hotels (Eva had adopted Hitler's parsimonious habits and liked to obtain even her postcards free), sent from the

Hotel Quisisana on Capri, she wrote: "We went to Capri after all—the journey to Taormina would have been too tiring for me. I've grown thin and very weak. . . ."

This illness is hard to explain and is belied by the photographs in Eva's album, which show her blooming with health, stroking the ears of a donkey in the narrow streets of Capri or climbing the slopes of Vesuvius. The registers of the Quisisana Hotel reveal that Eva Braun did in fact stay there, but nobody remembers whether any member of the party needed special attention.

The incident, whether attempt, accident, or mere panic, does not seem to have disconcerted Eva unduly. In her album she notes: "We make a tremendous impression on the Italians. I am courted and always referred to as *la bella bionda*."

CHAPTER THIRTEEN

I am "Miss No-Private-Life"

His Excellency Herbert von Dirksen was the bearer of a handwritten message from the British Prime Minister Chamberlain, Count Johannes de Welczec had come from Paris to convey a communication from Daladier, and from Washington, also claiming to have in his hands a letter from Roosevelt, there was Hitler's ambassador Hans Dieckhoff. But Hitler did not seem to be particularly eager either to read the letters or to see his three most important envoys during that September of 1938. He had already kept them hanging about several days, while he strutted like a chanticleer in the huge stadiums in Nuremberg. The Sudeten crisis that was to lead up to Munich was piling up thunderclouds on the political horizon, and the ambassadors were tired of waiting in the antechamber. Even Ribbentrop, however, did not dare to plead their cause. Eva Braun was present, as she had been in previous years, at this bayonet-and-swastika jamboree, and since she was staying at the Grand Hotel, the residence of the ambassadors, she broached the subject with her friend. "Chief, you shouldn't keep your people waiting like this. They've come such a long way to see you. Like master, like man . . ." Eva often used proverbs to illustrate her arguments.

Hitler was disposed that day to gratify her every whim. He reassured her, summoned his aide Wiedemann and, when he was sure that his Effie was out of earshot, ordered him: Wiedemann, send up those ass holes (*Arschlö*).

This incident has not been quoted in order to prove that Eva Braun sometimes dabbled in politics and played a part, even if an unobtrusive one, at the time of the pala-

vers that preceded Munich. She was no du Barry, no
Queen Louise of Prussia, no Mme. Chiang.

But it does not follow that, as Trevor-Roper claims,
"Eva Braun is a big historical disappointment." This author and those who have repeated his hasty judgment apparently lack comprehension of Hitler's character. This
man was not a libertine like Louis XV, and he was certainly not given to hiding behind a woman's skirts like
Frederick William III. Adolf Hitler submitted to nobody's
guidance, even at a tender age. Göring, Hess, Goebbels
had very little influence on him, and the reports of conversations at general headquarters show how far he opposed
and often ridiculed the ideas and proposals of Himmler
and the other party chiefs. Even Bormann was only there
to execute his orders and by all accounts rarely offered a
political suggestion. Eva Braun was influential in other
spheres as well, but her essential role was that of comforting Hitler by her physical presence, by the constant assurance of her devotion, by the simple fact that she was the
one person in whom he felt he could put complete trust.

"How do you think I handle the diplomats, Fräulein
Braun?" Hitler supposedly asked Eva, and her comment,
"Magnificently!" was perhaps a more gratifying reward
than the signatures at the bottom of the Munich pact. For
the details of her private life—and this may justify this
book—reveal an aspect of history quite distinct from that
based on collections of documents. Hitler never considered
Munich a victory and often declared to his intimates that
it was a semidefeat. "I hope," he complained on the eve of
his invasion of Poland, "that this time some clown won't
upset my plans."

Without digressing too far from the subject, it should be
said that no diplomatic crisis is more surrounded by legends than that of Munich. This should be realized because
the men who are today responsible for the destinies of the
free world too often base their highly inconsistent policy
on obsessive journalistic accounts of Munich, though admittedly they have at their disposal immense collections of
seized secret documents from the Nazi archives.

Hitler did not take his ambassadors seriously and had
an irrepressible aversion for the diplomatic career. "Our
ambassadors are complete nincompoops; they know nothing, understand nothing, and refuse to mix with the people
of the country where they are in residence," Hitler de-

clared to his intimates when, at table at Berchtesgaden, he started to pontificate on the state of things abroad.

Captain Wiedemann reveals that just at the time of the Munich crisis, Ribbentrop waited for weeks before being granted an interview by Hitler. The Führer requested his aide to find him pretexts for not answering the telephone when Ribbentrop wished to speak to him. In these circumstances, should great importance be attached to Ribbentrop's annotations on the seized documents? It is natural that for him a diplomatic compromise like that of Munich was an exploit, his first as foreign minister. But Hitler must have thought otherwise, for at the time of the occupation of the Sudetenland, General von Reichenau deplored: "My Führer, it is a big sacrifice for the troops to obey you and occupy these provinces without being able to fire a single shot." And another general near him insisted: "We wept, my Führer, when you forbade us to attack the Czech fortifications. . . ."

Eva one day was mentioning her visit to the Pope. Hitler had not raised the slightest objection to her taking part in an ordinary pilgrims' audience in the course of one of her annual trips to Italy. She had even had her photograph taken with the traditional black lace veil—which was for a woman with her vanity probably one of the chief attractions of an audience with the Holy Father. The mention of Rome elicited an anecdote from Hitler. The story, told to me by Eva's sister, who was present at the time, is absolutely authentic, for it is also quoted in *Hitler's Table Conversations*. One of the protagonists was an embassy counselor, a friend of Hewel. (As the man responsible for liaison between the Ministry of Foreign Affairs and Hitler, Hewel was a member of the intimate circle. In fact Hitler, who was very kindly disposed toward him, tried for a long time to marry him to Eva's sister Gretl and had promised Gretl to appoint him ambassador in Rome immediately after the marriage.) This embassy counselor was up on the dome of St. Peter's, in the company of an American lady, the wife of a White House official. The lady, after buying some postcards in the little office installed at the top of the dome, finally decided to look at the panorama. "Good grief," she apparently exclaimed, and Hitler, who understood English when he was so minded, used the original expression with a mocking air, "how dirty the streets of Rome are, how narrow and winding they are compared with our beautiful clean avenues in Washington. . . ." The German diplomat, incensed by this attitude, unceremoniously abandoned her by the balustrade and rushed down the stairs, for that day the elevator was out of action.

"This counselor was extremely discourteous," Hitler exclaimed. "It would serve him right if I shipped him off to some Chinese outpost. Our diplomats ought to have some training in good manners before they embark on political science. A pretty woman has the right to think and say whatever she pleases. She doesn't expect men to indulge in serious conversation with her but merely to devote themselves ardently to her service."

"Probably, my Führer, this was in fact what happened," Eva rejoined. "Your diplomat was perhaps courting the American lady too eagerly—you know what Italian sun and wine do to one—and she perhaps slapped him in front of everybody. This is how American women behave in films. . . ."

"Then that's even worse," Hitler laughingly decreed. "A good diplomat never displays his affections in public and must never undertake a conquest without being certain of success."

There is one indisputable proof that in 1938 Hitler was already preparing for an armed conflict with Czechoslovakia. The evidence is supplied by his first private will, which must not be confused with those he drew up later just before his suicide. The existence of this will is little known. It is handwritten and dated May 8, 1938; in other words, the morrow of the day when Hitler decided to use force for the solution of the Sudeten problem. He wrote the will in his private train after the meeting with his generals. It was deposited with the Minister Lammers at the Chancellery of the Reich. Hitler bequeathed his fortune— the amount is not specified—to the Nazi party with the proviso that the party should execute a number of legacies. The first and most important disposition concerns Eva Braun. Hitler had decided that a pension of a thousand marks a month should be paid to her for the rest of her life. This sum, even if one reckons that the present equivalent of its purchasing power is that of a thousand dollars, seems absurdly small—many Reno divorcees receive far more. But nobody else in Hitler's will is granted more, and only his two sisters, his brother Alois, one or two old collaborators, and a few others are entitled to similar sums. Hitler, who was extremely niggardly, was devoid of all practical judgment in money questions. To him a thousand marks still seemed a fabulous amount.

It can therefore be affirmed that in May, 1938, there was only one woman in Hitler's life and that this woman was Eva Braun. The will, which, it should be noted, is the first document of an official nature bearing Eva Braun's name, makes no mention of an infant or of any beneficiary who could be suspected of being Hitler's child. It can therefore be concluded that in 1938, he had neither a son nor a daughter, for, remembering his own difficult youth, he would not have neglected to provide for such offspring. He made legacies in this will to people who certainly interested him less than a child of his own blood, notwithstanding his views on the dangers of heredity. As for the need to keep the existence of a child secret, it was not operative in the drafting of a will destined never to be made public.

Eva herself ignored, if not the existence of this testament, at least the existence of any provision which concerned her and which would have confirmed in her eyes the validity of the love that Hitler bore her. The presence of this paragraph would have been for her a triumph a hundred times more precious than all the Munichs in the world.

Admittedly the tokens of her ascendancy were multiplying. After the purchase of the Bogenhausen villa and Eva's installation as mistress of Berchtesgaden, Hitler arranged for an apartment to be prepared for her in the course of the reconstruction of the Chancellery in Berlin. There was also the trip to Prague, immediately after the annexation of Czechoslovakia. Did Eva sleep in the Hradčani, the famous fortress of the golden city, when Hitler took possession of the capital? "She never mentioned it to me," affirms one of her sisters. "Besides, Hitler never allowed Eva to go into occupied territory; he refused to expose her to the slightest danger." This explanation is hardly valid, since Eva had accompanied him to Vienna. It is true, however, that the Hradčani was not equipped to accommodate so many people, and half the entourage had to sleep on improvised camp beds. In these conditions, a pretty woman would have felt considerably out of place. Yet there is the photograph taken by Eva showing Hitler surveying the main square in Prague from his window in the castle. She must therefore have been there for a short time at least.

Rumor has it that at the time of the tumultuous interview between Hitler and the Czech President Emil Hácha, the latter felt indisposed. Dr. Morell is said to have given him an injection of one of the products of his own invention that still further paralyzed the reasoning powers of the poor President, who was already half terrorized by Hitler's threats and the clattering of the sabers of his generals, who showed themselves ostentatiously at every moment.

Theo Morell had been appointed one of Hitler's personal physicians in 1937, an appointment—nobody has so far mentioned the fact—made thanks to Eva Braun, who was a close friend of Morell's wife Hanni nicknamed *Pralinchen*. The fat, good-natured doctor enjoyed a certain reputation in Berlin and Munich, chiefly because he specialized in the treatment of rich patients. For this reason, he was referred to as "Dr. Kurfürstendamm," after the smart Berlin street where his office was located. He had attended the Crown Prince and had served as ship's doctor on an ocean liner. But according to Hitler, his chief claim to fame was the discovery of a powder used to rid German soldiers of their fleas and other vermin. Eva had met Morell and his wife through the Hoffmanns, and it seems that her mother, Franziska Braun, considered the doctor a real magician. He had treated her successfully and had also cured Hoffmann of some pernicious complaint. It was therefore Eva who introduced him to Hitler and wangled an invitation for a weekend at Berchtesgaden. Hitler had some intestinal trouble at the time, and Morell prescribed a special treatment, consisting of powders and injections, that quickly eliminated the causes of the indisposition. Soon he managed to become Hitler's favorite medical man.

Eva's correspondence reveals that the Morells accompanied her on her journey to Italy and that they were present with her more than once at the Nuremberg Reichsparteitag. Eva wrote to her sister proposing that she should work for the wonder doctor. Ilse had been obliged to leave Dr. Marx by this time, at his request. The Jewish doctor realized that the association of the sister of the Führer's mistress with a Jew could only cause trouble for the Brauns, while he himself ran the risk of being sent to a concentration camp, this being a convenient way of disposing of those whose discretion was not to be trusted. Ilse greatly regretted his decision that they should separate. She still speaks with nostalgic admiration of the Jewish laryngologist, who emigrated to New York and never betrayed the Brauns' secret.

To work for Morell seemed to Ilse a betrayal of Dr. Marx, and she therefore refused—a refusal that probably saved her own life. The prospect of the three sisters surrounding Hitler would inevitably have intrigued the occasional visitor. For Gretl spent most of her time with her sister, and after flirtations or affairs with many of the Berchtesgaden clan, she finally married the SS general Fegelein, "Himmler's eye." Had Ilse become Morell's assistant, it might have been considered that Berchtesgaden had succumbed to "the Braun movement," as Göring once facetiously called it. This play on words was extremely distasteful to Hitler, who ordered his paladin to mind his own business.

In a letter dating from the end of August, 1937, Eva remarks that "Morell must be eternally grateful to me when he comes to the Berg," in other words to the Berghof. Further on she writes that if Dr. Morell wants to treat the Führer, he must be quick, because later on Hitler will be involved with his speeches and will no longer have time.

Thus, thanks partly to the support of Eva, who was always very ready to help her friends, but also by dint of intrigues, Morell succeeded in supplanting Dr. Brandt, Hitler's other personal doctor. By a curious twist of fate, Eva toward the end professed great admiration for Brandt and tried in vain to prevent his expulsion from Berchtesgaden or at least to palliate the effects of his disgrace. It may well be that Hitler was jealous of Brandt. The doctor was married to a delightful Olympic swimming champion, Anni Rehborn (before courting her, he had saved her saucy profile with a nose operation), but this did not prevent him from paying considerable attention to Eva Braun. At the end Eva became increasingly distrustful of Morell, whom she accused of poisoning her lover's system with his concoctions.

Morell, paralyzed, is known to have died in an American internment camp, while Dr. Karl Brandt was condemned at Nuremberg and hanged in Landsberg prison, in deplorable circumstances.

In Berlin, Eva was unable to move into her own apartment in the Chancellery before the beginning of 1939. Hitler had reserved Hindenburg's former bedroom for her. It had an enormous fireplace under a dusty portrait of Bismarck and heavy curtains over the windows, which the servants were not allowed to draw aside. This room and a boudoir communicated with Hitler's library but did not actually form part of the grandiose new buildings on the Voss-Strasse. Eva reached her room through the servants' entrance. Officially her position was again that of one of the numerous secretaries in the offices; she had to take her meals in her room and could not circulate freely in the official part of the building. She was rarely to be seen with Hitler, but she probably joined him at night, for Hitler always locked himself in his room when Eva was in Berlin. He himself admitted to his secretary: "I have a terror of staying alone at night." This childish fear explains why Hitler, when he was separated from Eva, was so insistent on prolonging his evenings indefinitely and often worked until daybreak.

When he took his meals with Eva, it was not at a large table like that at Berchtesgaden, in the social setting of an Austrian country squire's domain, but in his library, and always in the presence of two secretaries. When Eva asked to be invited to the sumptuous receptions organized by him or the high dignitaries of the party, or to the big balls of the season—and the Berlin season was brilliant on the eve of the world conflict—he invariably replied, "Effie, you're not made for such society life . . . you're too precious to me . . . I must protect your purity . . . Berlin is a corrupt city . . . you're like a flower . . . and the outside world is a dung heap."

Eva obeyed, but with constant grumbling. She was furious at seeing Emmy Göring photographed everywhere as "First Lady of the Reich" and never forgave her this usurpation. When Dr. Joseph Goebbels proclaimed in a speech that "Hitler was totally devoted to the nation and had no private life . . ." Eva never tired of repeating to all those she met, and that in Hitler's presence, while he looked on bleakly: *"Ich bin Fräulein Kein Privatleben."* (I am Miss-No-Private-Life.)

To make up for this, she harried the Berlin shopkeepers, buying all the most expensive goods and demanding immediate delivery. Her sister tells how one morning, very simply dressed like any little secretary doing her shopping during her half-hour lunch break, she went into Lederer, a store known all over Europe for its leather goods. She asked to see some purses. The assistant showed her a few cheap models. Eva waved them aside scornfully and indicated a splendid assortment in the window: a purse, umbrella, suitcase, traveling toilet outfit, and everything else. "Madam, it's real Madagascar crocodile skin, irreplaceable because of the currency shortage. It costs a fortune. In fact, it's only in the window for display because nobody can afford it nowadays."

Eva retorted icily: "I didn't ask you the price. I want that set immediately."

And as the salesgirl hesitated, Eva said to her: "Call the manager. . . ."

Finally, with her most regal air, she ordered: "Bring everything, this very afternoon, to the Chancellery of the Reich and send the bill to the Führer's private secretary."

Both manager and salesgirl began to tremble, the more so when Eva, after sweeping out of the shop, got into her black-and-silver Mercedes, piloted by a fair giant in SS uniform. The manager delivered the parcel at the Chancellery himself and accompanied it with a magnificent bouquet for which he paid out of his own pocket. Eva blithely related the incident and for some time everybody nicknamed her "Miss Crocodile."

The Mercedes, a 3.2 cabriolet, had been offered by the managing director of the Daimler-Benz company to Hitler, who had put it at Eva's disposal. For her twenty-seventh birthday, Eva had also received another car, which, though smaller, had greater sentimental value. It was one of the first Volkswagens. And although today people feign ignorance of the fact, it was Adolf Hitler who ordered the mass production of these small cars. He wanted to prove to the Americans that he was capable of following in the footsteps of Ford, the man who had encouraged him so much, morally and perhaps financially, at the outset of his career. Any German, starting with party members, could obtain a Volkswagen. Its delivery was ensured merely by the weekly pasting of stamps to the value of one or two marks in a savings book. Eva did not have to paste anything, of course, for the manufacturer gave her one of the prototypes.

Hitler's presents usually reflected other people's generosity. In this case, however, the generosity was deserved. The idea of the Volkswagen was basically his, and he took an active part in the production efforts and even designed a number of the car's features. Alas, the war prevented Eva from driving about in such a conspicuous car. The Volkswagen rarely left the garage in Berchtesgaden, and in her will, Eva bequeathed it to her sister Ilse. The Mercedes cabriolet she left to her father.

Eva Braun was no longer the schoolgirl waiting on the station platform in a little check coat with hood and cotton gloves bought in a sale. She now patronized one of the most distinguished dressmakers in Berlin, Fräulein Heise, her shoes came from Italy, her underwear from Paris, her sports outfits from one of the best fashion houses in Vienna. When she came to Berlin, she ordered dresses by the dozen and was extremely exacting during fittings. Her elegance would perhaps have made Paris society smile, but it dazzled the Nazi hierarchy.

It must be remembered that most of the notabilities of the regime were of modest origins and their wives lacked style, their tastes were undistinguished, their manners appalling, and, as often happens, they seemed even more awkward in their *nouveau riche* trappings. Eva eclipsed them all, and Hitler was immensely proud of her. "Look how elegant Fräulein Braun is," he would remark. He frowned, however, when Eva paraded in a model from Paris. "Did you buy it from smugglers?" he would ask. "We have no funds for such follies. Women insist upon buying foreign clothes, and refuse to believe that German products can be just as good. You always want French perfumes? But who invented eau de cologne? We did."

Eva was deaf to such reproaches, and in matters of fashion she went her own way. Hitler paid the bills, for ten years' salary from the photographer Hoffmann would have been needed to settle a single account. Eva sent all bills to Axmann or Bormann. Hitler often gave her cash, which eliminated recourse to a third party. He usually carried large sums, and when he felt so inclined, would draw a sheaf of hundred-mark bills from his pocket and put it in Eva's purse. She never directly asked him for money. More than once, in order not to importune Hitler or give the impression of being extravagant, she withdrew money from her savings' account to pay the dressmaker, no doubt hoping to be reimbursed later by Hitler.

Before she was given accommodation in the new Chancellery of the Reich, Eva stayed in the Adlon Hotel whenever she went to Berlin. This choice had been made by Hitler personally, for he did not want her at the Kaiserhof, where he stayed and which according to him was too crowded. Hitler was in the habit of taking tea every afternoon in the large lounge there while listening to light music. Naturally there was a swarm of pretty women who surveyed him from afar, openmouthed. The head waiter apparently made a fortune from the tips that these feminine admirers offered him in order to be placed as near as possible to the Führer's table. Some even ventured to come and offer him flowers or touch his hand. Hitler evidently did not think that this was a suitable place for Eva Braun, who was as jealous as a tigress of any female who came near her Führer.

In the spring of 1967, I persuaded Gretl Braun, after much coaxing, to accompany me to East Berlin, in order to visit the room where Eva stayed in the big Adlon Hotel. Only part of the building is still standing, but the hotel operates nonetheless. It is located at the corner of Wilhelmstrasse and Unter den Linden and is the only surviving prewar edifice in the neighborhood. The rest of the Wilhelmstrasse was practically razed to the ground. The room where Eva lived—although it is difficult, in spite of the evidence, to establish after twenty-nine years and so many changes that it is really the same room—has been transformed into a grill. But what desolation: The dilapidated walls have not been repainted for years, the tables are rickety, the floor is grimy and appears not to have been swept since the last communist holiday or so, and the tea is served in what seem to be test tubes that have been used in a laboratory. I don't think the East German government is deliberately responsible for all this; it is merely not interested in managing a luxury hotel.

During his intimate wartime lunches with Eva and the secretaries in his library on the Wilhelmstrasse, Hitler often broached topical questions. He talked about Churchill, whom he called "the eternal drunkard," and about Roosevelt, who for him was simply "the criminal." His judgments on the other statesmen on the international checkerboard were just as extreme. He declared that Ataturk was of Germanic blood and was a blue-eyed Kurd. Nobody was tactless enough to correct him by remarking that Kemal Ataturk was born in Salonica and that he had in reality ordered the massacre of a number of Kurdish tribes. It seems that nobody had ever told him that the Turkish dictator was, like him, the son of a customs official.

He would also expound his theories on the efficacy of repetition as an advertising technique—Hitler would have made an excellent Madison Avenue company chairman. "Fräulein Braun, why do you use your brand of tooth-paste?" "Because I like it," Eva replies. *"Falsch,"* Hitler announces triumphantly, "it is because you see that name everywhere—on posters, on theater programs, in magazines. The public must know in order to understand. That's why in politics we have constantly to repeat the same things. Then the people will realize that what we're saying must be true, since we say it over and over again."

At table, he was always reiterating his ideas on Jews. Eva Braun had grown up in a family where racial prejudice was taboo. Actually, Fritz Braun was a tolerant man for his era and his class; the proof is that he allowed one of his daughters to work so long for a Jewish doctor, even after the Nazis' rise to power. Yet Eva, during the sixteen years of her relationship with Hitler, and even in the darkest moments of the anti-Semitic persecutions, never intervened, even to plead for the lightening of a sentence. "It wouldn't have done any good," Ilse Braun claims in her defense. "I once interceded with Bormann for the release of Arthur Ernst Rutra, a Jewish writer whom I admired, from a concentration camp, Sachsenhausen, I believe. Bormann promised, in the presence of my sister Eva, to take the necessary steps immediately. A fortnight later he hypocritically announced: 'I'm sorry, but your protégé is dead. He tried to escape and the guards shot him.' I realized that any further intervention on my part would have the same results and I abstained, for my attempts to help, far from assisting the Jews, would have hastened their destruction."

It should not be forgotten that Hitler was not the inventor of anti-Semitism. It was there all the time, solidly established, particularly among the German bourgeoisie. In spite of this, Eva liked to read Jewish authors, and it mattered little to her that her favorite melodies should have been composed by musicians of impure blood. To convince her, Hitler repeated again and again, "The Jews aren't

Germans, they can't be Germans. They are my enemies and you must therefore consider them as such." Was there talk of concentration camps, of deportations? Eva Braun was no more concerned about the fate of Hitler's "enemies" than a Kansas housewife is grieved by the tribulations of the Congo or of the Arab refugees who, under their tents in the Arabian desert, have been struggling for existence for over twenty years.

Eva traveled widely in 1939. She had gone on a cruise with her sister and her mother—her father had refused the invitation—on one of the pleasure ships that went to the Norwegian fjords. These cruises, whose motto *"Kraft durch Freude"* (Strength Through Joy) was irreverently modified by some to "Joy Through Strength," were organized for the workers, under the auspices of a section of the party. They scarcely offered suitable accommodations for persons of good family who were guests of the Führer. Hitler, however, could not resist bestowing such favors— the cruises did not cost him a pfennig.

Eva was also invited to the Venice Film Festival, again at the expense of others. A telegram summoned her back urgently. August, 1939, was drawing to a close, and there was talk of war with Poland. Eva traveled in a first-class sleeper, but she noticed that the rest of the train was packed, that there were unaccountable delays, that the station platforms were black with people, and she also noticed that many troop trains passed them. These were the first symptoms of a mobilization in which, like almost all Germans, she had so far refused to believe.

Naturally she wanted Danzig to be German. She had given the Führer a birthday present of a set of gold-and-diamond cuff-links showing the swastika floating over the arms of the town of Danzig. Hitler wore them to the end of his life. But everything would be settled peacefully, she had assured her sister, with treaties and merrymaking.

Ilse had accompanied Eva to Berlin. Albert Speer, head of munitions, had offered the eldest Braun daughter a post as assistant, at Eva's request. Speer took the two young women to dine officially at the Chancellery. Hitler had relaxed his interdiction because Speer's invitation was a pretext that disguised the real reason for Eva's presence. It was a business dinner, at which Goebbels, Ribbentrop, Keitel, and others were present. Over dessert, Hitler turned to Ribbentrop and asked, "May I tell?" Ribbentrop, as proud as a peacock, smilingly raised his hand in assent. Then Hitler went on, "There will be no war. Tonight Ribbentrop is leaving for Moscow. We are going to sign a pact with the Russians."

Eva was near Hitler almost throughout the fateful hours that preceded the greatest war of modern times. Her album contains frightening photographs taken during the ten days with her little amateur's camera, and the captions written in her hand are even more so. There is Hitler on the telephone, listening to Ribbentrop's report of the signing of the pact. Hitler is also seen kissing Goebbels and Bormann and dancing for joy. Then there are the discussions and Eva's little note: "Poland is not prepared to negotiate after all. . . ." For Hitler had convinced her that it was the Poles who wanted war, with their intractable Ambassador Jòzef Lipski declaring in all the embassies on the Tiergartenstrasse that the German tanks were made of paper and that the Polish cavalry would be in Berlin by the end of the week. Finally, taken on Sunday, September 3, there are photographs of Hitler and his entourage listening to the radio, thunderstruck at the unexpected news: England was declaring war.

Eva Braun and her sister were present at the Kroll Opera when, on the morning of September 1, Hitler announced to the Reichstag and to the nation that he had invaded Poland.

"That means war, Ilse," Eva apparently said, "and he'll leave . . . what will become of me?"

When Hitler announced that he would wear his gray-green uniform unto death, Eva covered her face with her hands. In the fanatical excitement that reigned at that moment at the Kroll Opera, nobody except her sister noticed that she was crying. "If something happens to him," she finally said to her sister, "I'll die too."

The pandemonium of the *Sieg-Heils* and the Nazi hymns was interminable and the anti-Polish clamor was magnified still further by loudspeakers. But outside, the Berlin crowd was funereally silent, their faces were gloomy; the women hastened home pushing their children before them.

As they came out of the Kroll Opera, Dr. Brandt said, "Don't worry, Fräulein Braun, the Führer told me that there will be peace again in three weeks' time." Eva smiled, like someone who has just been offered a pain-killing dose of aspirin.

Yet that evening at the Chancellery she summoned the quartermaster, Kannenberg. "I heard Göring say," she announced to this stalwart gentleman, who was somewhat surprised by this unwarranted departure from Eva's usually unobtrusive role in Berlin, "that in the Hamburg docks there are some freighters loaded with canned foods, chocolate, wine, a whole heap of delicacies. Send someone immediately to collect provisions to be sent up to the Berghof. There must be big stocks, because we'll need them for a long time."

Kannenberg executed her orders. The provisions sent were indeed abundant and lasted for years. The Bavarian mob that pillaged the Obersalzberg in April, 1945, before the arrival of the Allied troops found a great many good things still in the cellars and the attics of the home of Hitler and Eva Braun.

CHAPTER FOURTEEN

Valkyrie

The Osteria Bavaria in Munich has remained a pleasant restaurant, although its original proprietor has died and its name has been changed to Osteria Italiana. The little garden with its temple-shaped niche containing a statue of the god Bacchus is welcoming, and it is still possible to sit at what was once Hitler's table, in the roof adjoining the kitchens. This was where for years he held his private court, met pretty feminine acquaintances, and, where later, as Chancellor, between a plate of spaghetti with tomato sauce or a sweet lettuce salad and an enormous glass of *Zabaglione* without Marsala, he decided the destinies of Europe.

A pretty English student, just twenty-one, fair-haired, six-feet tall, thin, with the wistful look of a Mary Stuart miniature, ate there regularly in the spring of 1935. The object of her studies in Munich has remained somewhat nebulous, for she did not know any German. But Emma the waitress was only aware of the regal tips she received from the English girl and docilely placed her at the table opposite the one to which Hitler had established a claim. The student had learned from Princess Stephanie of Hohenlohe, who was a friend, that Hitler dined sporadically at the Osteria. She ardently wished to make his acquaintance and knew that he was otherwise unapproachable. Her persistence was rewarded, for one lunchtime, Hitler, who was dining in the company of a few aides, was finally intrigued by the dreamy gaze that this child fixed on him unwaveringly.

"She's English," he was told by his aide Schaub, who, always anticipating his master's curiosity, had already made inquiries from the owner of the restaurant. (These details are gathered partly from the proprietor's daughter, who long ago sold the business. My other informant was the waitress, whom Hitler subsequently engaged as one of the cooks at Berchtesgaden, and to whom—playing at matchmaking even in the kitchens—he gave a generous dowry when she agreed to marry the man of his choice.)

Hitler invited the girl to his table that day. The conversation started slowly, because Hitler's English was still halting and the girl knew hardly a word of German. Later, she made rapid progress and was finally able to converse in that language, even with a slight Bavarian accent, without the least difficulty. Hitler was immediately captivated. He went into raptures over the slenderness of her figure, the delicacy of her features, the gold of her hair, and the cherubic softness of her skin, which had the radiance and the hue of the pale coral found in the Bay of Naples.

"Only English girls have such complexions; it must be the English rain, the walks in the English rain that produce this skin," Hitler told her, while the young student blushed with gratitude. Flat-chested as an Amazon under the thick folds of her blue sweater, she was as far removed as possible from the Chancellor's sensual tastes. Yet he straightaway pointed out to his entourage that she was the very embodiment of Germanic beauty, a racial masterpiece that confirmed his ambitious theory that the British nation was simply an annex of Germany. The aide-de-camp Brüeckner, less given to flights of fancy, once objected surlily: "And what if she's a secret service agent who's been planted under our very noses? One can't be too careful. . . ." Hitler started to laugh, hiding his eyes with his hand (this was a mannerism of his), and retorted, "My instinct would have warned me. I would never in my life shake the hand of a spy, even if he were one of ours and had saved an empire for me. This girl is a treasure. . . ."

So Adolf Hitler made the acquaintance of the Honorable Unity Valkyrie Freeman-Mitford,* daughter of the 2nd Baron Redesdale, a British peer. Referring to her as "Walküre," Eva Braun speaks of this girl in contemptuous and suspicious terms in the diary she kept before her second suicide attempt. She had good reason to be mistrustful. Of all the rivals that were mentioned to her at ran-

---

* Hitler called her "Lady Mitford" but she never had a right to this title.

dom, Unity was certainly the one who came closest to supplanting her. For after the first semi-fortuitous meeting at the Osteria, Unity Mitford became part of the Führer's life. She was to be seen everywhere—in Bayreuth, Berlin, Munich, even Berchtesgaden.

When Fritz Wiedemann, returning from an important diplomatic interview with Lord Halifax in London, went posthaste to the Berghof at Berchtesgaden, the Führer was too busy to receive him. He was strolling in the meadows with Miss Mitford. One photograph has survived of the Parteitag in Nuremberg, showing Eva Braun and Miss Mitford standing near each other in the stand reserved for Hitler's personal guests. Not only did Eva meet this hated rival more than once, but she was even ordered by Hitler to do her the honors of the house at Berchtesgaden. She always treated her with extreme courtesy, inevitably so, for the Braun girls felt themselves too well brought up to allow themselves the slightest vulgarity, particularly with this aristocratic foreigner.

Eva had many other potential rivals at this time. When she came to Berlin, where she had to stay isolated in her apartment overlooking the courtyard just above the kitchens of the Reichskanzlei, her friends and the secretaries, especially the beautiful Gerda Daranowsky, who, like all the women hovering around her Führer, was an object of extreme jealousy to Eva, took a malicious pleasure in telling her that Hitler had intervened personally in order to hush up a scandal involving the film star Brigitte Helm, that he was making eyes at the singer Maria Müller, that he had shown himself particularly gallant the other evening with Jenny Jugo at a reception for the "Kameradschaft der Deutschen Künstler" (the Stage Artists' Association) in the Viktoriastrasse, a function to which Eva was never invited, and that the following evening he had turned his attentions to Marika Roekk. He was also said to have had an affair with Margaret Slezak, the daughter of the famous tenor Leo Slezak, a rival of Caruso.

Ciano in his diary speaks of Sigrid or Sigi von Laffert as the favorite of the moment. How ill informed the Italian secret service was! Sigi was an aristocratic girl from Griefswald in the Mecklenburg region. Her parents, Oskar and Erika von Damaretz von Laffert, had lost their fortunes, and later Hitler supported them financially.

Sigrid met Hitler at a northern seaside resort, Heiligendamm, where one of his early collaborators, Putzi Hanfstängl, had a villa. Hitler, of course, showed a keen interest in her. The Baroness von Laffert was a seventeen-year-old with eyes as deep as the waters of the Baltic on a September morning. Viktoria, known as Tory, von Dirksen, who was her distant cousin, heard of the impression, perhaps only fleeting, that Sigrid had made on Hitler, and decided to introduce her into Berlin society. No doubt the older woman thought she would thus ingratiate herself still further with the Führer. . . . This was how things worked in Berlin.

The young baroness was soon noticed in the diplomatic drawing rooms. "She had a delightful bosom, long legs, and the smallest mouth in the world, with never a trace of lipstick," remembers Italian ambassador Alfieri. "She wore her ash-blond hair in braids coiled round her head like a crown." Wiedemann reveals that once when she was in hospital, he had to take her twenty-four red roses from Hitler. Shortly before the war, the Führer wanted to marry her to the ambassador Hewel—another indication of his vocation as a matchmaker. It is hard to see how this marriage could have pacified Eva, for Hewel formed part of the intimate circle, and Sigi would therefore have had the freedom of Berchtesgaden. But the baroness chose to live in Paris, where she married the son of Count Johannes de Welczek, the incumbent of the rue de Lille embassy, whom Herschel Grynszpan tried to assassinate on November 7, 1938, thus giving rise to the terrible "crystal night" anti-Jewish reprisals.*

I have come across a vague intimation that a lady by the name of von Laffert managed to penetrate into the bunker during the final days of the 1945 agony, because she had had some sort of liaison with one of the SS of the garrison. I have been unable to establish, however, whether the lady in question was the same Sigi, Countess Welczek, who had come to share the fate of the man whom she had once loved.

The American writer Musmanno states that "Sigi, long after the Nazi defeat, protested that she 'would never have married that despot. . . .'" These are the declarations

---

* Assassin Grynszpan shot Counselor vom Rath, mistaking him for the German ambassador.

that one makes when the despot in question has lost the war instead of winning it.

But I believe Captain Wiedemann, who was present at the following highly significant exchange. Hitler, who had invited Sigi von Laffert to have tea with him in Berlin, asked her, "Why aren't you married yet?" Sigi, giving him a look that was like a burning kiss, sighed, "My Führer, you know the reason . . . you know why. . . ."

Another, until now totally unknown, flirtation was the young, tiny, vivacious Princess Alicia of Hesse. Hitler was very fond of her because she spoke with a foreign accent —she was Greek.

At the Wilhelmstrasse, there was a moment when the possibility of a match between Hitler and Maria of Savoy, the youngest daughter of the King of Italy, was envisaged —perhaps as the result of another of Ciano's fantasies. It is difficult to imagine what little King Victor Emmanuel's reaction to the proposal must have been. The fact remains that Hitler's attention was discreetly drawn to the languorous glances that the princess cast in his direction when he visited the Quirinale, and he was assured that Maria considered him the incarnation of Lohengrin. Could the supposed attempt on Eva Braun's life in the Naples harbor be connected with this? Was the plan perhaps to dispose of the mistress in order to offer the vacant bed to the royal princess?

Hitler, in confidences to his friends, declared on several occasions that if ever he decided to make a marriage of convenience, he would wed the widowed Winifred Wagner, daughter-in-law of the great composer. He fondly imagined that a union of the names Hitler and Wagner, which were for him without parallel, would ensure the adoration of the masses until kingdom come.

Winifred was entitled to the name Wagner merely because in 1915 she had married Siegfried, the Master's only son. She was born in Hastings on June 23, 1897, of an English father, the journalist John Williams, and a German mother, Emily Karop. Even from an early age, her health was poor. She went to Germany to live with Karl Klindworth and his wife, who taught her to appreciate the music of Wagner. As early as 1923, she declared herself pro-Hitler. Prompted by his unbounded admiration for Wagner (he had himself tried to compose a grand opera at the age of seventeen) Hitler often visited Bayreuth. The children of Siegfried—Wieland, Wolfgang, Friedelind, and Verena—called him "Uncle" and addressed him with "*du*." Friedelind later sought refuge in England and expressed some very unflattering opinions on this childhood uncle. In order not to be an embarrassment to the organizers of the Bayreuth Festival, Hitler always went incognito to the little town. It was also rumored that Siegfried, the husband, did not approve of these visits. After his rise to power, however, Hitler became the official patron of the organization, and thanks to him, Mme. Winifred, whose husband had died in 1930, found herself rich and famous. Bayreuth again became the musical capital of Europe, as Richard Wagner had dreamed it would. It was there that Hitler spent the happiest days of his life as Chancellor, days during which, incredibly enough, he gave up all his political activities to listen to music. He invited notabilities, diplomats, journalists, members of high society. Eva Braun was among the guests several times, as was also Miss Mitford. Hitler did not stay at Winifred's, but in an isolated house; however, he often went of an evening, on foot and in civilian dress, to pay a friendly visit to the family. The festival continued during the war, at Hitler's express wish, and it is worth noting that Winifred's son Wieland was deferred from military service. Hitler's last visit to Bayreuth, however, was in the summer of 1940, when he was present, prophetically, at a performance of *Götterdämmerung*.

Unity Valkyrie formed part of what later became known, rather vaguely, as the British "Establishment." Her father was David Bertram Ogilvy Freeman-Mitford, second Baron Redesdale, nicknamed irreverently "Farve" by his children. He was a peer of the realm and a retired general. He rarely visited the House of Lords, but when he did it was to defend ferociously the feudal rights of the nobility. The family devise ran: "God Careth for Us," and he believed himself to be a direct descendant of Charlemagne.

He hated all foreigners, including Germans, the "Huns," but changed his mind when, thanks to his daughter Unity, he was received by Hitler on the occasion of the 1936 Bayreuth Festival. As a matter of fact, he and Lady Redesdale were charmed by the new Chancellor and dictator of Germany.

No one was surprised by these veerings of opinion, as

the Redesdales had the reputation of being "splendid eccentrics." Lady Redesdale, born Sidney Bowles, fought a permanent crusade against all the revolutionaries of all times and had baptized her children according to her romantic inspiration of the moment. But it is difficult to see why she named this daughter, born the fourth day after the beginning of the First World War, Unity Valkyrie.*

Unity was not the only one of the Redesdale children to lead a rather turbulent life. Diana, the eldest, became the wife of Brian Guinness, of the beer-and-stout multimillionaires, and because of her exceptional beauty was the darling of the society and fashion magazines. After her divorce from Guinness, her father for a time refused to see her. Then she took up fascism as a cause, following in Unity's footsteps and joining the British Union of Fascists, where she met their leader, Sir Oswald Mosley, whom she later married.

Nancy was famous for her biting wit and her practical jokes. She was the successful author of several satirical novels, such as *Love in a Cold Climate,* and of a biography of Louis XIV. After her marriage to the diplomat Peter Rodd she lived mostly in Paris. Pamela, more conservative, married an Oxford don and has been active in charitable causes. The only son, the Honorable Thomas Freeman-Mitford, amused himself in London and was not popular with his sisters.

Deborah, the youngest of the girls, married a son of the Duke of Devonshire during World War II. At the age of three she is supposed to have predicted that one day she would become a duchess. In due time her husband's older brother, the Marquess of Hartington, was killed in Normandy, making Deborah's husband the heir.

Hartington had married Kathleen Kennedy, sister of John F. Kennedy, who often danced with the Mitford girls when he was in London with his father the ambassador. Kathleen, Hartington's widow, died in 1948 in a plane accident in the South of France.

It is intriguing to realize that if Hitler had married Unity, as many believed he might, he would have become for a brief time related by marriage to the future President of the United States.

---

* The Valkyries or *Walküre,* daughters of Odin, were goddesses of Scandinavian mythology. They poured hydromel (mead) for the dead warriors and influenced the outcome of battles.

Unity and her younger sister Jessica were both crusaders, even as adolescents, but for opposing ideologies. Unity used to sing the *"Horst Wessel Lied"* and *"Deutschland über Alles"* in the park of the Redesdales' country house, while Jessica would retaliate by yelling the *"Internationale"* at the top of her voice. Unity would trace swastikas with her diamond ring on the windows of the reception hall and Jessica would scratch them out and replace them with the sickle and hammer. Unity had covered part of the library with portraits of Hitler and copies of *Mein Kampf*, while Jessica, on the other side of the room, displayed portraits of Lenin and Stalin and copies of Karl Marx's works.

Unity, called "Bobo" and also "Boud," had always admired Germany. She even refused to learn French at school or to go to a finishing school in Paris, as was the tradition. As a matter of fact, she had been expelled from one school, and later was politely invited to leave another institution for aristocratic young ladies. But her parents were not particularly upset. *"C'est l'age ingrat,"* commented Lord Redesdale. Even when Unity, presented at court to the King, tried to organize a pro-Nazi meeting among the debutantes, no one took her teen-ager pranks at all seriously.

To quiet her down, she was allowed to go to Germany. At first no one could believe that she had met Hitler, Göring, Himmler, and all the Nazi bigwigs so easily, but when she returned with photos and factual proofs, her parents were extremely impressed and flattered.

Not so the population of the village of Swinbrook, who protested indignantly when Unity walked down the main street, greeting everyone with *"Heil Hitler"* and a raised arm. She had the Nazi party insignia pinned on her blouse, and Jessica remembers that during a cruise, as the ship stopped in Barcelona, then still part of republican Spain, Unity escaped only narrowly being lynched by the indignant populace, at the sight of her Nazi insignia.

Diana shared her sister's exaltation. She went to Germany to join Unity and met Hitler. Her enthusiasm was so great, in fact, that she even characterized Julius Streicher, the monster later hanged at Nuremberg, as "a darling kitten." As for Unity, she once wrote a letter to the magazine *"Der Stürmer,"* directed by Streicher, trumpeting, "I hate all the Jews of the world."

Sister Nancy did not agree, and to eliminate any possibility of a marriage between Unity and Hitler, she invented a Jewish ancestor in the Redesdale clan and sent a forged family tree to Himmler.

Jessica, by then a fervent champion of communism, had a bolder plan. She proposed to visit her sister in Munich, be introduced by her to Adolf Hitler, and once in front of him, to take a revolver from her purse and shoot him down. But she admits in her memoirs that this was only a youthful dream. . . .

Jessica, nicknamed Dekka, was three years younger than Unity. And at the time her sister was flirting with Hitler, she fell in love with a nephew of Winston Churchill called Esmond Romilly. Even before she met him she was attracted because he also was a Red, and much to the alarm of his family he went to Spain to fight against Franco. Wounded, he returned to London, and only then Jessica was able to arrange for an introduction. It was successful, and soon she ran away from home, and the couple left clandestinely for Paris and then went to Spain. But they never managed to fight a second time with the international Red brigades—their main object was to get married. The elopement scandalized London, and soon sister Nancy and her husband Peter Rodd arrived in Bermeo, a port near Bilbao in the Basque country, aboard a destroyer of the Royal Navy, seeking to kidnap Jessica and bring her back to England. Eventually Jessica and Esmond married, returned to London, and then emigrated to the United States.

Esmond Romilly was killed at twenty-three during the war, and Jessica remarried and went to live in California. One of her books, an exposure of the undertaking business, *The American Way of Death,* became a much-talked-about best seller.

It is said that one day Unity with trepidation informed the Führer that her sister had become the black sheep of the family by fleeing to Spain to join the Bolsheviks. Hitler was not angry. He sank his head in his hands and sighed, "Poor child."

By this time Diana had decided to marry none other than Sir Oswald Mosley, the leader of the English fascists. For reasons that have never been explained, the Nazi party leaders never established direct contacts with their British counterparts. It was Unity who became the link.

She organized the wedding of her sister and Sir Oswald in Munich, not, as has been said, in Hitler's residence, but at the house of one of his friends. Hitler was not one of the witnesses at the ceremony, but he invited the newlyweds to dinner. He had a conversation with Mosley, of whom he said, "He's a very well-intentioned fellow." And Unity proclaimed extravagantly: "My brother-in-law, my Führer, will have to become your disciple."

Unity no longer concealed her intention of becoming the Egeria of the Third Reich. Although it was exceptional for a foreigner to enter the ranks of this ultrachauvinist organization, she solemnly received the party emblem. Hitler gave her an autographed portrait in a silver frame which she showed to everybody and placed on her bedside table even when she was traveling by sleeping car. Her auto was decorated with flags bearing swastikas and with the Union Jack. She declared that she was a modern Joan of Arc who was going to establish an indestructible union between the "Lord of the Seas" and the "Lord of the Land," between the King of England and the German Führer. Her very name Unity was a token of the success she was certain of achieving, she said.

Hitler, to the great consternation of his advisers (but who still dared to advise Hitler in those days?), took this fanatical girl very seriously. She talked to him about England, a country that he did not know and about which he had read practically nothing. (He once said that the only book about Great Britain that interested him was *Jane's Fighting Ships*, which contained information about the British naval forces.)

Unity had been acquainted with Winston Churchill, Eden, Chamberlain, Lord Rothermere, and had been presented at court. She told him exactly what he wanted to hear: that the government did not represent the country, that there was a strong nationalist movement, that the young people admired the Führer, that only the Jews wanted war, that they had bought the votes of the politicians, including Churchill, whom she called the grave digger of the Empire, that England and Germany, if they acted together, could rule the world. These were all things that his own ambassadors refused to tell him. Thus Hitler saw in Unity the irrefutable proof that he, with his instinct, was always right.

Did he envisage marrying her one day in order to consolidate this future union of empires? Or did he merely allow Unity to cherish this illusory hope? Adolf Hitler loved Eva Braun, or so he claimed. But this love or affection was subordinated to reasons of state, and it is quite possible that, like Napoleon who loved Josephine but married Marie-Louise, the daughter of the Emperor of Austria, Hitler might have wedded Unity Mitford if he could thereby have ensured the goodwill of England. Hitler always tried to imitate Napoleon except in his defeats. Unity boasted of the success at Munich, of the pact limiting a naval armament, of the Hitler-Chamberlain interview. She reassured everybody in Berlin by swearing that England, her native country, would never declare war—and Hitler believed her.

Then came September 3, 1939. Unity Valkyrie Mitford's world disintegrated like a reed hut in a Pacific typhoon. An hour after the radio announcement of the declaration of war, she went to see the Munich Gauleiter Adolf Wagner and gave him a big envelope with a wax seal, addressed to Hitler.

Wagner had other fish to fry that first day of the world war, and only opened the envelope after telephoning to Hitler, who was on the Polish front. Inside there was the party emblem, the autographed photograph of Hitler, and the most melodramatic of love letters:

> I am torn between my loyalty to you, my Führer, and my duty as a British subject. . . . Our two nations have thrown themselves into the abyss, one will drag the other after it. . . . My life is of no account now. . . .

By now Hitler was well versed in the reactions of young girls in the throes of despair, especially when he was its chief cause. He therefore ordered Wagner to go in search of her, to calm her . . . but Unity could not be found.

It was only on the afternoon of September 4 that the police were informed by the surgery department of the clinic in Nussbaumstrasse that an unidentified girl, suffering from a severe wound in the temple, had been hospitalized the day before after having been found on a bench in the Englischer Garten, the big park in the center of Munich. The young woman, who was carrying no papers, had fired two shots at herself. One of the bullets was still in the patient's skull and had paralyzed the whole nervous system. Her condition was desperate.

Hitler, warned of this, abandoned his generals to come to the telephone and order that Unity—whose identity had meanwhile been established by Wagner—should be attended by the best doctors, in the most luxurious room in the clinic, at government expense. He sent word to his Minister in Berne to break the news discreetly to Unity's parents.

The famous Professor Magnus treated the distinguished patient. She was temporarily out of danger, but an operation was necessary to extract the bullet that was still lodged in her temple. Hitler, on his sudden return from Poland on September 10, 1939, visited Unity, who gave no sign of recognition. He gave orders for the operation to be undertaken, but the surgeon was hesitant.

For months Unity lay in a state of coma, without speaking or seeming to recognize anybody. Hitler paid her another visit and continued to give orders for the princely treatment of the young woman, though she was theoretically an enemy subject. At his request, which must have caused her considerable disquiet, Eva Braun ordered flowers to be sent and attended to the purchasing of essential toilet articles for the patient, to her linen, and to various other details. She also persuaded Dr. Morell to take part in consultations with the doctors of the clinic.

All this created an atmosphere of mystery around Room 202, where Unity Mitford lay, after seeking refuge from reality. Hitler issued instructions that the utmost secrecy should be preserved. Fortunately the hospital staff were members of a religious order and were well trained in the respecting of discipline.

It was only in the spring of 1940 that Unity began to return to some semblance of normality. One can only give slight credit to a story told by Frau Schaub, the wife of Hitler's aide, who at the Führer's request often visited the patient. She affirms that she gave back to her the autographed photograph and the party emblem, and that Unity tore up the portrait and swallowed the emblem. She was only saved a second time by a miraculous intervention on the part of Professor Magnus. He still refused, however, to operate on her head, where the pistol bullet was still lodged. He argued that it was too dangerous, and that if

Miss Mitford died, it would be claimed in England that Hitler had caused his "mistress" to be "executed."

Finally, it was decided to send her back to her parents. A compartment on the Munich-Zurich train was prepared in such a way as to accommodate the patient and enable Dr. Reiser, who was to accompany her with a nurse, to operate during the journey in case of absolute necessity. An English doctor was waiting in Zurich. From there, the patient traveled back to England via Calais. She was subsequently operated on, but not a word was heard about her until the end of hostilities. It was only in 1946 that photographs of Unity appeared in the press. On May 20, 1948, the *London Times,* in unusually succinct terms, published an announcement of Unity's death.

But to all intents Unity Valkyrie Mitford had ceased to exist when the four o'clock train drew out of Munich station on the afternoon of April 16, 1940. Under the pretext of accompanying Dr. and Frau Morell—the doctor was to some extent responsible for the medical arrangements— Eva Braun had gone to the station to make sure that Unity was safely on board. To her this clandestine departure may have seemed a victory far more important than the capture of Warsaw was for Adolf Hitler.

CHAPTER FIFTEEN

"Tschapperl"

In her alarm, Eva Braun threw the cigarette she had only just lit out of the window of the special train—an imprudent gesture, for the wind might well have blown it back into one of the thirty coaches speeding away from Munich. Hitler, as was his wont, had come surreptitiously into the dining car, where Eva was sipping a drink with her friend Herta Ostermeyr. Hitler, however, was too overwrought to notice this infringement of his rules of conduct. "Fräulein Eva," he ejaculated, "I've had a narrow escape. I've just been informed that some infernal device has exploded in one of the pillars of the Bürgerbräukeller, where I have only just delivered my speech."

Every year Hitler traditionally delivered a lengthy harangue to his companions of the abortive putsch of 1923, the commemoration of which was a kind of Nazi Easter. This time, on the eve of November 9, 1939, despite the importance of the celebration, the first in time of war, he had been briefer than usual for some unexplained reason, and had left the beer-hall long before the scheduled time. In fact, Eva and Herta had almost missed the train, for they arrived at the station just as it was leaving, in advance of the scheduled departure time. The news of the attempt reached Hitler only when the convoy was already in the region of Augsburg. "The gods protect me," Hitler continued, "and I don't give a damn about these insects who tried to pester me. But it seems there are casualties, both dead and wounded. It's deplorable."

Eva, however, horrified by the idea of the danger to which her lover had been exposed, went to join him in his compartment and paid no heed to the remark about the dead and wounded. Seven Nazi dignitaries had been killed and sixty-three injured by the explosion of the time bomb. It was only the following day, when she telephoned to her sister from Berlin, that she learned that her father had been among the victims and was under observation in one of the hospitals of the town.

For Fritz Braun had suddenly changed camp, without even troubling to inform his family. On November 1, 1937, in other words only one or two months after the violent altercation with Eva because of the photograph published in a Czech magazine, when he swore that he would never set foot in her house again, he joined the ranks of the Nationalist Socialist Party. His identity card bore the low number 5,021,670, which was humiliating for the Führer's future father-in-law. However, much later, he had received through Eva, with whom he must evidently have made peace, a special green card, numbered 1,488, which included him among the veterans of the revolution. It was thanks to this card that he had been admitted to the Bürgerbräukeller, along with the earliest and staunchest supporters. After the explosion, covered with blood and dust, his uniform in tatters, he was extricated by the ambulance squads.

Eva Braun was naturally sad at the news of her father's misadventure, but at the same time extremely proud at having a father who had finally shed his blood for the Führer, her lover. She never knew that Georg Elser, also known as Eller, the man accused of having plotted this attempt for the British Intelligence Service, received preferential treatment in the concentration camps at Sachsenhausen and Dachau (where I met him). Elser claimed to have been paid by Himmler's Gestapo deliberately to plant the bomb in such a way that the explosion took place only after Hitler's departure. The aim was to strengthen the myth of the Führer's invulnerability and also to eliminate a few members of the party who were an embarrassment to Himmler.

Fritz Braun later explained his political change of front by the need to preserve domestic harmony and by the pressure exerted on him by the authorities, who would not tolerate a professor who was not a member of the party. The explanation is hardly convincing, for his attitude toward his daughter Eva never denoted such extreme solicitude, and as for the authorities, had he not formerly wanted to resign because he considered that the family

honor had been blotted? No, the real motive was that
Fritz Braun had decided that Hitler was after all a great
man, that he was the archangel come down from the heavens
to save and guide the great German nation. Braun subsequently admitted: "How could I believe otherwise with
Hitler liberating Austria, Czechoslovakia, Memel, and
later on conquering Paris, Warsaw, and Oslo?"

At the time of the trials that followed the fall of the
Third Reich, Fritz Braun denied having been the object of
special favors on the part of the Führer. He declared that
he had never received anything but a gold watch, a dog on
the occasion of his sixty-fifth birthday, and a fortnight's
stay at the Obersalzberg. He neglected to say that his wife
often resided there. Moreover, his daughters' photograph
albums show that in reality he went there several times,
and various letters and Eva's will suggest that he received
far more than a dog and a watch. The chief indication of
Hitler's goodwill, however, was his nomination—with the
rank of reserve army major—as director of the military
hospital that had been installed in the former Kurhaus at
Ruhpolding southeast of Munich. This was an appreciable
sinecure at a time when, for a peccadillo, a German was
sent to the white hell in Russia, and when life in the large
cities involved continual danger. Ruhpolding was bombed
only once by an absentminded English pilot, a raid that
appears to have scared Papa Braun considerably. Otherwise, thanks to the Führer, he lived for most of the war in
one of the most idyllic spots in Europe.

The elimination of paternal opposition appreciably
strengthened the position of Eva, who now reigned as un-
disputed favorite. Nobody else enjoyed her privilege of
being able to invite her parents or her sisters for protracted stays at the Obersalzberg. Gretl was entitled to her
own private apartment there. With Unity Mitford's departure, Eva had practically disposed of all her rivals.
After the summer of 1940, Hitler no longer went to the
Bayreuth Festival, thereby weakening his contacts with
Frau Wagner. In view of the climate of austerity with
which he now surrounded himself, he also gave up his
meetings with pretty theater and movie stars. His relations
with Eva became still more familiar, more conjugal, more
tender. The war, far from separating them, brought them
much closer together, for his stays at the Obersalzberg
grew longer and more frequent. It can even be said that

the more the war situation deteriorated, the more he took refuge at the Berghof, although as far as possible he avoided winter stays there, especially after Stalingrad. Perhaps so much snow reminded him too vividly of the disasters in Russia.

The Berghof staff realized that Eva was no longer an ordinary guest and called her *Chefin,* Wife of the Chief. In order to avoid indiscretions, she was never mentioned by name in public, but was referred to as "E. B." She had composed a monogram, which appears on nearly all her possessions, in the shape of a four-leaved clover. From time to time, to mock her, the company chanted *"Landesmutter"* at her, Mother of the Country, an appellation first given her by Hoffmann.

She always alluded to Hitler as the "Chief," or the "Führer," or sometimes as A. H. She never addressed him by his name or his title in public, but with the familiar *du.* Hitler also said *du* to her and increasingly used a Viennese diminutive "Tschapperl," which means little thing. He also called her "Veverl" or "Feferl," Austrian variants of Eva, as well as "Effie." Eva did not allow anybody else to take liberties with her first name. She had once forbidden Martin Bormann to call her Ewe, as he had sometimes tried to do with malicious intent, for this was supposed to be a Jewish form of her name, but he continued to do so in his correspondence with his wife Gerda.

Hitler would stroke her hand in company but otherwise always avoided giving any external indication of his affection. In the mornings he continued to act formally when he met her downstairs, greeting her ceremoniously and kissing her hand. When he knocked at the door of her room, in spite of the fact that he had direct access to it from his studio, he always inquired, "Fräulein Effie, are you dressed and visible?"

What was the nature of their sexual relations? Hitler never discussed the matter with others, and Eva Braun was extremely reserved, even a trifle mysterious, and very rarely broached the question with her sisters or her mother. The Braun girls, because of the atmosphere in which they had been brought up, did not like to speak about such things. This chapter was already in proof when I received from a person who alone is qualified to give evidence in this delicate domain a written testimony that enables me to give irrefutable information on the subject.

My informant decided to talk after twenty-two years of silence. (The American interrogators in the prisons of Nuremberg and Landsberg did not succeed, after thirteen months of effort, in extracting anything from her.)

According to this intimate source, sexual relations between Hitler and Eva Braun were perfectly normal. True, they were not of Latin intensity, but they could be defined as natural compared to those of any German couple. It must be borne in mind that Hitler was approaching fifty, that he was often away, and therefore separated from Eva, a large part of the time, that he worked late at night and often returned to his rooms exhausted after councils of war or important governmental discussions. Theirs was no honeymoon situation. Eva was a submissive and loving woman, but she did not have a flaming sexual temperament. The ladies of the Braun family give the impression of being very sober and reserved in this respect. When Eva confided in her friends, she spoke constantly of the anxiety that her lover's absence caused her, of her desire to see him, of her worries and jealousies, but rarely of any sexual deprivation or expectation.

Eva's mother confirmed to me that her daughter's vagina was "narrowly built." For this reason Eva was treated by a Munich gynecologist of repute, Professor Scholten, who was killed in a car accident while returning from Berchtesgaden in the company of Eva's friend Herta Ostermeyr. But Frau Scholten, his wife, remembers the treatments. Eva was operated on to remedy this peculiarity of her sexual organs, and the operation, which involved long and specialized medical attention, seems to have been successful.

Eva longed to have children, and being a good Catholic, would never have agreed to have an abortion. It is absolutely certain that she never submitted to such an operation and that she never had a miscarriage. Before receiving Professor Scholten's medical report, I interrogated all Eva Braun's acquaintances, and all swore to me that they had never noticed anything to suggest that Eva might have been pregnant at any time. There was never the slightest indication that her figure was filling out. On the contrary, it grew flatter every day.

Eva would have done anything to safeguard her pregnancy had she found herself in this state. This was for her the only justifiable reason for braving Hitler's anger. Hitler, relentlessly, said again and again: "We'll only get married after the war. Until then I don't want any children, no clandestine or illegitimate births. In time of war, I belong exclusively to my people."

Her intimate friend Herta assures me that Eva never entertained the illusion of being pregnant and never mentioned to her any irregularity in her monthly periods. She is convinced that if there had been any such lateness, Eva would have spoken of it, for she always confided in her and sometimes asked her for advice about feminine hygiene (Herta was the mother of two small girls).

How could Hitler and his mistress be certain that their lovemaking would not have such sequels? The problem was attenuated by the fact that their periods of intimacy were relatively rare. Hitler, whose aversion for venereal diseases is well known, could certainly utilize the normal contraceptives he had been taught to use while in the army. Since his doctors are all dead and Morell never made a precise statement on the subject, other than he was perfectly normal and "average" sexually, it is difficult to come to any definite conclusion. But one woman who was in their intimate entourage told me that she was certain that Eva used little capsules or pills, which were not taken orally (German medical science was not that advanced), but were nonetheless practical and reliable. These pills were commonly distributed to the German women who were serving in the army in Paris, the *souris* or *"Blitzmädel."* General Schmundt apparently demanded a certain quantity from army headquarters and had them sent to Berchtesgaden. Hitler himself gave public proof that he knew of the existence of such a method, since during a conversation at chief headquarters in Russia, he discussed the possibility of distributing the little magic capsules to the populations of the East in order to control their excessively high birth rate.

The mature Eva Braun of the war years, now unchallenged mistress of Berchtesgaden, was far removed from the chubby little girl fresh from boarding school who did not dare lift her nose from her plate of sausages. Favorite or mistress, she had acquired her own stature, she had become a personality surpassing all the other women of the Obersalzberg in charm, elegance, and self-assurance. She had grown more beautiful with time, the long waits and fears, the continual struggle against intrigues had veiled her gaze with a certain melancholy and made her look a little like one of the Florentine ladies painted by Leonardo da Vinci. She posed in the nude for one of sculptor Arno Brecker's most striking statues.

Traudl Junge, who first met her in 1943, recalls, "She was not a model from the pages of a fashion magazine and still less the personification of Nazi womanhood exalted in the Nuremberg parades. Her elegance was not a reflection of opulence but rather of good taste and discretion. She tinted her naturally fair hair to make it more golden, and she made herself up heavily, especially in our eyes, for we didn't even use lipstick then—it was considered unwomanly, un-Germanic. Her makeup was cleverly applied, though, and heightened her beauty. She moved gracefully—what a contrast to the other ladies of the hierarchy, who were elephantine in their gait! She must have had stacks of dresses and shoes; I never saw her wear the same outfit twice."

Her hobby was in fact collecting shoes, of which she bought great stocks in Italy. When she had worn them once, she would distribute them with royal liberality to her mother, her sisters, and her friends. To her great vexation, Hitler was always ridiculing the high Italian heels that were in fashion during the war. "One of these days," he would say, "Ciano will turn up here wearing heels like that." Eva also had a fantastic collection of gloves.

Her favorite perfume was Worth's *Air Bleu*. She shaved her superfluous hair, which was not customary among the German women of that time. She was extremely clean and took two baths a day. She preferred silk petticoats and matching silk brassieres and panties, if possible with a flower pattern. She hated wool or cotton underwear, which was quite common in those days. She never wore corsets, but suspender belts of silk, which Hitler's aides procured in large quantities from Paris. (Nylon lingerie was unobtainable at the time and therefore Eva never possessed any, despite the assertion of one overimaginative American historian.) She hated lace and preferred light, transparent underwear. Her nightgowns were on the short side and always of Italian silk.

Eva was very fond of jewelry, with the exception of pearls. She often wore a black dress whose extreme simplicity was offset by accessories such as a diamond bracelet or necklace. She always wore earrings, but her ears were not pierced.

The following is a partial reproduction of a list that she herself made toward the end of 1944:

Rings, one big and one small, bracelet of emeralds surrounded by diamonds, necklace and brooch, also of emeralds and diamonds, another brooch in the shape of a butterfly, emerald earrings, a marguerite-shaped brooch of diamonds and rubies, a solitaire diamond ring, a diamond brooch, a ring, a diamond watch, a brooch in the form of flowers, another diamond ring, jewelry of beryl, an emerald set consisting of a pin, a bracelet, a pendant, another ring and earrings, a gold bracelet set with sapphires and diamonds, a brooch and a necklace . . .

The list continues with about thirty more valuable pieces of jewelry, to which must be added a dozen or so fur coats, including one of sable and one of mink. It is a meager collection compared with the Marquise de Pompadour's jewel casket, but nonetheless impressive for a secretary who at the age of seventeen did not even have the means to buy herself a ticket for a dance. Officially Eva Braun was still a secretary, and in 1944 she resumed her activities with the photographer Hoffmann, having had herself drafted to work several hours a day in his office when she was in Munich. No doubt the job helped her to pass the time while Hitler was away at his military headquarters, but chiefly it afforded her exemption from the compulsory "civil mobilization" to which German women were subject. Hitler considered this measure very important and did not want to give the impression that he was prepared to allow exceptions. Hoffmann had to certify that the activities of the secretary Eva Braun at Berchtesgaden and in Munich were essential for the victorious continuation of the war.

Hitler insisted on this hypocritical preserving of administrative appearances. For instance, Eva had to refrain from using her car throughout the hostilities, and the visas and stamps on her passport prove that when she went to Italy, she had to obtain her currency through the normal channels. In a letter to her sister, Eva asks her to send some clothing coupons if she wants to receive a dress. This meticulousness, however, was in reality only a deceptive show.

"She had her hair done once a day," I was told by Milla Schellmoser, who was responsible for her waves, and whom I chanced to meet one day in the restaurant of the Turkenhof Inn near the Berghof. "She was often impatient and irritable. She was a perfectionist, but her tips seemed to me rather meager." Her personal hairdresser Bernhard states that he had to go to her apartment at the Berghof usually toward two o'clock in the afternoon, and that she never spoke of Hitler or of politics. Bernhard accompanied her to Berlin, where he stayed in the Reichskanzlei.

Milla Schellmoser later married Paul Roth, who was Hitler's barber. "He would summon me at midnight for a haircut, to which he attached the greatest importance. But normally he shaved himself," Roth attests.

Hitler's private habits were those of a modest bourgeois. He wore woolen underwear in winter, was constantly changing his shirt, dressed by himself, and took his bath alone. He had a horror of physical contact, like Porthos in *The Three Musketeers*. He would not even let himself be measured by his tailors, who had to cut his uniforms by guesswork. He slept in a nightshirt. Eva, despite her usual reserve about such topics, once confessed to a friend that she had tried in vain to convert him to pajamas. She related that the night of the invasion, June 5–6, 1944, he was awakened at the Obersalzberg while they were together. Hitler received the news jubilantly and full of zest, with the boast, "At last, we're going to meet our real enemies face to face." He got up and was about to rush to the drawing room to unroll his military maps, when Eva managed with difficulty to restrain him by pointing out to him that a white cotton nightshirt was not the fitting attire for the war lord of Europe.

With the passing of the years the mistress of Berchtesgaden had undergone a profound moral transformation. "I no longer recognized my sister," Ilse Braun affirms. This metamorphosis was according to Hitler's wishes. He had once said, "There is nothing finer than to mold a young girl's character. A woman of eighteen or twenty is as malleable as wax. It must be possible for a man to mark such a girl with his stamp. The woman welcomes this treatment."

So he had put his mark on her. "Eva had become arrogant, tyrannical, and lacking in tact toward her family. Living with the great of this earth makes one selfish, even cruel. She distributed her old dresses like a queen." These comments are taken from a private diary that Ilse Braun was keeping at the time. There is therefore nothing posthumous about them, and they were not forumlated for the sake of the cause.

In a letter to Ilse, who was always short of money, Eva promised to send her ten marks a month . . . ten marks! What generosity, what magnanimity! She claimed that she could not ask the Führer for anything for her family, that this "wasn't done." Perhaps in this way she wanted to repay the indifference and bad treatment she had received at home. One wonders whether the invitations to the Berghof, the distribution of dresses and shoes were not rather a satisfaction, a confirmation of her triumph, her own way of proving to her family that she and she alone of the three sisters had "made good."

Because Ilse was growing increasingly critical of Hitler's policies, Eva had forbidden her to broach such subjects at the Berghof and once had even declared: "If the Führer sends you to a concentration camp, I won't be the one to get you out."

The concentration camps were not a completely taboo topic at the Obersalzberg. Hoffmann had a whole repertoire of jokes about Dachau that greatly amused Hitler and Eva. Moreover, during the last years of the war, there were many Russian prisoners roaming in rags around the Obersalzberg. Gretl Braun revealed to me that after her marriage to an important SS officer, camp deportees came to work in her husband's house. When Eva's house in the Wasserburgerstrasse was slightly damaged during a raid on Munich in 1944, a slave worker from Dachau, who later told me of this episode, made some repairs there and claimed to have caught a glimpse of Eva Braun.

Once a conversation on the concentration camps and the treatment meted out to the Jews nearly took a dramatic turn. The following account of the incident was given by the valet Hans Junge, who married Hitler's private secretary Traudl Junge, née Humps, and after the wedding volunteered for service on the Russian front, where he was killed.

"Everybody sat down at table, with Henriette von Schirach next to Hitler. They were talking in low voices, but I was standing behind them and heard their conversation. 'My Führer,' Frau von Schirach was saying, 'I saw a convoy of deported Jews passing through the streets of Vienna. It was a heartrending sight, those poor creatures must be terribly maltreated. . . . Do you know about this, my Führer, and if so, why do you allow it?' " Hitler apparently did not reply, and after a long and heavy silence got up and left the table without a word to those present.

In her memoirs Henriette von Schirach, whose husband ruled Vienna, affirms that she was talking about Dutch Jews. The valet Junge may have made a mistake, but it is more likely that Frau von Schirach deliberately chose to make this geographical distortion. For logically the person responsible was her husband in his capacity as Governor and *Gauleiter* of Vienna—a capacity that Henriette allowed nobody to forget. (For example, she demanded that the curtain at the opera should not go up before she had taken her seat in the imperial box.) Her husband, then, should have been the first to prevent such crimes, of which he could not have been unaware. I for one still remember vividly my progress down the Mariahilferstrasse in Vienna, wearing a striped convict's outfit and handcuffs.

At all events the episode is authentic, and the Schirachs were practically expelled from Berchtesgaden. Eva Braun, however, who could not stand Henriette von Schirach (née Hoffmann), and who was glad to be rid of this one time, fleeing rival, gave a rather different reason for their banishment from the "court": "Schirach apparently wanted to go to America to visit his parents under the pretext of a peace mission. The Führer interpreted this request as a desire to make off and abandon him. And he was furious. He took advantage of the good days and now that things are stormy, he wants to desert. . . ."

Occasionally the table talk was slightly more amusing. "Sit up straight," Eva would reproach Hitler, "you're stooping like an old man. . . ."

"I've got some heavy keys in my pocket," Hitler defended himself, "and then don't forget that I'm lugging a whole sackful of worries about with me. . . ."

Then he added, "Like this we're better matched, Tschapperl. You put on high heels to make yourself taller, while I stoop to make myself smaller, and so we go well together."

"I'm not small," Eva exclaimed indignantly, "I'm one meter sixty-three, like Napoleon."

"Why Napoleon? You know how tall he was?" marveled Hitler, who was evidently ignorant of this detail. "How do you know?"

"But every educated person knows that," Eva replied. "I learned it in the convent." Whereupon Hitler went to fetch an encyclopedia from the library and immersed himself in the biography of Napoleon.

Eva, who once had taken no interest in politics, had now become a fierce partisan of Nazi domination. For her, the winning of the war was a foregone conclusion, and she did not brook the slightest criticism of the Führer in her presence. She shut her eyes to reality. When she was traveling by train toward the end of the war, she would ask for the curtains to be drawn, for she did not want to see the destruction in the towns and villages. She got up and left the room if a combatant—he could even be a childhood friend—who had returned from Russia started to describe the gruesome desolation of the front.

Yet she was prepared to argue with Hitler when specifically feminine questions were involved. For instance, she protested for a long time against the interdiction on dancing, which she claimed undermined the people's morale. Once when Himmler had ordered the closing of ladies' hairdressers, Eva persuaded Hitler to reopen them: German women had to have the possibility of making themselves beautiful to welcome their husbands or lovers when they came home on leave. She also obtained the repeal of a regulation forbidding housewives to buy food on the black market, "For when it's to feed their combatant husbands and their children, they are only doing their duty." Again, in Berlin, she had had to take the subway and noticed that officers in uniform kept their seats while she was standing. She complained of this to Hitler, who ordered that army officers should always show themselves gallant when using the public transport services.

Eva was gradually emerging from her obscurity. She attended Hitler's birthday celebrations on April 2, she was invited to the receptions given in Mussolini's honor at Berchtesgaden, she dined with generals. She queened it during Hitler's absences; she organized small parties and excursions, invited old friends, for example Beppo, Georg, his sister Kate, Mitzi, and of course traveled. She went regularly every year to spend a month at Portofino; her passport proves that her last trip there was in July, 1942. She refrained from visiting occupied territory except once, when she stayed briefly in Bratislava, the capital of what was then Slovakia. She never visited Paris. Hitler had invited her and had told her on the telephone, "You simply must come to the opera here, it's wonderful, and then we'll have a triumphal parade," but later he had changed his mind. The dangers of an assassination attempt even during an incognito stay in the French capital seemed to him considerable.

Hitler was always extremely anxious about Eva's safety. He would not allow her to ski for fear she might break a leg; she could not sunbathe too much because of the risk of cancer; she could never go out alone except under the surveillance of a criminal police official in civilian clothes; she always had to travel in the company of a relative or a friend; and later he begged her not to stay in a town where there was any likelihood of enemy bombing.* He insisted that Dr. Morell examine her lungs frequently, for he was afraid she might contract pneumonia because she was so thin.

Eva Braun, confident now of having achieved both the moral and physical conquest of Hitler, was no less solicitous about her lover's security. When Hitler was absent, she lived in dread of receiving news of his death on the front.

"Eva and I had gone swimming in the Königsee, near Berchtesgaden," Herta relates. "Suddenly the chauffeur appeared in a private car. Eva was immediately seized by a premonition, for we had to avoid using the car in wartime and traveled instead by the mail bus. The chauffeur announced the news of an assassination attempt but hastened to add that Hitler was only slightly injured. It was the afternoon of July 20, 1944. Eva, panic-stricken, rushed back to the Berghof and tried to telephone to headquarters at Rastenburg in East Prussia. It took a long time to get through. Eva was in a state of hysterics. At last, Hitler answered with the assurance that he was safe and sound and Eva said to him, 'I love you, may God protect you.' Eva

---

* But she owned a boat, which she kept on the Königsee, and often took some of the Bormann children out with her. Yet according to the children, despite their father's instructions, they refused to call her Eva or sister and insisted on Fräulein Braun.

was dancing for joy, leaping about, crying. Then we thought of General Schmundt's death. How should we break the news to his wife? Eva took refuge in her room.

"A few days later, Hitler sent her the uniform he had been wearing at the time of the attempted assassination. At the sight of the torn, bloodstained cloth, Eva nearly fainted. But she recovered herself, for she did not wish to lose face in front of the others, and went to hide in her room again, taking the tattered uniform with her."

There existed a collection of letters from Hitler to Eva Braun, many of them enlivened with drawings, and a little blue book into which Eva, always provident and orderly, copied the missives that she sent to her lover. The fate of these documents is wrapped in mystery. The family claims that they were destroyed at Berchtesgaden by an emissary sent by Hitler or by the housekeeper Margaret Mittelstrasse, but my inquiries have only elicited evasive answers.

They may have been seized by the American army intelligence services, along with the photograph albums and the private diary, or else destroyed by some impatient soldier looking for souvenirs who had no use for meaningless papers written in German. It is also possible that these documents are being hoarded by people who hope one day to turn them to good account.

By pledging to preserve the anonymity of the possessor, I have been able to study two of the letters written on the occasion of the July 20 attempt. I did not have the possibility of photographing them, but only of making notes while examining them. Hitler's letter, which was typewritten, but not by a secretary, for it contains typing errors, ran roughly as follows:

My dear Tschapperl,

I'm fine, don't worry, just a trifle tired perhaps. I hope to come back soon and so be able to rest, putting myself in your hands. I greatly need tranquillity, but my duty to the German people comes before all else. Don't forget that the dangers I run are nothing compared to those of our soldiers at the front. Thank you for your proofs of affection and please thank your very honored father and your gracious mother for their good wishes. I am exceedingly proud, I beg you to assure them, of the honor of enjoying the devotion of a daughter who belongs to such a distinguished family. I've sent you the uniform I was wearing that ill-fated day. It is a proof that Providence protects me and that we need no longer fear our enemies.

With wholehearted affection

The letter is signed with the initials A. H., which were undeniably in Hitler's hand, and there is a large drawing, in which Hitler's draftsmanship is again unquestionable, showing the ruined building after the explosion of the bomb.

Eva's letter, on blue paper with the monogram EB in a four-leaved clover in one corner, but without an address, reads:

My love,

I am beside myself. Desperate, miserable, unhappy. I am half dead now that I know that you are in danger. Come back as soon as possible, I feel slightly crazy. Here the weather is fine and everything seems so calm that I feel ashamed. What a tragedy about Schmundt, I don't dare talk to his widow. You know, I've always said so, that I shan't go on living if anything happens to you. From the time of our first meetings, I promised myself to follow you everywhere, even in death. You know that my whole life is loving you.

Your Eva

Eva Braun was never aware that *"Operation Walküre"* included an attempt on her own life.

The first try by von Stauffenberg dates from July 11, 1944. The colonel flew to Berchtesgaden carrying a briefcase with military documents but also a time bomb made in England. He planned to kill Hitler, Göring, Himmler, Eva Braun, and everybody else there. But Himmler did not appear for the meeting, and the conspirators decided to postpone the attack.

The next "H" Day was planned for July 15. Stauffenberg and a fellow conspirator, General Fromm, were ordered to Berchtesgaden. But Hitler changed his mind and flew unexpectedly to his headquarters in Rastenburg. If he had stayed at the Obersalzberg, Stauffenberg planned to place the bomb under the dining table between Hitler and Eva Braun.

CHAPTER SIXTEEN

"Smoke gets in your eyes . . ."

Hitler had a very low opinion of Americans, based largely on his favorite Hollywood gangster movies. Although he read voraciously, he had neglected works on America, a country that he judged inconsistent, and he was convinced that American soldiers were incapable of holding a gun properly. Even after the invasion, he explained his reverses by the fact that the commanders of the United States military forces were all more or less of Prussian origin—Eisenhower, Spaatz, Nimitz, and, by adoption, Patton. When he first heard about the WACs, he rubbed his hands and announced, "I'm going to send them our most seductive SS; then we'll have fine children after the battle." He nonetheless sympathized when he heard the inaccurate rumor of the closing down of the Metropolitan Opera in 1942: "It's deplorable, a cultural debacle." He despised Roosevelt, whom he considered a puppet whose strings were pulled by sinister interests. Stalin, on the other hand, was in his eyes a genius, even though a terrible one. He showed himself indulgent toward Churchill. He once assured Eva Braun that at the end of the war he would not have him executed but would allow him to live under surveillance in a place where he could daub canvases to his heart's content. Hitler spoke of his own retirement, which he had resolved to spend painting and writing a book of memoirs. "Eva and I will be married and will live in a beautiful house in Linz, and I promise you, there won't be a single uniform there, nothing to remind one of the war." According to Eva's sister, they had even bought land near Linz and also in Munich for retirement homes.

There was, however, one period of American history that deserved his admiration: Prohibition. "Only a young nation could venture to take such a drastic but such a necessary step." Hitler was a militant teetotaler, although he did not forbid the members of his entourage, even Eva Braun, to drink strong liquor. He had many other aversions besides. He hated traveling by boat, for he was not a strong swimmer and suffered from seasickness; he refused to go horseback riding; he had sworn never to ski again; he was a strict vegetarian, as has already been mentioned; and he never listened to the radio. His greatest fixation, however, was about the mortal danger that resulted from smoking. "Before going into retirement," he informed Eva's sister, "I shall order that all the cigarette packets on sale in my Europe should have on the label, in letters of fire, the slogan: 'Danger, tobacco smoke kills; danger: Cancer' " (In this matter he was far ahead of his time.)

He often told how he had given up this vice himself as a young man in Linz, when he realized that the money he spent on cigarettes deprived him of many evenings at the theater. "I was on the bridge that crosses the Danube and I said to myself, 'Enough of this,' and I threw my cigarette into the yellow waters of the river. I've never smoked since."

He wanted to save others from smoking. The council meetings, the long conversations around the fire, the receptions where he was present were real torture sessions. Hitler had even ordered the removal of the ash trays from all the rooms of the Berghof, and one of the Braun sisters swears that he did not hesitate to inspect the ladies' room to make sure that nobody was smoking there in hiding. Eva promised to abstain and gargled all the time in order not to betray the fact that she nonetheless practiced this vice secretly. One evening, according to Ilse, when Hitler had gone up to his room, Eva lit a cigarette in the company of her sister, Goebbels, and Dietrich. But Hitler made a sudden reappearance. In her panic, Eva, who was standing at the bottom of the stairs, hid her cigarette by sitting on it. Hitler gave no sign of having noticed anything and went off again after five minutes. But the cigarette had gone on burning; it had made a hole in her woolen skirt, burned through the petticoat, the underthings, and had begun to attack Eva's tenderest parts. She did not flinch, but for several days afterward Eva chose to stand up most of the time despite Hitler's solicitous efforts to make her sit down.

Hitler's hatred of tobacco was so strong that he had even destroyed a photograph of his enemy Stalin because it showed him smoking.

Once he had proposed a strange bargain to Eva's sister Gretl, whom he called "Colibri" because she was the youngest: "Give up cigarettes, and I'll offer you a villa."

"My Führer," Gretl candidly argued, "a villa would be a great joy to me, but only one, whereas smoking gives me twenty little satisfactions every day, satisfactions that last and multiply."

He had also promised the ladies who went for a month without smoking a gift of a Swiss gold watch and some jewelry. Eva obtained her reward and so did about twenty other women, but Eva's sisters Ilse and Gretl and her intimate friend Herta forfeited theirs. "This was because the others cheated," Herta reveals, "whereas we confessed to our weakness."

Whenever Hitler thundered against tobacco, Eva Braun's habitual protest was to hum nonstop one of her favorite American songs, sometimes in English and sometimes in her own German adaptation. The song was "Smoke Gets in Your Eyes . . ."

Some people consider an aversion for alcohol, meat, tobacco, and hunting as proofs of human virtue. But how should Hitler's excessive affection for his dogs be interpreted? He once invited to the Berghof the surgeon Sauerbruch, who was deservedly considered the best in Europe. Hitler's motive was to have his dog Bella operated on.

His tastes in animals were highly inconsistent, however. He found horses stupid, disliked boxer dogs, kept away from deer, tortoises, and chicks, whose smallness did not conform to his ideas of grandeur, and was allergic to cats. He had a passion for Alsatians, dating from 1921, when he had been given one. Since at the time he had no room to keep the dog, he had been obliged to house it elsewhere, but it ran away and came back to him, and forever after he was devoted to the breed.

Hitler had two favorite topics on which he would discourse before his audience at the Berghof. The first concerned his sweeping projects for the reorganization of the conquered territories, "for great men do not exploit the world, they form it." For example, he predicted that after the war he would settle Germans in princely style in the towns of the East and force such native inhabitants as he had not massacred to struggle for an existence in the fields. His other topic was the incredible intelligence of his dogs, Bella the magnificent, Muck, another outstanding specimen whose only fault was an excessive liking for bitches, and above all Blondie. "She learns everything, follows me like a shadow, is courageous, faithful, and attentive. Do you know that Bella eats grass—I must have a supply brought in when I'm in the bunker. And although it's always dark in the bunker, Bella knows exactly what time it is."

Eva Braun, not to be outdone by her lover, was constantly singing the praises of her dogs and organized demonstrations to show how well trained they were.

For whole evenings, the only subject of conversation at the Berghof was the mating of Blondie. Hitler, as has been seen, tried to marry off everybody, including his dogs. To this end he invited Gerdi Troost, Professor Troost's widow, to come for the weekend with her male Alsatian. Blondie unfortunately gave him a hostile reception. She seemed to share the distrust felt by Eva Braun, who was not overjoyed at Frau Troost's visit, for she had been told that this lady once used to flirt with Hitler. Blondie preferred the courtship of a fox whom she had met in the fields. Frau Troost departed with her Alsatian, leaving Hitler very crestfallen at the fiasco. His hopes revived a little at the report that Blondie was associating with a stray German shepherd. She grew fatter, but in the end Tornow, who was in charge of the kennels, had to admit that appearances were deceptive. "Perhaps that dog was underfed . . . oh, this war . . ." Hitler lamented. Or perhaps Blondie had a premonition of what would happen to her puppies.

Eva adored children, but did Hitler like them as much as his dogs? "Certainly," Paula Hitler assured me. "My brother always sought the company of youngsters. He couldn't resist their imploring little hands." One of the secretaries who worked for him for a long time told me that he even wished to adopt Harald Quandt, Magda Goebbels' son by a first marriage. Traudl Junge gives a rather different picture. "I wouldn't be a good father," Hitler apparently confided to her. "I don't want to have children. The descendants of a genius are beset with enormous difficulties in life. They're expected to show the same abilities as their famous parents, and they very rarely succeed. Indeed, they are mostly cretins."

In Eva Braun's twenty-three albums, there are several hundred snapshots showing Hitler and Eva in affectionate attitudes with small boys and girls. Hoffmann often took pictures of Hitler with children because this was an infallible recipe for political publicity. Eva's photographs, however, which were not destined for diffusion, prove that they spent a good part of their time in the company of youngsters. This was understandable in the case of Eva, who, since she could not have children of her own, satisfied this maternal wish with those of other people.

Her friend Herta often wondered whether the real motive for her frequent invitations to the Berghof lay in Eva's desire to create for herself an illusion of motherhood through the company of Herta's two little daughters, Ursula and Gitta.

The almost constant presence of these children at the Berghof, a mass of widespread hypotheses, the paradox of Hitler, so intent on conquering the world, having his photograph taken all the time with these little girls, the striking resemblance of young Ursula, known as Uschi, to Hitler and Eva Braun, all this aroused my perplexity for many years.

When planning this book, I had considered devoting a whole chapter to this unknown daughter of Hitler, but the idea proved to be unfounded. For months on end I meticulously examined registry records, compared the dates of Hitler's stays at the Berghof and in Munich, consulted midwives, without being able to establish any filiation. I met Uschi, who today works for a tourist organization in Madrid. There is no longer any trace of a resemblance. The same is true of Gitta, who lives in Austria.

The photograph albums were not an amateur's hobby for Eva, but a part of her life. She was irrevocably condemned to be ignored by the world, to exist on the unknown side of the moon, and she found this exclusion from notoriety hard to bear. She therefore prepared for the future, for history, by collecting photo after photo, thus creating the irrefutable proof of her existence. At the time of her suicide and earlier, as she wrote her will, she gave precise instructions for the preserving of these albums. Moreover, she had also had copies of many of the photos made, which she distributed as birthday presents to her relatives and friends. After her death, the small number of personal photographs that were known to the general public—nearly all of them with erroneous identifications—came from these gift albums.

Eva's father and mother no longer mentioned the question of marriage, which had lost some of its importance in a country now in the full throes of war and destruction. Yet Eva still suffered, as Herta recalls, from the realization that her position was terribly ambiguous. Coming as she did from a narrow-minded bourgeois family, influenced as she still was by the principles inculcated in her at the convent, a faithful Catholic in spite of everything, she could never be completely happy outside the marriage state. Her renunciation was a sacrifice, a sacrifice that continued to weigh heavily upon her. A small incident related by Wiedemann reveals her pusillanimity in the domain of moral conventions. The aide had suggested that he should accompany her to a party given by Princess Stephanie of Hohenlohe at the castle of Leopoldskron near Salzburg, once Max Reinhardt's home. "But I can't accept, Captain," Eva Braun replied wistfully, "as you well know, I'm not a married woman. . . ." Fritz Wiedemann, a soldier of the old school, frankly admits that he would have refused to invite Eva Braun officially to his house in the presence of his wife.

Eva never spoke openly of marriage to Hitler. She was too shrewd to bore him with jeremiads. She merely turned his mind to the subject by singing pertinent tunes. Thus when she wasn't humming "Smoke Gets in Your Eyes," she invented variations on love and marriage, first in English and then in German, using her favorite melody, "Tea for Two."

Hitler listened to her complacently, indifferent to the innuendoes and disregarding the fact that the composers and librettists of these songs were hardly paladins of Nazi ideology.

CHAPTER SEVENTEEN

The Picture of Dorian Gray

The days followed each other in sad and monotonous succession at the Berghof in 1944. Hitler demanded unbroken tranquillity and even refused to attend the movie showings, which had to be held in the cellar. He denied Eva permission to organize a concert with Maurice Chevalier. The Berghof cooks produced deplorable menus, but between meals the guests could raid the kitchens for whatever they fancied. There were cigarettes, real coffee, and cognac to be had there, a fact that amply justified the journey to Berchtesgaden.

April 20, Hitler's birthday, was also celebrated very quietly, with Eva, in a black dress, presenting Hitler with gifts laid out on a flower-decked table. Hers to the Führer was a black dressing gown with gray trimmings, as well as permission for the dog Blondie to keep her master company for the whole day.

Not wishing to marry his favorite, and having had little success with his bitch Blondie, Hitler nonetheless wished to have a marriage in the family. By 1944 the signs of an Anglo-American invasion of the Continent were multiplying, and he suspected that soon there would be no further occasion for festivities at Berchtesgaden or elsewhere. He therefore arranged a brilliant match between Eva's sister Gretl and Fegelein, a general of the SS. This Fegelein was the liaison officer between Himmler and Hitler, which was already remarkable, and in addition he was a great friend of Martin Bormann (they got drunk together almost every night), which was extraordinary.

Gretl was dazzled, the family was delighted at the honor, for an SS general was an important personage, and Eva was touched by this proof of her lover's interest, the more so because the fact of being Fegelein's sister-in-law considerably strengthened her social position. She could now be presented everywhere, and go out and travel with her brother-in-law. Moreover, being very resourceful and unscrupulous, Fegelein managed to procure her dresses, perfumes, and furs even in the most impossible circumstances.

This marriage had not been easy to arrange. Fegelein was a magnificent specimen of a male who had all the females of Berchtesgaden at his feet and who considered any woman who refused to sleep with him a mortal enemy. At the same time he was extremely ambitious and the prospect of being the Führer's brother-in-law, even morganatically, was highly attractive to him. From the moment of his marriage, he flaunted this new position with such arrogance that even his friend Bormann, who had placed him in Hitler's entourage, became worried.

Gretl, with her giddy temperament, was not overparticular in the matter of men. The photographs in her sister's albums show her with a hundred different boys, and it seems that she rarely refused a flirtation. She even fell in love with an American diplomat. Hitler had originally wanted to marry her to Heinz Hoffmann, the photographer's son, but had not succeeded. Hoffmann himself, because of his increasing drunkenness, had been banished from the "court." Then Hitler's choice fell on another SS of his entourage, Fritz Darges, but he showed himself recalcitrant. Hitler, furious, packed him off to the Russian front. The next candidate was Walter von Hewel. He was a remarkable man who long enjoyed Hitler's confidence and who seems to have been perhaps the only disinterested and loyal member of his entourage. He had fought at his side in the Munich putsch and shared his captivity in Landsberg prison. He was an excellent diplomat ("One has to be," he used to say, "to become an intermediary between Hitler and Ribbentrop") and kept Hitler informed about foreign politics. His diplomatic instincts, however, seem to have warned him against a union with Gretl. He married somebody else and committed the unpardonable sin of not inviting Eva Braun to the wedding. This blunder and other intrigues incurred the wrath of Hitler, who banished him for a long time from his presence. But the faithful Hewel came back to join him at the end in Berlin, where he met his death.

As for Eva's other sister, Ilse, she was married in 1942 all alone in Breslau, with none of her family present, after giving up her dream of conquering Bruno Mussolini, whom she idolized. Her husband was a Dr. Fucke-Michaels.

Hans Georg Otto Hermann Fegelein, who was thirty-seven at the time of his marriage to Margareta Franziska Bertha Braun, was the son of the proprietor of a riding school in Munich, which still exists. At the Berghof those who dared to mock him said that he had started life as a stable boy and that his marriage bed should be straw litter. He was an accomplished horseman, and had taken part in numerous equestrian competitions, where he had carried the German colors to victory by winning several cups. The SS organization had absorbed this handsome young man, who was still more irresistible in flashy uniforms that, although hardly in accordance with military tradition, dazzled the common people by their extravagance. He had been decorated with the Knight's Cross with Oak Leaves, a high distinction. Fegelein, however, had obtained it for having mercilessly pursued the partisans in Slovakia, against whom he had organized fierce repressions, and for having accomplished a mission in the concentration camp of Theresienstadt. Indeed when drunk he admitted with admirable candor that he was a coward and had not the slightest desire to fight seriously.

With his brilliant dancing, his social gaiety, he had seduced Gretl. Before his marriage, however, he had declared all over the Berghof that she was a "stupid goose," and it seems strange that she should have remained unaware of this.

The civil wedding took place on the third of June, 1944, in the Salzburg town hall, with Bormann and Himmler as witnesses, but the reception was held at the Obersalzberg. Hitler invited the Braun and Fegelein families and fifty or so other people to lunch at the Berghof and even made a short speech over dessert. Then the whole party went up to the Kehlstein for a real celebration, the only one that ever took place in this mountain house that Hitler very rarely visited. He went there only twice during the war, and Gretl's wedding was the last occasion.

The Kehlstein, which today is called "The Eagle's Nest" or sometimes "Hitler's Teahouse"—another invention, for Hitler never went up there for tea—looks like a blockhouse and is situated a few yards from the summit of the Kehlstein peak, which is 6,017 feet high. All around is an Alpine paradise. Bormann had built it with party funds, at an estimated total cost of thirty million marks, and offered it to Hitler as a birthday present. The idea was that he should meet the kings, presidents, and dictators of his acquaintance there in complete tranquillity.

To put the building there at all involved an amazing feat of construction. It is reached from the Berghof by a fantastic tarred road which winds up around precipices for almost four miles and which cost two years of building efforts and the death of twenty-odd workmen. The road leads to the entry of a tunnel bored in the mountainside, nearly 13 feet high and 142 yards long, with walls covered with Italian tiles. Then comes an elevator, all gilded, with a ventilator and piped-in music, equipped with a red plush chair for the Führer placed in front of a mirror imported from Venice. But Hitler felt uneasy in this elevator; he was always afraid the cable would break or be cut. This mistrust explains his rare appearances at the Kehlstein. It was also said that he had difficulty breathing once he was up there because of the altitude.

The elevator deposits the passengers in a relatively small lounge, which leads to the dining room. The rooms are of fairly modest proportions with the exception of the tearoom, which is built of Carrara marble and has an enormous hearth in the center. Its Gothic windows look out over Bavaria, while from the room designed for Eva Braun, one can see Austria. The rest of the house comprises a studio, two rooms with bath, two kitchens, a room for the SS guards, and an enormous basement. A magnificent terrace allows one to bask in the sun and in winter can be transformed into a heated veranda. A generator taken from a U-boat provided electricity.

It was Eva who had insisted on elaborate marriage festivities. "I want this wedding to be very beautiful, as though it were mine," she had said. She had even hired a small amateur band composed of SS guards, who were a sorry sight in their creased uniforms and whose playing was even less inspiring than their appearance. This was the only time that Hitler allowed dancing in the house during the whole war. The wedding photographs, which show Eva dancing and singing, and which were sold by Hoffmann in every part of the world after the catastrophe, give the illusion that Eva Braun's life was one long party, which is far from the truth.

Hitler retired early, but for once Eva danced and enjoyed herself all night long. Bormann had downed so much schnapps that he had to be transported back to his chalet in a litter. The champagne, which needed no chilling, flowed freely. There was no talk of politics, although the Normandy invasion was due to take place in a matter of days, and everyone knew it. The guests had completely forgotten all their cares. Yet it was a Kafka-like celebration. The dancers, shut in a luxurious stone prison on a mountaintop, were nearly all condemned to death. The execution of their sentences would take place within the next twelve months. For a number of them, for example the actor Heini Handschuhmacher, it did not take that long. He met his death a few weeks later during an air raid on Munich.

The beautiful "Daran," the secretary who had married General Erhard Christian, remembers having said to Ilse Braun in the course of these wedding festivities, "Hitler is only a shadow of his former self."

Hitler had indeed aged greatly. His hair had turned gray ("My hair is white not because of my enemies but because of my generals," he had said), his hands trembled, and his eyesight was steadily dimming. Eva Braun was constantly having to bring him his steel-rimmed spectacles, for she alone knew how to present them to him in such a way that he could slip them on rapidly with his left hand. To enable him to conceal this weakness from those who came to see him, special typewriters with enormous letters had been constructed, ancestors of the TelePrompTer, which enabled him to read documents in public without glasses. He blinked in an unpleasant way, and his complexion was waxlike. His valets wherever he went brought along suitcases laden with Morell's medicines.

Whenever he was away, Eva was full of anxiety. "I got a shock when I saw the Führer again the other night. He's become an old man and he looks so grave. How is he?" she asked his secretaries on the telephone. "I can't ask Professor Morell; I distrust him, I hate him. The Führer must be very worried. He never talks to me about these things, but my instinct tells me that he must be suffering."

Bormann complained to his wife that Eva's telephone

calls and letters to Hitler depressed the Führer. "She sees everything in black and now argues with everyone."

From the time of Gretl's wedding at the Kehlstein, Hitler's physique deteriorated steadily. He refused to admit this fact, and the entourage, to flatter him, admired his vitality. Goebbels distributed thousands of propaganda photographs of a vigorous, athletic Hitler. But it was like the portrait of Dorian Gray, except that in this case it was not the picture but the man that was falling into decrepitude.

The assassination attempt of July 20 aggravated Hitler's state still further. His left hand was seized by a tremor ("It's lucky," he remarked to his secretaries, "that it's not my head that's started to tremble"), and he suffered from constant headaches. Then he grew hard of hearing. A specialist was summoned from Berlin, a Dr. Giesing, who discovered that both membranes of his ears were damaged. An operation was necessary and was successfully undertaken. After this, Hitler went through a long period of depression. He no longer took any interest in anything, not even in the military situation. He only emerged from his torpor to telephone to Eva. Half crazy with worry, she insisted that she should join him at the front, to look after him. But Hitler was adamant, for he did not wish the troops to reproach him for such a privilege—they who for years had been obligatorily separated from their families.

Later, he confessed to Traudl Junge: "I'm no longer afraid of death; it will be a deliverance for me. For since my youth, misery and anguish have been my constant companions."

It was Hermann Fegelein, the "left-handed brother-in-law," who, on his return from his honeymoon with Gretl in Austria in the castle that he had received as an appanage from Hitler, was put in charge of the investigation into the plot of July 20. He was choking with indignation and talked of having the whole general staff of the Wehrmacht shot. What incensed him was not so much the attempt on his "brother-in-law's" life as the realization that the conspirators might at the same time have sent that magnificent and unique individual, the Gruppenführer Hermann Fegelein, rocketing sky-high.

He had his own reasons for his strong attachment to life. His wife, already pregnant, had returned to Munich to keep her sister company, while he had a mistress at the Obersalzberg, a Berlin actress whose red hair inflamed men's hearts. She had had a child by him but did not even have the means to buy it clothes, for Fegelein did not provide for her in any way. Finally Bormann sent her packing.

Then one night at the Berghof a guard who was innocently going his rounds surprised Fegelein in bed with one of the chambermaids. The scandal was hard to hush up and Bormann had once more to use his influence in favor of his protégé. In order to conceal the incident from Gretl, he found a thousand pretexts for keeping her away from the Berghof.

With the enemy at the gates of the Reich, the atmosphere at Berchtesgaden was becoming nightmarish. Eva listened to the radio every evening solely to know whether the region was threatened by an air raid. Suitcases and bags were kept in readiness for a descent into the cellar in the event of a warning. The whole of Berchtesgaden was wrapped in an artificial smoke screen in order to mislead the enemy pilots and to foil parachute commandos, for Hitler believed that an attempt would be made to capture him, as he had had Mussolini abducted.

Trenches had been dug in the whole area and a vast bunker built under the Berghof. Access to it was by a staircase of sixty-five steps cut in the rock, which led down from the main drawing room. The bunker comprised a room with a bathroom for Eva, another for Hitler, various other rooms, a defense system with redoubts, shelters, cupolas, salients and ramps, a kennel for Blondie, and ramifications that led to an exit on the opposite slope and thus provided an escape route if the Berghof was surrounded.

Eva was always unwilling to take refuge in the bunker. Hitler would telephone from his headquarters on nights when there were air-raid warnings and insist that she should go down to the shelter. When she was at her house in Munich, he wrung his hands and paced about like a caged lion. "She's brave, my Eva, but rash. She'll be crushed under the debris in her little house. I beg her to go to my apartment, which is much more solid, but she's so obstinate. . . ."

It was her turn to worry when she was at the Berghof and Munich was being bombed. She immediately telephoned to all her friends to ask for news and wanted to go into town. Hitler would not allow her to do so. Once, however, when she was told of the death of people whom she knew, she absolutely insisted on being driven into Munich, which was ablaze. She returned to the Berghof disheveled and in tears and gave Hitler a pathetic account of the tribulations of the civilian population. Hitler listened with a somber, wrathful expression, and comforted her with talk of vengeance and retaliation, of a new bomb that was capable of annihilating whole cities in a few seconds.

This vision of a stricken Munich, which was to be subjected to further and much more violent bombing, or perhaps her lover's first allusion to that atom bomb which the scientists were busy perfecting, explains the drastic decision that Eva Braun made on October 24, 1944. She made a handwritten draft of her will. She was then only thirty-two years old. The document was written in her house in the Wasserburgerstrasse and she used her sister Gretl's writing paper. She crossed out this name and substituted Eva at the top of each sheet. The document was extremely simple: There is the word WILL, followed by the names of the beneficiaries and a meticulous list of the jewelry, dresses, documents, and other objects that she was bequeathing to them. The signature was simply Eva Braun.

A few days later, Eva went to Ruhpolding to see her parents. "I'm going to join my Führer," she told them, "for I want to be near him in the hour of danger. Perhaps we shall never see each other again."

"I've made my decision," she said to her sisters. "I know I shan't die in my bed."

Her sister Ilse noted in her diary that that Christmas night, 1944, she had a nightmare in which she saw her sister on a pyre, smiling, but surrounded by rats. Then a wall of flame hid her from sight. . . . She woke up with a start. Enemy planes were bombing the town.

CHAPTER EIGHTEEN

Into the inferno

The Führer's unique flag, with its flames and steel, its swastika lost in the middle of arabesques, which Hitler had designed himself in pale imitation of the English Royal Standard, was not flying on the new Chancellery of the Reich. Eva Braun started to tremble and apathetically ignored the gaping holes in the buildings and the barricades whose construction had been started not because of any belief in their future necessity (since Napoleon, no enemy had marched victoriously into the capital on the Spree) but out of bravado to prove that the intrepid inhabitants were prepared to come down into the streets. Eva was seized by a single apprehension: What if Hitler was no longer in Berlin but had left for one of his new headquarters, at Ziegenburg or Bad Nauheim?

She was soon reassured when she entered by the gateway of the old Zossen Palace, for the Wilhelmstrasse archway was impracticable because of a yawning crater in the roadway. The Führer was there, but the custom of flying the banner to show his presence in the seat of government had been abandoned. Was this to hoodwink enemy airmen who, knowing he was there, might attack Berlin even more violently, or because it was feared that the population of the city—the widows, the orphans, the crippled, homeless and starving—might come demanding relief? Or was it simply because Hitler was hiding in shame at having reduced this time-honored capital to such a massacre-ground?

Nothing could keep Eva at Berchtesgaden after she heard the news that Hitler had had to be operated on by Professor Eicken for a tumor in a vocal cord. He was unable to speak, and Eva, who could no longer hear him on the telephone, had been seized by panic at the thought that it might be cancer. Moreover, she wanted to be with him for Christmas, which was only a few weeks away. Hitler had come by train for the operation from his headquarters in the Taunus known as the *Adlerhorst*, or eagle's nest. He had kept the carriage blinds lowered during the journey in order not to see the destruction along the way.

He was in conference, and Eva went up to her apartment, where she immediately rang up to order a new dress for Christmas from her dressmaker, Fräulein Heise, whose workrooms had been destroyed in the bombing but who had found temporary accommodations elsewhere. Eva was not unaware of the military situation or indifferent to the country's misfortunes. She had seen, along the Wilhelmstrasse, the blasted facade of Dr. Goebbels' Propaganda Ministry, the ravages at the Ministry of Foreign Affairs, the destruction of the Radziwill Palace, once the seat of Hindenburg's chancellery, and she had been told that the fabled Kaiserhof Hotel was about to collapse any moment like a card house.

"But did the women of Coventry give way to despair?" she asked. What if a great deal of territory had been lost? It was territory that the Germans had conquered once and could conquer again. So the German cities were threatened? But what reason was there to believe that their inhabitants would be less capable of resistance than those of Stalingrad? Eva, it is true, was beginning to feel fear gripping her, but how could she admit it when a man like Field Marshal Keitel promised a grandiose victory for Christmas ("We'll be at Antwerp, and the American army will be wiped out"), and when the man who in her eyes was the greatest military expert of all time was always saying to her, "Evi, Evi, I've never been so certain of victory as now." Her credulity and her optimism, her naïveté and her fanaticism were in no way exceptional. Millions and millions of Germans thought and acted just like her, like Eva Braun, the very prototype of the young German woman. Had she behaved otherwise, Hitler would have banished her from his presence long before.

She therefore continued to live peacefully in her apartment according to the established routine: summoning the hairdresser, walking with her dogs in the Tiergarten, dining in private with Hitler. Christmas came and went. Hitler clinked glasses with her on New Year's Day and wet his lips in poor champagne. The paladins of the Third Reich who had ignored her so superciliously now courted her as a queen.

But the German forces did not reach Antwerp for Christmas; instead the Russians invaded Silesia. Eva only realized this when she received a telegram from her sister Ilse. FORCED TO FLEE FROM BRESLAU . . . An official car went to fetch Ilse from the Schlesien Bahnhof on the morning of January 21, 1945. The young woman was haggard after three sleepless nights. She was carrying nothing but a small cloth suitcase, having abandoned and probably lost all her possessions. The train was packed, and the faces of all the passengers were marked by fear and exhaustion. The chauffeur took Ilse to the Hotel Adlon, then the most luxurious in Berlin, where Eva had lived before moving into the Chancellery. Ilse found it hard to adapt herself to such grandeur. How could one still accept living in material abundance? Eva rang her up and, as though she were greeting a society friend who had come casually to spend the weekend in the capital, she apologized for not having met her at the station. "I'm so sorry not to be able to put you up at the Chancellery, but it's full of soldiers and we're rather short of space, but naturally you're dining with us this evening. . . ."

Eva was extremely well dressed, with her hair freshly set. Supper was served in the library by white-gloved valets, off silver dishes. Hitler excused himself at the last moment: He had to attend a staff conference. The two sisters took advantage of his absence to smoke, but Eva, as a precaution, sprayed the room with a French perfume that irritated her sister. Ilse began to moan about the war, the Bolshevik invasion, her separation from her husband.

"By the way," Eva interrupted her, "why isn't your husband in the army? You know, everybody must contribute to the common effort. . . ."

Ilse, distressed and tearful, lamented: "I've nothing left to put on, and my beautiful furniture, my books . . ." But Eva assured her nonchalantly: "Don't worry, 'Olsche,' in a fortnight's time you'll be back home in Breslau, I have this from reliable sources. Did you lock up your house well? Then you've nothing to fear. . . ."

Ilse, unable to contain herself any longer, burst out: "You wretched creature, wake up, open your eyes to reality. Breslau is lost, Silesia is lost, Germany is lost. Do you realize that hundreds of thousands of people are choking the snowy roads, fleeing from the enemy, who is ravaging and carrying off everything? Your Führer is a fiend, he's dragging you into the abyss with him, and all of us along with you."

It was Eva's turn to rage: "You're mad, crazy! How can you say such things about the Führer, who's so generous and who told me to invite you to stay at his house at the Obersalzberg until you return to Breslau. You deserve to be lined up against the wall and shot."

Suddenly Eva flung open the window as though she needed air. She put her hand on her heart and sank into a chair, fainting. For some months she had been complaining of heart palpitations, real or imagined. This attack was the long-term aftereffect of the suicide attempt of May, 1935, when she had swallowed twenty sleeping pills. It may also have been brought on by her use of numerous tranquilizers which Dr. Morell prescribed for her and which she took constantly. Soon Eva regained consciousness and Ilse kissed her good-bye. She was never to see her sister again.

Later Ilse went all the same to the Obersalzberg on an armored train of the Wehrmacht, ensconced in the mail van. Eva regained her health and celebrated her birthday on February 6 with her sister Gretl, brother-in-law Hermann, Martin Bormann, and the Morells. "Hitler was there the whole evening," writes Bormann to his wife, "in a radiant mood—Eva looking all the time for dancing partners."

Yet she had to leave Berlin on the ninth of February, for the Führer had told her that she must take charge of things at Berchtesgaden. "I shall be leaving for the front any moment," he said, "and here you're in everybody's way. We have grave decisions to make. . . ." He softened and added coaxingly, "Tschapperl, I worry about you so much with these air raids. Don't you think I have enough troubles as it is? Go to the Berghof, at least I'll be easy in my mind then—and my dear, I absolutely forbid you to come back to Berlin. I promise you that at Easter we'll be together again. . . ."

And the ever-present Bormann, by order of Hitler, had to go and make sure Eva and her sister were on the so-called vegetable train that left Berlin after midnight.

Eva let herself be convinced, because she wanted to

take her two dogs back to Munich, put certain possessions in safekeeping, see her family and friends, and above all celebrate her birthday a second time at home. She had no desire to be deprived of this satisfaction, for after all, a celebration was a celebration. Unfortunately Munich was bombed that night, and the festivities had to be postponed until two days later. The company again included Gretl, visibly pregnant, Herta, some aunts, a number of friends, even some colleagues from Hoffmann's, Anny Brandt. It was gay, it was warm, it was touching; the little villa in the Wasserburgerstrasse had become an oasis in the storm. Eva was proud of the Führer's gift, which he had given to the chauffeur of the car to present during the party, thus creating a small surprise. It was a pendant of topaz, surrounded by diamonds.

The merrymaking continued until the early hours. It was then that Eva announced her decision not to take refuge at the Obersalzberg. No, she was going to return to Berlin, she wanted to be at Hitler's side, whatever happened. . . .

"That's jumping into the lion's mouth; it's crazy," her friends protested, and for hours they tried to dissuade her. But Eva was stubborn by nature and did not abandon a decision once she had arrived at it. "Death matters little to me—I know the end that's in store for me, I've known it for the past year. Hitler has forbidden me to return, I shouldn't. But nothing can stop me," she said.

Herta, her good friend, then proposed to share her fate and leave Munich with her. "No, Herta," Eva decreed, "your place is with your husband, who will come back one of these days, with your children, just as my place is with HIM."

Gretl also offered to accompany her. "You've got to give birth to a child, and mind it's a boy, for the Braun girls are born unlucky. . . ."

It was not so easy, however, to move about in February, 1944. The roads were congested, the trains were running hopelessly late, confusion reigned. Eva telephoned to Bormann, who refused to help her. The Führer had given strict instructions that she must go up to the mountains. Bormann spoke gravely, but probably he was delighted to be rid of Eva for good in this way. He was reckoning without the Braun spirit of initiative, however. Eva went to Daimler-Benz, where the cabriolet reserved for her per-

sonal use had been garaged since the beginning of hostilities. "The Führer has summoned me urgently to Berlin; I
need the car." The staff could only acquiesce and even detailed Eva's former chauffeur Jung to drive her. He was
free at that moment and naturally preferred piloting Eva
to the risk of being thrown into battle at any minute. The
car had to be painted dark gray in order to camouflage it
better and make it look like a Wehrmacht vehicle. Thus
the journey was accomplished on February 23 despite
great difficulties and a dive-bombing attack by a British
plane.

When Hitler saw her, he tried to scold her, but his joy
was apparent to those present. The whole evening, he repeated to his assistants, "I'm so proud of Fräulein Braun.
What devotion! I've known her for a very long time, but
do you know that it was years before she allowed me to
pay for so much as a taxi fare. She had no telephone at
home, and she used to wait late into the night, asleep on a
bench in her office at Hoffmann's, in order to be sure that
I could get in touch with her. . . ."

Eva rarely went down into the bunker that month of
March, and Hitler merely held his military confabulations
there to avoid being disturbed by the air-raid warnings. He
had decided to defend his capital on three fronts. Others,
it is true, took a different view of his position. "One can
go from one front to the other by subway," they quipped,
"our communication problem is solved." Eva herself joked
with the secretaries on the subject: "One can follow the
battles on the subway plan map. . . ."

The grandiose Reichskanzlei building was relatively un-
damaged except for a few cracks in the facade and some
blocked passages. I should like here to give a brief sketch
of the setting of the final scenes of this drama, as it remained fixed in my memory when, in my capacity as a
foreign journalist, I was admitted into Hitler's study a few
weeks before the attack against the Russians in 1941.

One must imagine a huge trapezoid bounded on the left
by the Hermann-Göring-Strasse, a street which stretches to
the Brandenburger Tor and which today, under a vague
name, roughly constitutes the frontier between the two
Berlins. The base of the trapezoid was the Voss-Strasse
and its right side the Wilhelmstrasse. The main entrance,
which consisted of a vast courtyard with pseudo-Ionic col-
umns, was in the center of the building not far from the

famous balcony. There were several other gateways, one of them reserved for the military and another for the party. I went in by the Voss-Strasse gate and was immediately confronted by an immense gallery, said to be modeled after the one at Versailles, which had Gobelin tapestries hanging on the walls, Persian carpets on the marble flagstones, and genuine Italian Renaissance furniture. A lobby led to the main drawing room, with a ladies' sitting room on the right and the movie theater and concert hall on the left. Three enormous glass doors opened onto the garden, which had a pond, floodlit at night, and a huge greenhouse on the other side. Opposite the pond was the winter garden, which was Eva's favorite haunt. One could have breakfast there in the morning or receive visitors. Hitler's private quarters were on the second floor, as were those of Morell, Bormann, Colonel von Below, and General Burgdorf, while other officials had accommodations on the first floor. The minor personnel lodged in premises on the Hermann-Göring-Strasse side, where there were also the garages, the quarters of the chauffeur Kempka, and the washrooms of the SS guards.

Hitler's study was not far from the winter garden. An eagle perched on a swastika, with the initials A. H., all in concrete, surmounted the door, which was framed by two other beasts of prey, living in this case—SS on guard duty. There was another stone eagle inside, and the vast room was decorated with swastika reliefs on the walls. This study was an imitation of that of Mussolini at Palazzo Venezia, with the difference that when one went into Mussolini's study, one had the impression of being in a cathedral. The frescoes on the walls, the beauty of the marble, the chiaroscuro effects of the light filtering through the great curtains of the balcony window, the disorder on the table where papers were piled around a lamp—all this dated from another century. In Hitler's study, on the other hand, despite the Gobelins, the valuable paintings, such as the famous portrait of Frederick the Great, and the carpets, one always felt one was in barracks, in the general's office maybe, but nonetheless in barracks. The curtains of the windows overlooking the garden were gray and were embroidered with the initials "A. H."

Mussolini customarily sat facing the entrance but never gave any sign of having noticed the arrival of a visitor, who waited, ill at ease, at the far end of the immense room. Hitler, however, sat in a black chair facing the windows and with his back to the door. There was not a single paper on his heavily carved desk of solid oak. There was a pen-and-ink stand, a blotter, a telephone, a bell, and two heavy paperweights—nothing else. As soon as a visitor came in, Hitler got up and went to welcome him, immediately availing himself of that hypnotic charm which seemed to paralyze the reasoning powers of his generals and ministers.

The bombing and then the shelling by the Red army soon destroyed a good part of the Chancellery, and the pictures, tapestries, and furniture were taken down to the shelters or stowed away safely elsewhere. Hitler's study remained intact, however. When I saw it on my return to Berlin, a few weeks after the city's capture by the Russians, I noticed that only the stone eagles had been demolished. Of course the soldiery had broken up all the fittings, staved in the chair, shattered the table, lacerated the curtains, scrawled names and obscene signs everywhere. Hundreds of documents, which today would rejoice the hearts of archivists, were strewn all over the floor, torn and rendered illegible by muddy boots.

The main bunker was situated in the center of the Voss-Strasse. It had sixty rooms and six exits, of which three opened onto the street. Because its concrete vault was only ten feet thick, Hitler did not feel safe there, the more so as it had been built in haste and water had seeped through to a depth of several inches in some of the passages. He had invited the "mothers and children of Berlin" to take refuge there. Later, it was transformed into a hospital. A section was reserved for government personnel, for until the end there were more than six hundred people employed in the Chancellery compound. There were also a number of padlocked storerooms that contained quantities of the good things of this world—tobacco, canned foods, chocolate, liquor, bacon, as well as medical supplies. There was enough to withstand a year's siege.

Hitler had had a personal bunker built for himself that lay to the right of the trapezoid, under the site of Hindenburg's old chancellery. There was access to it through the right wing as well as through a gallery that opened onto the garden. A concrete pillbox protected this entrance and the ventilation system. The reinforced concrete ceiling was approximately twenty-six feet thick and even reached thirty-three feet in places. There were thirty-seven steps leading down to the Führer's Bunker, as it was called, and the construction was on two levels, the lower reserved for Hitler and the upper one assigned to his immediate suite. The bunker had only been finished at the end of January, and its concrete was still damp and its atmosphere foul. It communicated with the main Voss-Strasse shelter through a labyrinth of passages.

At first Eva went down to the bunker only when there were air-raid warnings, but then she gradually started to transport some furniture and personal effects to these lower regions, and at the end of March, she installed herself there permanently.

It is not proposed to give here an exhaustive description of the last two weeks of Hitler's life. Hundreds of books have already been written on this subject. My aim here is merely to relate the salient episodes of these days of agony as Eva Braun lived through them. They were described to me by three women who escaped alive from the bunker: Traudl Junge and Gerda Christian, the secretaries, and Liesl Ostertag, the faithful servant.

Eva followed Hitler about like a shadow. She was worried because he seemed to have become a living specter. "Morell is poisoning you; don't take any more medicines," she begged him. He himself admitted, when it was proposed that he should join the troops and attempt to fight his way out: "I can't hold a gun anymore; I'd collapse immediately, and then who would give me my quietus?" Eva was afraid that even if the battles proved victorious, Hitler would die of exhaustion. She attended a grandiose press conference where General Heinz Guderian denounced the Russian atrocities. Eva, unnoticed and unidentified by the journalists, was shaken by the stories of rapes. Was that the fate that awaited her if she were taken prisoner? Hitler had told her: "If we're captured, we'll be put in cages and hung up in the Moscow zoo."

All this did not prevent Eva from being in excellent spirits when she telephoned to her sister and her friend Herta for Easter. Guderian left and was replaced by General Hans Krebs, a friend of Bormann. Operation Seraglio, the transfer to Berchtesgaden, was proposed, and Eva jumped for joy. Then Goebbels triumphed with his "Friday the thirteenth, which will bring our enemies bad luck." Roosevelt died (he in fact died on the twelfth, but because of the time differences and the delays in transmission the news was only announced on the morning of the thirteenth), and this death was immediately compared to that of Empress Elizabeth of Russia, which saved Frederick II *in extremis*.

In the elation of the moment, Eva even ventured to reproach her lover: "Your uniform is grubby. Just because you think you're another Old Fritz [a nickname for Frederick the Great], that's no reason for being as dirty as him." But then came the news of the capture of Vienna. "A pity," Eva commented, "you had a magnificent collection of old weapons there. . . ." The Russians had crossed the Oder, but Eva was assured that the German resistance had stiffened at Frankfurt-on-the-Oder and so stabilized the situation on April 18.

Four letters written by Eva Braun during these fateful days have survived and are here transcribed for the first time. They reveal her state of mind far more clearly than any oral testimony or any other written account and so make it possible to get a close and accurate view of this turbulent drama. These letters, along with Hitler's two wills and the marriage contract, are the only absolutely incontestable documents that came from the bunker. They therefore have inestimable historical value.

The first letter is dated April 18, and appears to be without significance. Eva is writing to her sister, confiding to her a few of her countless daily worries: "It's still chilly, look after yourself. I rang up last night. Just imagine, the dressmaker is demanding thirty marks for my blue blouse, she's completely crazy, how can she have the face to charge thirty marks for such a trifle? . . ."

The next day, April 19, after returning from what was to be her last walk in the Tiergarten, where the avenues were almost leafless because of the fire bombs, and the swans from the lakes had long since been devoured by the starving Berliners, she wrote to her best friend and only real confidant, Herta:

Berlin 19 April 1945

Dear little Herta,

Heartfelt thanks for your two dear letters and belated greetings in writing for your birthday. When I rang you up, the connection was so bad that I wasn't able to express these best wishes by word of mouth. I wish you a quick and happy reunion with your Erwin, which I'm sure must be your dearest thought and desire. Let's hope his birthday letter arrives all the same. It can't have got lost.

I'm so glad you've decided to keep Gretl company at the Berghof. Since Traunstein was bombed, I'm no longer so sure that you're safe at Garmisch. Thank God my mother is joining you tomorrow. Now I don't need to worry anymore.*

We can already hear the gunfire from the front and of course we have air raids every day. From the east or the west, it just depends. Unfortunately I'm obliged to present myself at each warning because of the danger of flooding. My whole life is spent in the bunker. As you can imagine, we're terribly short of sleep. But I'm so happy, especially at this moment, at being near HIM. Not a day passes without my being ordered to take refuge at the Berghof, but so far I've always won. Besides it's now impossible to go through the front lines with a car. But when everything has resolved itself, there will certainly be the possibility of us all seeing each other again. There's been a real foul trick with Brandt, he's responsible for it, that is. I can't go into more details here. The secretaries and I have taken up pistol shooting and have become such champions that no man dares accept a challenge from us.

Yesterday, I probably telephoned Gretl for the last time. From today on, there's no way of getting through. But I have unshakable faith that all will be well and HE is more optimistic than ever before.

What is Anneliese doing? She wasn't able to flee because of the factory. I offered the Berghof as a refuge to her and her aunt, in his name. And where is Ilse? Write again if it's possible, I beg of you. Perhaps the letter can be sent by plane, Captain Bauer is always making trips to Bavaria. Frau Bormann will also know how a letter can be despatched.

Where are Käthl, Georg and Beppo, and how is Gretl? Please write quickly and at once. Forgive me the

---

* Gretl, who was pregnant, had taken refuge with Herta at Garmisch-Partenkirchen. She decided to go with Herta and her mother to Berchtesgaden, but they arrived just in time to be present at the pillaging of the Obersalzberg, which had been attacked from the air. They left the following day.

style of this letter, which is not up to scratch, but I'm in a hurry, as usual. With my fondest regards to every-body,

Ever yours,
Eva

N.B. The photo is for Gretl. One of the sausages [puppies] is destined for her. Would you please tell Frau Mittelstrasser that the Austrian chambermaid, by orders from above, must be given leave to go home. But only for a limited time. I imagine a fortnight at the most. Convey my regards to her at all events.

In a few words, Eva describes the strategic situation: the guns are audible; the telephone is no longer operating; escape by car is impossible; there are air raids galore. But she is happy because she is near him, and every day in the bunker is a victory for her. She speaks of Hitler as though he were a god. She underlines "his," writes "he" in capi-tals, and talks about orders "from above" as though they came from the emperor. And she believes that there will be a rainbow after the storm. She even attends to domestic affairs at the Obersalzberg and gives orders for the house-keeper. The maid must be given leave. But not more than a fortnight, mind. . . . On the eve of the cataclysm, Eva Braun writes as though, in two weeks' time, everything would be back to normal and they would be having tea at the Obersalzberg, and so the maid must be available. In January, in Berlin, she had said the same thing to her sis-ter Ilse, a fugitive from her home in Breslau, which Ilse was not to see again for twenty-three years.

The photograph is of Blondie and her puppies. Eva had indicated with an arrow the one destined for Gretl. This snapshot is the last photographic document dating from Hitler's lifetime that has survived from the bunker.

The allusion to Karl Brandt Herta failed to understand. Was Eva thinking of Morell, who deserted the bunker? This is unlikely, for Morell only left the day after this let-ter was written. It has been surmised that Brandt had again incurred the Führer's displeasure by presenting him with a defeatist memorandum on the situation.

Eva and the secretaries practiced pistol shooting every day in the courtyard of the Ministry of Foreign Affairs, where everything was in ruins, by aiming at the fanlights and the statuettes in the garden. Hitler had first made sarcastic comments about this activity: "As though I hadn't enough worries with the enemy and my generals, I now have to run the risk of being shot down by Eva or Traudl or Gerda." But Goebbels' propaganda, which dramatized the bestial rapes perpetrated by the Russian soldiery, required that women should learn to handle weapons.

Hitler celebrated his fifty-sixth birthday on April 20. He looked ninety. Eva offered him her portrait in a jeweled silver frame, an admirable piece of work that she had ordered as early as the preceding summer. Mrs. Kannenberg, the wife of the house intendant, offered a painting of Hitler's mother, Klara, which was immediately hung in the bunker. All the important personages of the regime are there, their uniforms rather creased, it is true, and prudently stripped of decorations, but their grandiloquence quite unimpaired: "Victory, fidelity, steadfastness." Admittedly they tried to persuade Hitler to flee. Ribbentrop begs Eva: "You alone have any influence on him, if you tell him you want to seek refuge, he'll do it for you." Eva refused. "It's not for me to decide, but for him."

And yet historians ventured to write after her death that Eva Braun was an insignificant character, without influence, unworthy of history, when according to Ribbentrop she was the only person capable of forcing Hitler to leave Berlin.

Hitler dined alone with Eva and the secretaries. There was talk once more of going south. "Impossible," Hitler declared, "if I left I'd be like a Tibetan lama turning an empty prayer wheel. I have to force a decision here in Berlin or else plunge into the void." Eva accompanied Hitler to his room and then returned and proposed to the secretaries that they should have a party. A celebration was a celebration, and she did not want to be deprived of a single one. They went up to her apartment in the Chancellery, which was still intact. Only the furniture had been carried down. They decorated a table, and other guests arrived, even Bormann, and also Morell, although he was preparing to leave Hitler for good the following day. There was no air attack, only the rumbling of the guns. Somebody brought an old phonograph on which the remaining record, *"Blutrote Rosen erzählen dir vom Glück"*

(Blood-red roses tell you of happiness), was played over
and over again. Eva danced inexhaustibly.

Then heavy detonations were heard, and the sky turned
red. This was Stalin's birthday present: The Russian army
was at the gates of Berlin.

The following day there was a general exodus. Morell,
Ribbentrop, great and small alike—all disappeared under
one pretext or another. Hitler saw Hoffmann once more
and begged him to take Eva with him, but to no avail. Eva
refused. Two of Hitler's secretaries also left.

They were Johanna Wolff, who was his secretary for
twenty-five years, and Christa Schroeder, who worked for
him for twelve years. Johanna has remained religiously
faithful to Hitler and even refuses to speak of the past to
an outsider. Christa Schroeder collaborated with a French
officer on a book entitled *Douze ans auprès d'Hitler*.

Subsequently, she bitterly repented its publication and
tearfully begged forgiveness from her former colleagues
and friends. "All sorts of statements were put into my
mouth; I was alone and intimidated." The publishers indis-
criminately gathered all that had been told and invented
about Hitler and incorporated it in this largely fictitious
composition. This was a pity, because much of what
Christa related could have been extremely interesting.

The sun was shining on Berlin on Sunday, April 22. But
the inmates of the bunker were unaware of it; they had
lost all count of time and no longer knew whether it was
night or day. Hitler summoned his two remaining secretaries, Traudl and Gerda, as well as Konstanze Manziarli, the
cook who prepared his dietetic meals. Eva Braun was also
present. He spoke almost in a whisper, his eyes lowered,
his face shaken by a nervous tic.

"Get dressed immediately, ladies. In an hour's time, a
plane is going to take off and convey you south. Everything is lost, irrevocably lost."

A long silence. Then Eva Braun went up to him, smilingly put her face close to his, and said to him like a nurse
to a patient, "But you know very well that I'm staying
with you. So why are you trying to send me away? . . ."

Then Adolf Hitler did something that nobody, not even
his closest friends, not even his servants, not even Eva's
sisters, had ever seen before in all these sixteen years. He
kissed Eva on the lips.

The secretaries and the cook, probably all three secretly

in love with Hitler, announced without consulting each other: "We're staying here."

Hitler looked at them and insisted: "I order you to leave."

They shook their heads. Hitler clasped their hands and remarked, "Oh, if only my generals were as brave as you."

Then he left the room, leaning tenderly on Eva's shoulder and ignoring the officers who were waiting in the anteroom to take their leave of him.

That same evening, while the ring of fire was closing in on Berlin, Eva, like a character in one of the romantic films that were her passion, wrote her first farewell letter.

Berlin 22 April 1945

My dear little Herta,

These are the very last lines and therefore the last sign of life from me. I don't dare write to Gretl; you must explain all this to her with due consideration for her state. I'm sending you my jewelry, to be distributed according to my will, which is in the Wasserburgerstrasse. I hope that with this jewelry you'll be able to keep your heads out of water anyway for a time. Please come down from the mountain, for it's too dangerous a place for you should all be lost. We're fighting here to the bitter end, but I'm afraid this end is drawing dangerously near. I can't describe to you how much I'm suffering personally on the Führer's account.

Forgive me if this letter is a little incoherent, but G.'s six children are in the next room making an infernal racket. What else should I write you? I can't understand how all this can have happened, it's enough to make one lose one's faith in God!

The man is waiting to take this letter.

You have my most affectionate and kindly thoughts, my faithful friend! Say hello to Father and Mother, they should go to Munich or Traunstein. Regards to all the friends. I shall die as I lived. It's no burden. You know that. With fondest love and kisses,

Yours,
Eva

P.S. Keep this letter to yourself, until you hear of our fate. I know this is asking a lot of you, but you're brave. Perhaps everything will still turn out happily, but *he* has lost faith, and as for us, we're hoping in vain.

This letter—badly written and full of mistakes but nonetheless moving—from a young woman in her early thirties who claims that she will die as she lived, with detachment and without regret, but who betrays herself in the last line when she hopes that in spite of everything all will end well, gives irrefutable evidence of Hitler's state of mind that Sunday, the twenty-second of April. He no longer believed in anything.

The following day, Monday, April 23, Eva nevertheless decided to write to her sister Gretl. She did so with solicitude, for her sister was pregnant, the baby was expected any moment, and she wanted to be gentle with her.

Berlin 23 April 1945

My dear little sister,

How sad I am that you're going to receive such a letter from me. But it's inevitable. Every day, every hour, the end may be upon us, and I must therefore use this last opportunity to tell you what still remains to be done. First of all: Hermann isn't with us. He left for Nauen to gather a battalion or something of the sort. He wants to fight his way out in order to continue the resistance in Bavaria, anyway for a time. As for the Führer, he has lost all hope of a happy outcome of the conflict. But all of us here, myself included, still believe that while there's life there's hope. So I beg of you, hold your head high and don't despair. There's still hope. But naturally we're not going to let ourselves be captured alive. The faithful Liesl refuses to abandon me. I've proposed several times that she should leave. I should like to give her my gold watch, but unfortunately I've bequeathed it to Miezi. Perhaps you could give Miezi something of equal value from my jewelry. I'm sure you'll find a satisfactory solution. I want to wear the gold bracelet with the green stone until the end. Then, it can be removed and you must wear it always as I have always worn it. It's also destined to Miezi in the will, so make another substitution. My diamond watch is unfortunately being repaired. I'll write the exact address at the bottom of the letter. Maybe you'll be lucky and manage to retrieve it. I want it to go to you, because you've always admired it. The diamond bracelet and topaz pendant, Hitler's gift for my last birthday, are also for you. I hope my wishes will be respected by the others.

In addition, I must ask you to attend to the following things: Destroy all my private correspondence and above all the business papers. On no account must Heise's bills be found. Also destroy an envelope addressed to the Führer which is in the shelter, in the safe at the villa. Please don't read it. I want you to make a water-resistant packet of the letters from the Führer and the copies of my replies (blue leather notebook) and bury them if need be. Please don't destroy them. I owe the Heise firm the enclosed bill. There may be other requests, but not for more than 1,500 marks. I don't know what you propose to do with the films and albums. At all events, please only destroy everything at the last moment, except for the private letters and the envelope addressed to the Führer. Those you can burn immediately.

I'm sending you at the same time the wherewithal for food and cigarettes. Give some coffee to Käthl and the Linders too. Give the Linders some of the cans from my cellar. The tobacco is for Papa. The chocolate for Mama. There's chocolate and tobacco at the "Berg." Get them to give you some. Now I don't know what to think anymore. For the moment, I'm told that the situation has improved, and General Burgdorf, who yesterday gave us only a 10 percent chance of salvation, today declares that there's a 50 percent chance of victory. So you see! All may end well.

Has Arndt arrived with the letter and the case? We heard here that the plane was late. I hope Morell delivered the jewelry to you. It would be terrible if something had happened. I'm going to write to Mother, Herta and Georg, if possible, tomorrow. That's enough for today. Now, my dear little sister, I wish you lots and lots of happiness. And don't forget that you'll certainly see Hermann again.

With most affectionate greetings and a kiss from your sister

Eva

N.B. I've just spoken to the Führer. I think today he's taking a much less pessimistic view of things than yesterday.

The watchmaker's address: SS Unterscharf. Stege-
mann SS Lager Oranienburg evacuated to Kyritz.

Here again is apparent the mad optimism of this
doomed creature who, following Burgdorf's insane predictions, in spite of everything still expects a miracle. Burgdorf even offered mathematical probabilities, as for a
horse race. Eva makes arrangements for the disposal of
her private papers, but wants this done only at the last
possible moment. She becomes once more the queen of
Berchtesgaden who royally dispenses provisions and finery.
She even indulges in romanticism when she asks her sister
to wear the bracelet all her life, as she has done, without
considering that her sister, to feed her baby might well be
obliged to sell these things for a crust of bread. She does
not wish future generations of Germans to know about
her dressmaker's bills; she is already thinking about her
place in history and does not wish to give the impression
that Eva Braun was a frivolous person.

These are incontestably the last words we have written
by Eva Braun. Were there other letters that are now lost,
destroyed, or jealously hidden away? Probably not. There
was no lack of time for writing in the bunker. But the atmosphere was so unreal, so unnatural, that nobody wanted
to write and so be reminded that there was an outside
world with which one could still establish contact. Eva
herself had announced that these were her last letters. She
entrusted some mementos to her maid, the faithful Liesl,
but no written messages. A letter from Eva Braun involved a certain danger, it could compromise the person
on whom it was found. Moreover Eva, probably at Hitler's
order, wanted to avoid the risk of such a document falling
into enemy hands. A letter supposedly written by Eva, a
"pompous, adulatory" letter, was said to have been entrusted to the woman pilot Hanna Reitsch. This is pure
invention. Hanna Reitsch denied to the author personally
that she ever saw or received such a missive or any kind
of message from Eva Braun.

A macabre feature of this last letter is Eva's revelation
that she has given her diamond watch to be repaired by a
deportee (expert watchmakers were nonexistent in Berlin
at this time, for they had all gone to work in precision fac-

tories, and only an SS man guarding KZ prisoners at Oranienburg was in a position to get a watch repaired).

Thus the last words known to have been written by Eva
Braun, by a grim coincidence, or perhaps by an underlin-
ing of destiny, speak of a concentration camp.

CHAPTER NINETEEN

The wedding gift

Blondie the bitch had finally brought four puppies into the world—or more exactly, into the underworld. The father was a greyhound belonging to one of the officers. Hitler had named the finest of the litter Wolfi and had promised the others to friends, one of them being reserved for Gretl, also about to become a mother. The family was huddled in a box, which was placed first near the lavatories and then transferred by Hitler to a corner of his bedroom. Nearly all the time, Hitler had a puppy on his knees, which he stroked interminably as though to conceal the trembling of his hands.

Eva decided that these poor animals should take some air. She therefore went up to the surface with Traudl Junge and Gerda Daranowsky Christian. (Eva and Gerda had abandoned their rivalry and become friends.) "La Daran," as she was still called, was pale because of her prolonged stay in the bunker, and this pallor—for she did not make herself up as Eva continued to do—enhanced her dazzling beauty.

Hitler, under the pretext of keeping an eye on his dogs, accompanied them, but did not go out into the garden. He merely looked out of the glass bay, and then, seized by some strange curiosity, he went to a window overlooking the Wilhelmstrasse and gazed for a quarter of an hour at the people who were running across the street and the small square opposite the Kaiserhof.

Eva, Gerda, and Traudl went as far as the garden of the Ministry of Foreign Affairs while Blondie pursued her puppies, who were playing carefree games around the bomb craters, completely insensible to the uproar of war so close at hand. The young women smoked, Eva especially lighting one cigarette after another. There were still trees in the Ministry garden, and the spring sun was coaxing out the young leaves.

The following day, April 24, Eva tried to go for a final walk in her favorite avenue in the Tiergarten, but the Russian shells that were exploding close by forced her to turn back. This was the last time that she saw the light of day.

A sixth woman had come to live in the bunker. This was Magda Goebbels—blond, vivacious, and dressed as for a ball. She, her husband, and their six children had installed themselves in the room that Professor Morell had abandoned. Eva welcomed her with open arms, for they were all sisters in adversity. Magda proclaimed histrionically that she too would be faithful unto death and had pinned the gold emblem of the Nazi party on her blouse, in the opening between her breasts.

As we have said, the Führer bunker had two levels, the upper one, where the secretaries and aides had their accommodations, and the bunker proper below. This was a rectangle bisected by a wide corridor that served as an anteroom. At one end of this corridor, there was the gallery that led out to the garden, with an unfinished concrete pillbox at the exit. At the other extremity was the stairway leading to the upper level and from there to the entrance in the right wing of the Chancellery. The anteroom was cluttered with antique furniture that had been brought down from the palace, and old masters hung on the mildewed walls. On the right, there was first of all a door leading to a small room that served as a clothes closet and then a compartment that housed the sluice controlling the water flow. Next came a so-called map room, where military conferences were held. From here a door opened into Hitler's bedroom, which had access to his sitting room. This, in turn, led to the study, which was therefore adjacent to, but did not communicate with, the conference room (see plan). Only from Hitler's study was it possible to penetrate into the bathroom, whose taps were of gilded metal, and from there into a little private boudoir and finally into Eva's bedroom, which she had furnished comfortably and hung with draperies. This room had no door onto the corridor, so that to reach it, Eva had to enter the study, then cross Hitler's sitting room, the bathroom, and the boudoir. Next to her room, at the end of this part of the bunker, were the communal lavatories.

On the other side of the central corridor, opposite the conference room, was Professor Morell's room, now occupied by the Goebbelses. Behind lay the room of the surgeon, Dr. Ludwig Stumpfegger, and next to this was the infirmary. From it, a small lobby led to the antechamber. Then came the telephone switchboard and behind it Bormann's room. Right at the end of the corridor were the electric generators and the ventilation apparatus.

Hitler's bedroom was furnished only with a camp bed, a small table, two chairs, and the dogs' box. The conference room contained nothing but a large table and benches. The anteroom was more welcoming, with carpets on the concrete floor and Italian sixteenth-century paintings hanging everywhere. A brown rustic-style bench stood against the wall, and there was a large table surrounded by chairs and another bench on the side opposite the door leading to the conference room.

Hitler's entourage had thinned out pitifully. Apart from those already mentioned at the beginning of this chapter, it now included only Zander, Bormann's assistant, Fegelein, Eva's brother-in-law, the ambassador Walter Hewel, who had come to share the fate of the friend who had disowned him, Colonel Nicolaus van Below, the other military aides, Admiral Voss, General Eckhardt Christian, husband of the secretary Gerda, Generals Krebs and Burgdorf and their aides, Lorenz, from the Ministry of Propaganda, who was in charge of the information services, the pilots Bauer and Bets, Rattenhuber, the Gestapo head of security, and his assistant, and another pretty woman, with eyes as blue as the sea—Fräulein Else Krüger, who was Bormann's secretary. Of course there were also the servants and other minor personages, including a little operator of the shortwave radio who was ready to sleep with everybody, and various SS of the protection services. Indeed, both bunkers were swarming with idle SS, so loaded with machine guns and hand grenades that one would have thought that the enemy was not up above, two subway stations away, but here below ground.

Julius Schaub had left, but at Hitler's orders. After burning all the Chancellery documents, he was going to do the same in the Munich apartment and at the Obersalzberg.

Efforts were still being made to persuade Hitler to leave for Bavaria. But by now the question had become an academic one. On April 25 the Berghof was bombed and partially destroyed, and the rest of the little "capital" was severely damaged. After the raid, the local inhabitants rushed into Hitler's house and started pillaging frenziedly.

Messengers of disaster were continually arriving: The Russians were everywhere, in both the northern and southern quarters; they had passed the Imperial Palace, taken the Anhalt Station, the nerve centers of the Wehrmacht, Maybach I at Zossen, and Maybach II at Wussdorf. Tempelhof was captured on the twenty-fifth, and the Russians joined up with the Americans on the Elbe. There was only the little airport of Gatow left: all the other routes were cut. The radio station and its antennas had been destroyed; only a telephonic cable made it possible to communicate with the outside world, and this was destroyed on April twenty-sixth. Göring's communication, proposing his immediate take-over in terms that Hitler interpreted as an ultimatum, had been relayed two days before by this cable. Göring was promptly arrested in his villa at the Obersalzberg. While Hitler was fuming, Goebbels was laughing like a child. Oh, if only his fat rival had also been pulverized during the air attack on the Obersalzberg. . . . Eva herself could not suppress her satisfaction. This was a well-deserved punishment for that haughty Emmy Göring who wanted to usurp the title of "First Lady."

Nevertheless, Eva lamented at all these desertions: "Why have they all abandoned you? Where's Speer? He was your friend. But he'll come—I'm sure of it, I know him."

On the morning of April 25, although it must be remembered that there were neither mornings nor evenings in the bunker, a man in SS uniform, with a pleasing face but an ambiguous smile, made his appearance. It was Albert Speer, who had managed to land on the north-south roadway axis in the Tiergarten just before the victory column where Napoleon III's cannon captured at Sedan were triumphally displayed. Eva kissed him with tears of joy in her eyes. "I knew you'd come. You would never abandon the Führer."

Speer sheepishly admitted that he was leaving the same evening. Eva knew nothing of his machinations against Hitler, his attempt to asphyxiate everybody in the bunker.

Hitler was vacillating between hopes of certain victory and the most abject defeatism. He spent his time poring over general-staff maps, when a subway plan, as Eva joked, or any aerial photograph of the district, was sufficient for a study of the front.

What was he hoping for? Recently I could not refrain from asking Traudl Junge this question. "He said that the outcome of a battle depends on the last battalion, and quoted Kuhnesdorf and Waterloo as examples," she replied. He believed that if he could resist the Russians before Berlin, he would electrify the Germans, as the Russians had been rallied by Stalingrad. He still had appreciable forces in Norway, Italy, Czechoslovakia; there would be time to muster them around the capital and so prolong the war. Meanwhile the Russians and Anglo-Americans would go from incident to incident until a conflict between them would become inevitable. Then he, Adolf Hitler, would be the arbiter.

The occupants of the bunker, Eva especially, had grown so accustomed to the idea that the world above no longer existed that the arrival of outsiders seemed to them like a landing by Martians. The last visitor to the bunker was Hanna Reitsch, a blond young woman who was a test pilot. She considered herself the leading air ace of the Reich and wanted to form a Nazi kamikaze corps. She had accompanied General von Greim, whom Hitler was about to appoint as Göring's successor. It is not entirely clear why Fräulein Reitsch took part in this desperate flight. In any case, she had not originally been detailed to fly the machine. A sergeant piloted a Focke-Wulf 190 from Reichlin to Gatow, with Hanna Reitsch, who was tiny, squatting in the back. From there, Greim placed himself at the controls of a Fieseler Storch, a small observation plane, but just as he was coming down to land on the north-south axis, in other words, on the Charlottenburg parkway, he was wounded by a Russian bullet. It was then that Hanna Reitsch seized the controls and accomplished the feat of bringing down the plane. The Americans later accused her of having been summoned to Berlin to fly Hitler clandestinely to Argentina.

The idea of an escape by Hitler existed only in Hanna Reitsch's mind. Later she wrote that she wanted to throw herself at his feet and persuade him to seek safety while waiting for the hour of his return, as Napoleon had returned from Elba. Otherwise she, the constant nymph, would die with him. For Hanna Reitsch loved Hitler madly, fanatically.

Hitler, however, listened only perfunctorily to these projects. He had no use for another Unity Mitford; those times now seemed very far away. And Hanna Reitsch made a horrifying discovery. A woman was living with Hitler, a mistress of long standing whom he declared he loved. She concealed her profound disillusionment and even kept Eva Braun company in the evenings, but she decided that she did not wish to die for a man who had betrayed her love. She left on the night of April 27–28, and was therefore spared the humiliation of being present at the announcement of Hitler's and Eva's marriage. As she took off in the darkness, flying an Arado 96, she noticed the mysterious presence of another machine on the roadway, a Ju 52.

With all this coming and going, nobody had attached much importance to Fegelein's absence, though his arrogance had antagonized everybody. Even Hitler found him irritating, for during councils of war he would get up and talk a lot of nonsense. The evening of Hitler's birthday, after carousing immoderately in his sister-in-law's room, he took an army officer's uniform and, throwing it on the ground, trampled it underfoot, shouting: "German generals, all cowards." When he was quiet, it was only because he was with the feminine members of the staff under some pretext or other, bluntly proposing that they should join him in his bed.

On the evening of April 26, Eva Braun was talking to Hitler, Goebbels, Magda, and the rest of the company in the Führer's study. Goebbels had proposed to hide Eva, his wife, the children, and the women secretaries in the Italian embassy that stood at an angle to the Tiergartenstrasse, in order to protect them from the risk of a sudden incursion by Russian soldiers into the bunker. In the midst of this discussion, an orderly called Eva to the telephone. It was her brother-in-law, Fegelein. "Eva, I'm safe here in Berlin-West. Listen, you must leave the Führer, in a few hours it will be too late to escape from Berlin. Don't be stupid; it's a matter of life and death. I'm going to join Gretl, a father must be near his child. . . ."

Eva was horrified. "Hermann, come back to the bunker immediately. Otherwise the Führer will think you've betrayed him; he wants to talk to you. . . ." But Fegelein had hung up. Why did he call her? Probably he felt that she had a top secret *laissez-passer*.

Eva said nothing to Hitler, but he was informed of this incident by the official who listened in on all conversations. He said to Rattenhuber: "Fetch me that fellow."

What both Eva and Gretl did not know was that Fegelein kept an apartment on the Bleibtreustrasse near the Kurfürstendamm. The Gestapo, however, was in the know. Rattenhuber's assistant, Hogl, first interrogated the aides-de-camp of the SS general, and then, in a gray Mercedes followed by a military car full of police, he arrived at 5 P.M. outside Fegelein's house. He found him in civilian clothes, obviously all prepared to leave.

A suitcase was found containing 217 pieces of silver, a diamond watch belonging to Eva, two chronometers, one Universal and one Omega, an International watch, another watch-chronometer, two pairs of gold-and-diamond cuff links, several bracelets, fifty Swiss "Vreneli" gold pieces, 105,725 marks, and 3,186 Swiss francs. The Gestapo official was not particularly concerned with the fact that a number of these pieces of jewelry probably came from a concentration camp. He merely noted that the Swiss francs revealed Fegelein's intention to escape into neutral territory.

There was also another fact. Fegelein was not alone. A small but provocative Hungarian lady was with him, and the rumpled bed suggested certain conclusions. She was the wife of a resident diplomat. She spoke French, and declared that she was rich and that Fegelein hoped to start life afresh with her in Switzerland. The superintendent telephoned to the bunker. The answer was peremptory: "Arrest him and shoot him if he tries to escape."

Eva, as soon as she heard of this, interceded with Hitler: "He's young, his wife is expecting a baby, the only one in the family. You can't make it an orphan. . . ." Hitler was mollified. He merely summoned the brother-in-law to his study in uniform, accused him of cowardice, tore off his epaulettes and his Knight's Cross, and sent him off to a room in the main bunker, which had been converted into a cell, to teach him a good lesson.

Destiny, however, had not finished with Hans Georg Otto Hermann Fegelein, born August 30, 1906, at Ansbach, who found himself cooped up in this way in the bunker on the morning of April 28, 1945. That afternoon, another fateful cable came into Lorenz's hands. It was a Reuter bulletin transmitted by the Swedish radio: Himmler, then in Denmark, was reported to have proposed negotiations for peace and to have proclaimed himself Hitler's successor in his turn. The Führer, beside himself with rage, cast about for a scapegoat and of course lit on Fegelein. His private papers were examined and apparently contained proof of Himmler's conspiracy. Fegelein had wanted to go to Switzerland to start peace talks.

Hitler gave immediate orders for his execution. He said to Eva, "He's a traitor, there must be no mercy, remember Mussolini and Ciano." Eva, impressed by this historical parallel, offered no further opposition. "You are the Führer; family considerations no longer count." She had meanwhile been informed about the suitcase full of jewelry, some of it hers, and about the Hungarian mistress, and now felt only animosity for her brother-in-law. In the bunker the news was received with general apathy. Death today or death tomorrow, what difference did it make?

Besides, Eva Braun had been busy since that morning. For her this twenty-eighth of April was the day of days. After nearly seventeen years of humiliations, waiting, frustrations, she had at last reached her goal—she was about to win Hitler forever.

"Tonight, we're going to weep," she had told Traudl, who at first had misinterpreted the words. Was she already talking of suicide? No, Eva had shut herself in her room with little Liesl, and her hair was being done, dresses were being ironed, all kinds of mysterious preparations were afoot.

Toward eight o'clock in the evening, or perhaps it was more like ten o'clock—who was still keeping count of time?—Hitler inquired whether Traudl Junge had rested long enough: "For I want to dictate something to you. . . ." As she crossed the anteroom to go to Hitler's study, she noticed that the table had been elaborately decorated: a tablecloth with the initials A. H., the silver dinner service, champagne glasses. There was no shortage of champagne in the bunker, nor of food either. Traudl could not help noting mentally that the last time she had gone up to the surface, she had seen a dead horse in the middle of the Wilhelmstrasse, and some women who were cutting chunks of this carrion, happy to have some food at last.

Hitler usually dictated directly into the machine, but on

this occasion he asked Traudl to take her shorthand pad. "My Political Will," he announced, and Traudl held her breath. She was taking down history. The dictation was long, with Hitler impatiently leaving the room every few moments. He made no corrections, although normally he niggled over every phrase, recast whole passages, and hesitated a quarter of an hour over a comma. Still he went on dictating. He began: "My Private Will," and then came the phrase that made Traudl Junge jump. "Though I did not think, during the years of the conflict, that I could assume the responsibility of founding a family, I have now decided, at the end of my life's journey, to marry the young girl who, after years of faithful friendship, freely chose to share my fate in a city already almost completely besieged."

This was what Eva had meant when she spoke of tears —a wedding! This explained the champagne, and naturally Traudl did not point out to the Führer that he was exaggerating slightly when he claimed that Eva had come to join him in a beleaguered town. In February, Berlin had not yet been threatened.

Traudl was not present at the ceremony. She had to go into the small room near that of the Goebbelses to type out the documents. Hitler went into the conference room, where Eva was waiting, counting the seconds, along with the witnesses and the guests. There were Bormann, Goebbels, Magda, Gerda Christian, Konstanze Manziarli, General Burgdorf, General Krebs, and Axmann, the head of the Hitler Youth, who had come down to the bunker between two battles. It had been planned to start the proceedings much earlier—it was by now nearly midnight— but it had been difficult to find a justice of the peace to marry them. When Walter Wagner was finally discovered fighting in the Volkssturm near the Friedrichstrasse, he had none of the relevant documents with him and had conscientiously gone home to fetch them. It was not easy, however, to move about in what was left of Berlin. An armored car had to be requisitioned and countless detours made.

Eva did not have her grandmother's brocade dress that she so often wore at Berchtesgaden. She had to make do with a long gown of black silk taffeta, with a very full skirt and a high neck. It was one of Hitler's favorites. She wore a gold bracelet set with tourmalines and a diamond watch, as well as a topaz pendant and a brooch pinned in her hair. Hitler was in uniform as usual.

The formalities were brief. The wedding rings were too big. They had been hard to find. Nobody in the bunker had wanted to give up a ring, for gold was precious in case of flight. Finally they were obtained from the Gestapo treasury. Quite possibly they were rings confiscated from gassed victims. The next day Eva sent hers to her friend Herta. A photograph of this ring will be found in the documentary part of this book. Hitler kept his on his finger.

Eva, like all young brides overcome with emotion, made a mistake when signing the marriage certificate. She started to write *B,* for *Braun,* then crossed it out and for the first and last time in her life wrote *Eva Hitler.* The registrar was just as excited and signed his name wrongly with a double *a.* Goebbels and Bormann added their signatures as witnesses. The time was just before midnight.

A quarter of an hour earlier, a corporal had fallen, his body cut in half, in the Tiergarten sector, at the approaches to the canal. He had been fighting for three days in defense of his Führer. His name was Hans Braun and he was Eva's first cousin.

It was thought for a very long time that Eva Braun was married on the evening of Sunday, April 29. Traudl Junge, however, distinctly remembers that it was Saturday the twenty-eighth, just before midnight. Yet the marriage certificate is dated the twenty-ninth. Why? The reason is childishly simple. Wagner, under the combined influence of emotion and champagne, placed one paper on top of the other without realizing that the ink was not yet dry. The result was a blot that obliterated the date. He therefore decided to retrace the figures, but before doing so, with a bureaucratic respect for formalities, he looked at his watch. It was then thirty-five minutes past midnight, in other words, already the twenty-ninth, and without thinking, Wagner changed and wrote the date more clearly as the twenty-ninth. All this is apparent if one examines the original certificate, which is in the Eisenhower Library in Abilene, Kansas. Many historians have merely inspected photostats of photostats and have not noticed these details.

Hitler gave his arm to his newly wed bride, and the company passed into his study for the wedding feast. He even drank a little Tokay wine and joked with the guests.

Eva was radiant, although Hitler had not kissed her at the ceremony. She talked of dancing and merrymaking. She ordered the phonograph to be fetched with the one remaining record, *"Red Roses,"* and then went out into the corridor with Hitler to receive the congratulations of all the staff. Hitler gave signs of impatience and went to see what Traudl Junge was doing. Eva had given orders for some champagne and cakes to be taken to her. Hitler stayed with his secretary until four in the morning, waiting to sign the documents. He completely disregarded the fact that outside and in the other bunkers small parties were being organized in honor of his marriage. He joined the guests once more and discussed politics uninterruptedly with Goebbels and Bormann. At midnight the little Liesl had laid out the blue silk Italian nightdress on her mistress's bed beside Hitler's short white nightshirt, which was crude and badly sewn. It was only toward five o'clock in the morning that Hitler and Eva found themselves alone.

Nobody will ever know what happened during that belated wedding night. It is certain, however, that Eva did not hear the early-morning firing from the courtyard, in the direction of the conservatory. Her brother-in-law, Hermann Fegelein had been shot "like a dog" by a platoon of SS. This was Adolf Hitler's wedding gift to his bride.

CHAPTER TWENTY

The last sacrifice

Liesl had brought her mistress some good coffee. It was already midday of Sunday, April 29, but what reason was there for waking her up earlier? Eva was pale, very pale, for it was an age since she had been in the sun.

"May I offer you my sincere congratulations, *Gnädiges Fräulein*," the maid said. Then, correcting herself with a blush, "Oh, I beg your pardon, I mean *Gnädige Frau*."

Eva looked at her with great condescension: "Oh, Liesl, you need have no qualms about calling me Frau Hitler; there's documentary evidence now."

She doubted that they were destined to die that day. Before leaving her, Hitler had told her that there was a last hope, the arrival of General Wenck, for which he was desperately waiting, as Napoleon waited for Grouchy at Waterloo. He also had another motive for postponing the moment of his suicide as long as possible. He wanted to die on May 5, like Napoleon.

Thus for two days and two nights Eva Hitler was the first lady and *Führerin* of the Third Reich. She called back Liesl, who was tidying the bathroom, and said to her, "Liesl, dear, I've a last service to ask you. When I'm no longer with you, I want you to go to see my friend Herta in Munich—not immediately but whenever it's possible and there's no longer any danger. Give her my wedding ring and this nightdress—they'll be easy to hide. I know I can trust you. Take this ring in memory of me. . . ." Liesl, moved to tears, kissed Eva's hand.

There was a lot of noise in the corridor, but it was only the Goebbels children imitating the rattle of machine guns and the explosions of grenades. They were playing at war. As soon as they saw Eva, they all came to kiss her, for they had grown attached to the young woman. Then, no doubt remembering their mother's instructions, the girls curtsied and the boy stood to attention. *"Wir gratulieren, Tante Eva . . ."*

For them, whether married or no, Hitler was Uncle Adolf and Eva the kind aunt. Every evening, while their mother drank quantities of Martell brandy, it was Eva who kept them company, sometimes seconded by the secretaries and by Hanna Reitsch during her brief stay there. Eva told them stories, but the kids preferred explanations of what was happening above ground. "The wicked bandits are trying to destroy everything, but Uncle Adolf will get on his white horse and give them the lesson they deserve."

There were five girls and one boy, Helmut, who, at the age of nine, knew how to make a report like an officer and could diagnose the origin of every bomb blast that shook the bunker. Heide was five, Hedda six, Hilde seven, and Holde eight. Then, with a bigger gap, came the eldest, Helga, who was twelve and who had an inkling of what was really happening. She did not believe in the "big journey" that was promised them and the excursion to their favorite beach in Pomerania. Frau Goebbels did not know that her child by a first marriage, Harald Quandt, had already been taken prisoner by the Russians.

To put the children to sleep, Eva, often harmoniously accompanied by Traudl, "Daran," and Konstanze, sang Brahms' lullaby for them:

"Tomorrow, if such is His will, the Lord will wake you once more. . . ."

Traudl had slept late. The drafting of the wills had exhausted her. Now, on reflection, she found these wills somewhat ridiculous. What did Hitler have to leave and how could the bequests be carried out? The legatees were probably dead already. In his private will, Hitler instructed Bormann to make financial provision for "a modest but comfortable existence for my sisters and my wife's mother," as if Bormann, even if he survived, would be in a position to do so.

Traudl had ventured to ask Hitler, while she was putting fresh paper in her typewriter: "Don't you think that National Socialism will outlive us?" "No," Hitler had decreed categorically. "The German people have shown themselves unworthy of my movement. In a hundred years' time, maybe, another genius will take up my ideas again, and National Socialism will rise again from its ashes."

Traudl Junge shared with Hitler and perhaps Eva a secret to which nobody else in the bunker was a party: the nature of the last scene of this drama. Hitler, drawing his inspiration from Wagner and from the opera libretto that he had himself composed at the age of seventeen, had dictated to Traudl:

> I and my wife, in order to escape the ignominy of flight and capitulation, have chosen to die. It is our wish to be immediately cremated on the spot where for the last twelve years I have accomplished the greater part of my daily task in the service of my people.

On the basis of information from certain inmates of the bunker, who have perhaps subconsciously amalgamated what they really saw with what they have subsequently read or heard, it has constantly been claimed that Eva and Hitler decided to have their bodies burned because of the horrible fate that Mussolini and his mistress Clara Petacci suffered in Piazza Loreto in Milan. Nothing could be farther from the truth.

The news of Mussolini's capture and execution reached the bunker on the evening of Sunday the twenty-ninth. As there was never a wire-photo machine in the bunker, Eva and Hitler cannot possibly have seen the pictures of Mussolini and Clara hanging naked by their feet at a service station, even if such photographs had been transmitted that evening, which is very doubtful.

The only news that reached the bunker was that received on a simple amateur short-wave set, which merely picked up the Stockholm radio broadcasts. I examined the minutes of these broadcasts and found that the report of Mussolini's death was succinct and contained none of the macabre details. It was received with indifference in the bunker, according to Traudl.

Hitler had taken his decision much earlier: The final disposition in his will that has just been quoted was signed at four o'clock in the morning on Sunday, April 29, but had been dictated to Fräulein Junge the preceding evening a little before eleven o'clock.

Traudl Junge went up into the main shelter, where she

made her way with difficulty along the damp labyrinthine passages, looking for some food for the Goebbels children. "It was a world peopled with zombies," she recalls, "whose only thought was to laugh and sing. They had appropriated some liquor reserves and were stuffing themselves on rolls and caviar. An erotic fever seemed to have taken possession of everybody—everywhere, even on a dentist's chair, I saw bodies locked in lascivious embraces. The women had discarded all modesty and were freely exposing their private parts."

The SS went out only to go on "Whore" patrol, in other words, to collect women, who were being tracked in the besieged zone and who, attracted by promises of food, coffee, and drink, dresses and jewelry, or simply because they too were thirsting for love, agreed to take part in the bunker orgy. They were tossed from one compartment to another like magazines that everybody wants to read in turn.

Toward six o'clock Hitler summoned his faithful followers. He was in his study, which was screened off from the anteroom by a red velvet curtain with gold fringes. The room was just over twelve feet wide and between nine and ten feet long. The ceiling, no doubt for safety's sake, was thicker than elsewhere, and its lowness made the room oppressive. On the right there was a writing desk against the wall, under a portrait of Frederick the Great by Anton Graff. This was Hitler's talisman. These last days he frequently declared: "Beside him I'm just muck. . . ." The picture was the only personal possession that he wanted to be kept; everything else—statuettes, clothes, ties, diaries, his fountain pen—had to be destroyed so that the enemies would not be able to boast of such trophies in their museums.

Against the wall opposite the red curtain was a sofa, or more exactly, a padded bench, in front of a square table surrounded by three chairs. To the right of the sofa stood a small table, on which was a *Volksempfänger* (radio). At the end of the left-hand wall, beyond the door leading to the bathroom and Eva's room, the heating and ventilation apparatus was installed. The portrait of a fine-looking woman hung on the wall: it was Klara, Hitler's mother.

"Wenck will never come now," Hitler told his visitors. "Unless some miracle happens, my wife and I are going to die. I have already given orders for the disposal of our bodies. I am waiting for news of the safe delivery of at least one of the three copies of my will that Lorenz, von Below, and Zander have been trying since this morning to hand over to Doenitz and the others, for I wish to avoid chaos, and Goebbels refuses in spite of my orders to take over my functions. . . ."

He then gave the ladies some glass phials, sealed with copper. Himmler had procured large quantities of them. It was cyanamide. He apologized to Gerda and Traudl: "It's not exactly what I would have wished for a farewell present."

Eva had long had one of these lethal phials in her possession. She was acquainted with its effects, which Brandt had explained to her a long time ago. She therefore paid no heed to the conversation. She was not afraid. Naturally she was in a state of nervous anguish and prostration like everybody else, but the idea of death no longer troubled her. She had grown accustomed to it, for her decision had been reached and her farewell letters sent long before. She spent the rest of the evening singing her favorite tune, "Tea for Two," and playing with the Goebbels children.

The others talked about the effects of cyanamide. "It's better to fire a pistol into one's mouth," General Krebs declared. "Of course," Hitler replied, "but if I miss, who will dispatch me? And besides, I don't wany my Eva's pretty face to be disfigured . . . I couldn't shoot at her." Goebbels inquired whether the phials might not have lost their deadly effect with time. Hitler was seized by doubts. The poison had been supplied by Himmler, a traitor. . . . Six days before he had banished Morell, whom he had accused of wanting to send him to sleep with his injections so that he could be transported against his will out of Berlin. Hitler ordered: "Call Stumpfegger."

This was Dr. Ludwig Stumpfegger, the bunker surgeon. He proposed that one of the phials be tested on the dog Blondie. Hitler agreed and then was beset by another doubt: Stumpfegger belonged to the SS. What if, by order of Himmler, he substituted a good phial for an ineffective one? Another doctor, Professor Haase, was summoned. It was he who forced the liquid down the Alsatian's throat. And so Blondie died, whom Hitler loved above all else, perhaps even more than Eva Braun, and from whom he never wanted to be separated. Otto Günsche, a member of his body guard, took the box with the dead bitch and the living puppies up into the garden. He killed the puppies, who were still pressing against their mother's cold teats.

"The thirtieth of April," Traudl Junge recalls, "began quite normally except that Hitler had got up early, contrary to his habit. Eva stayed in her room until midday."

At six o'clock in the morning Hitler had summoned SS-Brigadeführer Mohnke, who was virtually the commander of the remaining combatants outside. His report was disastrous: "Everything will be over in twenty hours' time. . . ." Was Mohnke wrong in his forecast, or was he deliberately misleading Hitler? Field Marshal Vassili Chuikov, who was directing the attack and who was to be hailed as the conqueror of Berlin, was at this same moment telephoning to Moscow, as he records in his memoirs: "There's no possibility of taking Berlin for May Day." The same evening, this thirtieth of April, he remarked morosely to his superior, Marshal Georgi Zhukov: "There's no question of capitulation in a matter of days. . . . The struggle will be a long one."

Hitler lunched with Eva, the secretaries, and Konstanze Manziarli. Werner Schwiedel, the valet who was serving at table, related that the conversation was banal. After the meal, Traudl accompanied Eva to her room. She feigned nonchalance, but did not want to be left alone. They chatted fitfully. Then she went to a cupboard and took out her fine silver fox coat. "Frau Junge, I want to give this to you in memory of me. I've always liked having well-dressed people around me. Take it, and I hope it will give you much pleasure." In the emotion of the moment, it did not occur to Traudl how incongruous it would be to emerge from the bunker wearing a fox fur coat. Eva kissed her and said, "Good-bye, try to get out of here. Maybe you'll succeed, in which case say hello to Bavaria for me. . . ."

Hitler had sent for his last disciples to wish them farewell. He kissed Magda Goebbels, and shook hands with the others. Eva and Frau Goebbels also kissed each other. Then Hitler and Eva retired into the study. Günsche, the "gorilla," his machine gun slung from his shoulder, ushered everybody out of the anteroom into the corridor.

There were nonetheless thousands of women in Germany who would have envied Eva Hitler's fate, had they known about her. I am not speaking of the concentration camps, where the inmates were dying like flies, but of the ruined towns, where German women, trapped like ani-

THE LAST SACRIFICE 231

mals, were suffocating and helplessly watching their children being disfigured by bombs; of the roads where they were fleeing despite the cold and the snow, traveling hundreds of miles across rivers and forests; of the seas where they were drowning when the refugee ships sank under bombardment; of the homes where they were being killed and savagely raped. Everywhere, exposed to cold, hunger, and outrage, they would have welcomed a comfortable death like that of Eva Hitler as a relief and a deliverance.

Bormann, Hewel, and General Krebs were in the corridor. Goebbels was standing outside the door of his room. Linge, the valet, was sitting on the stairs near the entrance to the bunker.

Magda Goebbels, as though transported, rushed toward the door of the anteroom in an attempt to see Hitler, but the imperturbable Günsche barred the way. Then she shouted, "My Führer, don't abandon us, we'll all die without you . . . come back . . ." And she retired sobbing to the little room that served as an infirmary. Arthur Axmann, who had just arrived, wanted to rush in to say good-bye to Hitler, but Günsche was again impassable. Axmann then went to join Goebbels.

Traudl Junge was on the upper floor of the bunker, where she was giving the Goebbels children something to eat. Suddenly a sound echoed along the damp concrete, its sound magnifying to a rumble. "It's a bomb that's dropped just on top of us," the little expert Helmut declared.

He was wrong. It was not a bomb but a shot. It did not occur to Traudl to consult her wristwatch, which she had forgotten to wind up since the previous day. But then nobody in the bunker was concerned with time. Later, 3:30 P.M. was fixed as the hour at which the pistol was fired, but this was purely arbitrary. It could just as well have been 3:22 or 3:37 P.M.

Goebbels, after a few seconds' hesitation, advanced to the door of Hitler's study and opened it. Günsche, Bormann, and Axmann followed him. Linge penetrated into the death chamber only much later.

Eva Braun was at the left end of the sofa, with her head resting in the corner and her left hand trying to touch Hitler's arm. She was wearing her dress with the rose at the corsage. Her hair was freshly washed and carefully dressed. Her face was expressionless but beautiful. Her small pistol was lying on the pedestal table near a red stole. The broken phial, which looked so like lipstick, had fallen to the ground. The air reeked of acid fumes, and there was a smell of almonds.

There was also a stench of powder, for Hitler, who was sitting at the right end of the sofa, had shot himself with his 7.65 mm. caliber Walther pistol. Another 6.35 mm. caliber pistol lay unused on the table, beside a phial of the poison, which was still intact. Hitler had fired at his right temple. The blood was running down from a minute hole, over his cheeks, his freshly pressed uniform, around the Iron Cross pinned on his chest and down onto the sofa. He was very pale, with his right hand hanging down and the other resting along the back of the sofa. A jug lay overturned on the table, and the water was still flowing out and forming a pool around the pistol.

Günsche, with Linge's assistance, wrapped Hitler's head in a blanket. Dr. Stumpfegger came hastening to certify the death, and he and Linge carried the body up and out by the emergency exit that led directly into the garden. Bormann tried to follow with Eva, but she proved too heavy for him, and it was Otto Günsche who rendered this last service.

The two bodies were placed beside a concrete mixer near the small observation tower of the bunker, the construction of which had never been completed. It was dangerous to venture any farther because of the shell shrapnel. Kempka, the chauffeur, had procured forty gallons of gasoline. They were poured over the two bodies, which were placed side by side, feet toward the bunker. Hitler's dark trousers, with military braid stripes at the side, and his thick shoes were visible. Eva's legs had been covered with a blanket, and only her black suede Ferragamo shoes protruded. Eva was on the Führer's right, as for the marriage ceremony. For her it was the suttee, the final sacrifice. Berlin in flames was the pyre, and the Russians firing their "katuschka" mortars provided the funeral march.

Bormann, Linge, Günsche, Dr. Stumpfegger, General Krebs, General Burgdorf, Dr. Goebbels (who soon succumbed to the strain and disappeared), and a few SS were present—a small company compared with the hundreds of thousands who had sworn at Nuremberg to follow their Führer even in death. Kempka threw a flaming torch onto the gasoline and the flames rose in a violent, greedy dance. A smell of burning flesh spread through the air, as in the vicinity of a crematory oven in a concentration camp. The bodies were consumed slowly, and until five o'clock that evening it was still possible to distinguish the fine features of Eva, who seemed to be asleep.

CHAPTER TWENTY-ONE

The ashes are cold

The fate of Eva Braun's corpse, or of her ashes if her body was completely cremated, remains a mystery.

Over the years, the Russians have replied only reluctantly and with contradictory explanations to requests for information. They affect such great indifference over Eva Braun's end that it merely increases the inquirer's incredulity. The Soviets are past masters in the art of preserving and exposing the dead and had there been anything to preserve, they would certainly not have missed the unique opportunity of enhancing their triumph by displaying the bodies of Eva Braun and Hitler in Red Square before the people of the USSR.

Recently published, *The Death of Adolf Hitler,* a little book by the former Soviet intelligence officer Bezymenski claims that the charred remains of Eva and the Führer were found by Russian agents on May 4. Research is supposed to have proved the identity of the corpses. Yet this story remains largely unsupported by real evidence—and why did the Soviet authorities wait over twenty years to make their findings public?

Despite inquiries, counterinquiries, official versions, testimony after testimony, and a steady flow of publications, what happened that Monday, April 30, 1945, is still one of the great enigmas of contemporary history.

Kempka affirms that after the cremation, he and Rattenhuber buried the two bodies in a crater near his little house at the other end of the garden. Other informants speak of a communal grave. The ashes of Hitler and Eva Braun are said to have been mingled by the SS with those of Blondie and Wolfi, who had also been cremated. There is mention of a trench just near the entrance to the bunker and also of the destruction of the bodies with a *Panzerfaust*. The cremation took place in the greatest secrecy, in order to conceal the fact that Hitler was dead. It seems that the cook Konstanze Manziarli prepared Hitler's potato puree and fried eggs as usual that evening, so that nobody would be aware of his absence. But she, the secretaries, and many others knew that the couple had committed suicide. How is it possible that, if not out of a sense of duty, at least out of morbid curiosity, after so many years of having lived close to this man, for whom they had been prepared to face almost certain death, they did not try to go up—if only to see the pyre for a moment during the long hours of the cremation? Did it not occur to these women, who considered themselves Eva's friends, to say a prayer on the spot where the flames were consuming her?

"Hitler's death," Traudl Junge explains, "was like the end of a state of collective hypnosis for us. Suddenly we discovered the light; a mad desire to live, to revert to our former selves, to return to a normal human state took possession of us. Hitler no longer interested us, in fact, we felt a violent hatred for him. In the confusion of the bunker, his death, his funeral were merely a negligible, an insignificant detail. . . ." *

Today the trapezoid of the Chancellery of the Reich is nothing but a huge lawn surrounded by barbed-wire entanglements, which, because of its position alongside the wall that divides Berlin, is inaccessible to the ordinary visitor. There are turrets with police armed with machine guns and the area is said to be mined. There is no relic of the past except that on the spot where Eva Braun's body is supposed to have been cremated, a hump of earth still marks the entrance to one of the underground shelters.

In the spring of 1967, as mentioned before, I persuaded Gretl Braun Fegelein, now Frau Berlinghoff, to visit the Wilhelmstrasse zone with me. I was amazed that Eva's sister had never thought of laying a few flowers, even a humble bunch of violets, which would certainly have passed unnoticed, on the spot where her sister's ashes must have been interred. When I suggested it to her, I must admit with the idea of taking a photograph, she reacted with ex-

---

* One of the secretaries believes that Eva's ashes were thrown into the Spree River and Hitler's cremated remains were put into a box and given to Axmann. Where the box is hidden is a great guarded secret, obviously.

treme indifference, an indifference that was also shown by the other members of the family when I mentioned the incident to them.

Contrary to what is generally supposed, Hitler's suicide was not followed immediately by an epidemic of hara-kiris in the bunker. Even Goebbels, who alone had remained faithful and had proclaimed that he would not live on a minute after his beloved Führer's death, thought only of negotiating at first. At 2:46 on the night of May 1, a German emissary presented himself at the front lines of the 102nd regiment of the 35th Soviet division, with a request for an interview between General Hans Krebs and the Russian commander in chief. At 3:30, Field Marshal Vassili Chuikov received the Nazi general, who immediately announced: "Hitler committed suicide yesterday, April thirtieth."

"I know," bluffed the Russian, who in fact knew nothing at all but, like all eastern Europeans, was extremely suspicious of diplomatic maneuvering. Krebs gave a wealth of details, presented copies of the wills, and cryptically explained the nature of his mission. He wanted Goebbels to be recognized as Hitler's successor and himself and the other inmates of the bunker to be given a safe-conduct so that they could go north and join Doenitz, and in exchange he promised armistice negotiations. He tried to persuade the Russians that the only way to prevent Himmler from making a separate agreement with the Anglo-Americans—an agreement detrimental to Russian interests—was to allow Goebbels to take in hand the effective government of what remained of Germany and to make it clear that he alone would conclude peace with the Russians. These negotiations constitute one of the least known and most intriguing episodes of the end of the war, and one for which the Russian Field Marshal's rather imprecise account is the only source of information.

It is interesting to note that Krebs made a number of mistakes when speaking of Hitler's death. He had a *lapsus linguae* and declared that Hitler died during the night of April 30 to May 1. Then he forgot himself and talked as though Hitler were still alive. He revealed that the body had been burned during the night of April 30 to May 1 but breathed not a word about Eva Braun. It seems extraordinary that a negotiator, even a clumsy one, should not have tried to surprise his audience still further with the dramatic account of Eva's life and death.

Krebs's mission failed, and he returned to the bunker at 1:55 P.M. The occupants of the shelter, whose last glimmer of hope had been strengthened by a lull in the fighting, now had to face the inevitable: give themselves up to the Russians or attempt to escape.

Goebbels, the victim of his own propaganda, ordered his wife to seek escape with the children from the Bolshevik monsters. But Magda Goebbels refused, and, freshly made up and with her hair impeccably combed, a black woolen dress outlining her still youthful figure, the gold party emblem now pinned on her left breast, went into the little room in the bunker where the children were playing. Heide, the youngest, was suffering from tonsillitis and had been put into the little infirmary bed, but her sisters and her brother came to see her constantly.

Only Liesl Ostertag, the humble maid of peasant origin, who had never been a Nazi in her life, tried to make Frau Goebbels change her mind. She proposed that she take the children with her to her home in the country and hide them there until the storm had abated. But again Magda refused. The time for real sacrifice had come. She now intended to give proof of her devotion to the Führer, the man whom she had loved as passionately as she had hated her own husband. Magda Goebbels had gone mad.

She was accompanied by Dr. Stumpfegger, but it was she who wielded the hypodermic syringe containing strychnine. She began with Heide, who offered no resistance. Magda went into the next room. "We are going away. You have to be given an injection for the journey," she announced, and administered the strychnine to Hedda and Hilde. Then she decided to smoke a cigarette and chatted nonchalantly with the other children before completing her sixfold matricide. Only Helga, the eldest, suspected something and resisted. She had noticed that her younger sisters had slumped to the floor. Dr. Stumpfegger pinned her arms behind her back and immobilized her. Magda finished her work with calm determination.

A surprisingly large number of the Nazis who were in the three bunkers managed to escape thanks to the chaos that reigned during the last hours of the Berlin battle. For those who believe in divine justice, nothing could be more incomprehensible, for many of these people were responsible in varying degrees for a multitude of crimes, ranging from Auschwitz to the massacres in doomed Berlin. But everything is forgotten with time, everything is pardoned, even Auschwitz. Yet who could ever forget this unnatural mother, turned fiend, destroying her innocent children?

What is remarkable is that not a single SS, not a single general, now freed from the Hitlerian incubus, those SS and those generals who had set themselves up as heroes and shining examples of manhood, should not have tried to disarm this mother, tie her up and expose her to the Soviet bullets, to save the innocents.

Magda, an hour after the death of all her children, took poison, with Hitler's name on her lips. Her husband Joseph Goebbels committed suicide that evening in his Ministry of Propaganda. General Krebs, having failed in his mission, shot himself in the brain, and General Burgdorf followed suit.

Traudl Junge joined a group commanded by Otto Günsche that tried to slip through the lines. On her way out of the bunker, she passed for the last time in front of Hitler's room. The uniform coat and gold-braided cap were still in the cupboard . . . She went into Eva's room. The silver fox coat was there, with its lining bearing the initials E. B. in the shape of a four-leaved clover. But Traudl took nothing with her.* Günsche's party included Gerda Christian, Else Krueger, and Konstanze Manziarli, Martin Bormann, the pilot Bauer, who had wrapped Hitler's portrait of Frederick the Great under his shirt, Stumpfegger, Kempka, Rattenhuber, Linge, and Axmann. Mohnke, Hewel, and Admiral Voss were also in the group. Everybody was in civilian clothes, and the women were wearing trousers. According to Kempka, Bormann was killed by an explosion at the corner of the Friedrichstrasse, near the Admiral Theater. (I know the spot, for I once had my office there.) Kempka, however, is not a trustworthy witness. Stumpfegger was killed, as were Hewel, Rattenhuber, and many others. Konstanze Man-

---

* Traudl Junge was able to escape the bunker but was captured by the Russians in Berlin, and was released and interrogated by the Americans at the Nuremberg trials. Beautiful Gerda Christian crossed the Russian lines, her face hidden by a bandage. Gerda, who had become Hitler's secretary by chance, as she was a beautician and model for Elizabeth Arden in Berlin, says today: "None of the secretaries have married again. After Hitler, no other man would ever interest us."

ziarli was taken prisoner by a Russian patrol. It is thought that she swallowed the contents of the phial that had been Hitler's parting present, in order to escape being raped.

At 12:05 on May 2, after the capitulation of the SS, the soldiers of the Russian Eighth Army penetrated into the Chancellery garden without firing a single shot. Private Tchurakow is supposed to have discovered the smoking bodies of a man and a woman in a trench. How could they still be burning after forty-eight hours? A mystery. Shouts of hurrah went up, and photographs were taken of the man, who was in uniform and still had a moustache (why had it not burned?). Then the soldiers' thoughts turned to other things—to the pillaging of the bunker, to drinking and celebrating the victory with all the brandy and champagne the fugitives had abandoned there.

I do not doubt for a moment that Eva Braun and Hitler are dead, although Marshal Zhukov speaks of an Arado plane that left Berlin *in extremis* on the afternoon of May 2, and although the fate of the Ju 52 noticed by Hanna Reitsch at the time of her take-off has never been explained.

The evidence of Traudl Junge, whose extreme good faith is beyond question, and all the other circumstances provide conclusive proof of their death. What remains open to doubt is the moment and the method of its occurrence.

It can immediately be ascertained that nobody, absolutely nobody, was present at the suicide. The only people who claimed to have seen Hitler and Eva dead were Goebbels, Axmann, Günsche, Bormann, and later Linge. Kempka saw only a body in uniform whose head was wrapped in a blanket. The same is true of the few others who were present at the cremation. Traudl Junge, Gerda Christian, Else Krueger, and all the rest learned the circumstances of Hitler's death only indirectly, and often the account, in its successive transmissions, was inaccurately embroidered.

Bormann is missing and Goebbels is dead. Only Axmann has been in a position to evoke the past. In his statements and his memoirs, however, he shows himself extremely reticent and seems at pains to avoid going into details.

The information that exists is based largely on the accounts of three servants: Günsche, the "gorilla," Linge, the valet, and Kempka, the chauffeur. These were no ordinary servants, however, but brutal, ignorant SS men, with a limited intelligence and gangster pasts. Their capacity for observation was extremely restricted. Were they qualified to be the recorders of history? Were they versed in ballistics, medicine, and toxicology? Their chief function was merely to transport the bodies, and in the haste and confusion of the moment, did they not blindly accept what Bormann and Goebbels announced to them? It should be remembered that for the SS, with their innate respect for discipline, the word of a superior was law.

Moreover, their accounts are nothing but a series of contradictions. Kempka places the moment of death at one o'clock in the afternoon. Günsche corroborates this claim and in addition affirms that Hitler took poison. Axmann states that Hitler fired into his mouth. Linge insists that he aimed at his temple, and a committee of experts in the service of the German Federal Government agreed with Linge on this point.

"Hitler's whore is dead!" This is how a peasant woman who was crossing the street announced the news she had heard on the radio to Ilse Braun, whom she did not know. Eva's parents also learned of the marriage and its sequel from a radio bulletin. Herta did not immediately communicate this rumor to Gretl Braun, who was living with her at Berchtesgaden in daily expectation of her baby's birth.

The family was almost relieved to know that Eva had met her death in this way. They had feared a worse fate, with the Russians in Berlin. Moreover, Eva had chosen her destiny, and had she stayed alive, she would have been a serious handicap to them at this zero hour when every German was trying merely to escape being engulfed by the catastrophe.

The Braun family had to pay dearly for this kinship Eva had forced on them and for the luxurious stays at Berchtesgaden. There were interrogations by the Americans followed by persecutions by the German authorities. The father was deprived of his pension and fined. He was refused work and assistance, and his furniture, houses, and bank savings were confiscated. There was also the strong hostility of the general public. Their neighbors ignored them, their friends made themselves scarce, insulting and threatening letters were sent to them. Most Germans now claimed that they had never in their lives been Nazis and professed bitter hatred for Hitler. Since, however, a lingering fear of retribution prevented them from attacking the Führer directly, even after his death, many decided to make Eva Braun's memory the scapegoat for Hitler's crimes. The press was full of imaginary accounts of orgies, corruption, and depravity. Then there was also the fake diary. Eva Braun's name was never printed without an accompaniment of mudslinging.

But everything passes. The father succeeded in exculpating himself and spending a peaceful old age, the sisters managed to rebuild their lives. With the revival of their pride and vitality, the Brauns have started to side with Eva once more, to defend her openly. Ilse, alone and without financial resources, got a tribunal to condemn the forgers of the private diary attributed to Eva. After this victory, she chose to retire from the scene and let people gossip as they pleased.

The mother today speaks proudly of her daughter, who died "Frau Hitler"—in other words, an honest woman. She seems to attach little importance to anything else.

Many of Eva's friends are dead. Brandt was hanged and Morell died miserably in 1948 at the Tegernsee, after his liberation from a camp. Others chose to disown Eva or heap insults on her name. Some thought it wiser to keep silent about the past lest they say something that could be unfavorably interpreted. Herta, her close friend, her only friend, has kept alive the memory of Eva, who for her is a saint and a martyr.

The Polish deportee from Dachau concentration camps who worked for a time in the little villa in the Wasserburgerstrasse returned there after the liberation with his comrades. They started to pillage the place, until one of them, seeing the address on a letter, remembered that the owner, Eva Braun, had been named as Hitler's wife. A monster sale of souvenirs was organized for the American soldiers, and when the dresses and underwear ran short, fresh supplies were procured from elsewhere and palmed off on the GIs in vast quantities as "owned by Hitler's concubine." The American commander finally placed an officer in charge of the house and put an end to this strange traffic.

Gretl Braun, widowed, accompanied by her friend Herta, had hidden the photograph albums, amateur films, letters, jewelry, and other mementos in the park of her husband Fegelein's castle, Schloss Fischorn, at Zell-am-See in Austria.

Later she met a German refugee to whom she took a great liking. Whatever the nature of their relationship may have been, the man persuaded her to reveal to him the secret of the whereabouts of the documents that had belonged to her sister. The ingenuous Gretl, out of love or in the hope of financial gain, which she urgently needed, took him into her confidence. The German was a C.I.C. agent of the American Third Army. The films, albums, pages of the diary, and other documents, whose nature seems to have been kept secret, were all sent to Washington. The films were exploited. The albums were found to contain photographs of Martin Bormann, the only ones in existence at that time. Thousands of reproductions of them were immediately made and distributed to the government and to the secret services throughout the world. It was decided to keep the albums. Then their existence was forgotten, and so it was that I chanced to find them in a corner of the American archives.

On May 4, the SS flooded the Berghof with gasoline and set fire to the place. Shortly afterward, at six in the evening, units of the 101st Airborne Division of the American army followed by French detachments commanded by General Leclerc appeared on the scene. The villas, barracks, installations, and the remains of the Berghof were gradually destroyed by the Americans and then by the local authorities. Today, there are only ruins left, and even the stones are disappearing as a result of souvenir hunters' activities.

The Platterhof has been turned into an elegant inn for the U.S. Army. American tourists abound. On an average three hundred of them come to the Obersalzberg every day, for this is for them one of the chief tourist attractions in Bavaria. The ruins of the Dachau concentration camp near Munich also draw many visitors.

The Türkenhof Hotel near the Berghof has been re-opened by Therese Partner, the daughter of the former proprietors. The food is bad but the decoration stylish. There are symbols glorifying Nazism on the walls, and the proprietress, if she is well disposed, will tell you anecdotes of the good old days. She owns a gold mine, the entrance to the bunker, which one can visit for a mark. People sometimes look for the hidden treasures of Eva and Hitler, and even try to dig through the rock in their search. An American couple was once married in Eva Braun's bedroom.

The Kehlstein house, the "Eagle's Nest," is intact and can be visited in fine weather. The German government has supplied the necessary transport facilities, the gold elevator is functioning, and the view from the top is magnificent. One can eat lunch on the terrace or where Hitler and Eva Braun took their meals, or sit in the chimney corner, where Eva liked to gaze into the fire.

Nothing has changed except that a cross has incongruously been stuck on the top of the mountain and souvenir stalls have been set up everywhere. There are postcards evoking the past, plates with Hitler's portrait, and all manner of knickknacks for sale.

Do the three hundred thousand tourists who visit the Obersalzberg every year do so out of simple curiosity, to pass the time, or is it already a pilgrimage? It is too early yet to say.

Gretl's daughter Eva was born on May 5, the day on which Hitler had wanted to die like Napoleon. Today she is a fine upstanding girl. She is the image of her father Hermann Fegelein, but she never mentions him, for the name Fegelein is anathema for the Braun family.

When I showed her photographs of the past, she laughed. "Mother, that Hitler looks a real clown. How could you talk to him without bursting out laughing?"

Like most members of her generation, she is quite unconcerned with the past. Maybe she is waiting until it is possible to form an opinion in Germany without having to take into account the reactions of the Russians or Americans.

I checked her birth certificate, which confirms May 5 as the date of her birth. In spite of some gossip, Gretl was not living anywhere near Hitler when her daughter was conceived, so there is not the slightest possibility of his being the girl's father.

Young Eva was engaged to a charming young man with whom she was deeply in love. He was killed in a car accident in Italy. Eva bought the car, had it repaired, and since then has used it constantly. Strange creatures, these Braun girls.

The Mother Superior of the convent in Simbach, where Eva was educated, asked me: "But did Hitler love her?" I was unable to answer her question at the time. Since then I have given it much thought.

There are many different kinds of love, that of Othello, who strangles Desdemona, that of Napoleon, who sacrifices Josephine to an empire, that of long-married couples who never stop bickering, that of Italian films, that of a head of state who adores his wife and yet, by pressing a button, can decide the atomic destruction of the world. What love was Hitler, that egocentric par excellence, able to offer? This is a question for psychiatrists. But however limited this love may have been, Hitler offered it to Eva. He offered her the only kind of attachment, the only tenderness of which he was capable.

It was not for love that he married her. He had remained extremely bourgeois, and he wished to regularize a situation that he had always found distressing. He wanted to keep a promise which he had made to Eva and which it would now cost him nothing to fulfill. He wanted to give her this last joy, perhaps to console her for Fegelein's execution, but chiefly to reward her (he could after all not give her a medal as he had done with Frau Goebbels) for following him even in death.

I think, however, that this marriage was also determined by another factor. Hitler, who was well versed in propaganda, wanted to leave the Germans a vision both human and heroic of their Führer: an Adolf Hitler who was so madly loved by a woman that she took part in his Viking funeral.

Had he loved Eva normally, he could have saved her life. One word from him, and she would have been carried, bound hand and foot if need be, out of Berlin. Eva chose her fate of her own free will; this is undeniable. But it was Hitler's wish that she should die. It was no suicide. It was in a sense murder.

Did Eva Braun love Hitler? It is for the reader to decide. But whatever verdict he may reach on this hapless woman, he should remember that Eva Braun was merely a symbol of the German nation during the tumultuous period of its history from 1929 to 1945. Like Germany, Eva gave herself blindly to an abnormal man, like Germany she believed in him, like Germany she allowed herself to be totally guided by him, like Germany she venerated him like a god and loved him like a father, and like the Germany of that time, she descended for him and with him into hell.

Index

ABOUT THE AUTHOR

NERIN E. GUN, a freelance journalist and writer, was born in Rome of Turkish and Italian parentage. Educated in France and Germany, he entered the newspaper field in Berlin at the start of World War II and was eventually imprisoned at Dachau. He was rescued by the United States Army while under sentence of death.

He became a United States citizen in 1946, and is now a correspondent for many important European magazines. He is the author of two previous books, *The Day of the Americans* and *Red Roses of Texas*.